8-27-92

Dear Margaret,

Welcome back - Have a Significant year.

Love,

-R

SIDNEY AND BEATRICE WEBB

Indian Diary

edited and introduced by
NIRAJA GOPAL JAYAL

Oxford   New York
OXFORD UNIVERSITY PRESS
1990

Oxford University Press, Walton Street, Oxford OX2 6DP

Oxford New York Toronto
Delhi Bombay Calcutta Madras Karachi
Petaling Jaya Singapore Hong Kong Tokyo
Nairobi Dar es Salaam Cape Town
Melbourne Auckland

and associated companies in
Berlin Ibadan

Oxford is a trade mark of Oxford University Press

First published 1987
First issued as an Oxford University Press paperback 1990

British Library Cataloguing in Publication Data

Webb, Sidney
Indian diary.
1. India. Description & travel 1905–1916
I. Title   II. Webb, Beatrice, 1858–1943
III. Jayal, Niraja Gopal
915.404356
ISBN 0–19–282748–0

Library of Congress Cataloging in Publication Data
Data available

Printed in Great Britain by
Richard Clay Ltd.
Bungay, Suffolk

Contents

Acknowledgements

This project could not have been launched but for the encouragement and assistance of Nisha Puri, Alan Ryan and Anatol Lieven, to all of whom I am most grateful. In the course of preparing this manuscript for publication I have also incurred numerous other debts, at least some of which I would like to acknowledge here. For clues to obscure references in the text, and for the loan of useful material for the footnotes, I would like to thank Vishalakshi Menon, Benoy Mukhopadhyaya and my father, Madan Gopal. Drafts of the introduction have been read, re-read and corrected by Gurpreet Mahajan, Sucheta Mahajan and my husband, Rakesh Dhar Jayal. To them I am particularly grateful. I would also like to record my gratitude to Manosi Lahiri, who toiled in friendly labour to prepare the map which decorates the front endpapers of this volume, and to Sangeeta Goel, who typed my manuscript with care and speed. Finally, the Oxford University Press has been most patient in the face of constantly unmet deadlines.

A Note on Spelling

Throughout the text of the Diary variations occur in the spelling of Indian names and place-names, as well as, occasionally, in other words. Most of these have been retained in the form in which they appear in the manuscript. Some examples:

Hindu, Hindoo
Arya Somaj, Arya Samaj
Guru Kula, Gurukula
Mohammedan, Mahomedan, Mohomedan, Muhammedan, Muhamedan
Maulvis, Moulvis, Mulvis
Sanscrit, Sanskrit
Brahman, Brahmin
Benares (usually Banaras)
Muttra (usually Mathura)

Introduction

If there is any one quality which distinguishes the Webbs from their intellectual and political peers it is surely their indefatigable and unrivalled talent for institution-building. They were the pioneers and architects of an alternative tradition which has in no small way contributed to the changed face of society and politics in modern Britain. This tradition includes a vast and impressive complex of institutions which were, in greater or lesser measure, the brainchildren of Sidney and Beatrice Webb—the Welfare State, the Labour Party, the Fabian Society, the London School of Economics and the *New Statesman*.

Their towering intellectual and political presence was nevertheless attended by strange contradictions. Despite their anti-establishment politics they dined with prime ministers and cabinet ministers oftener than with trade unionists. Their socialism, too, was ironically maintained by Beatrice's considerable private income, which allowed her and Sidney to concentrate their energies on the propagation of their 'creed' (socialism) and the advancement of their 'craft' (social investigation), free from the cares of earning a livelihood. Moreover, the 'firm of Webb' was a remarkable partnership of—in the eyes of their contemporaries—two curiously ill-matched individuals: one, the handsome and wealthy Miss Potter ('Too beautiful, too rich and too clever', moaned Sidney, her despondent-suitor); the other, the unprepossessing Sidney Webb, a middle-class clerk in the Colonial Office with every conceivable social disadvantage and little to commend him besides a strong memory and a sharp intellect. It turned out, however, to be a most fruitful partnership, running into many thousand printed pages ('our solid but unreadable books', wrote Beatrice), service on many royal commissions, and some parliamentary and governmental work. In addition to this legacy, Beatrice left behind in fifty-seven hand-written exercise books a diary spanning seventy years, kept from the age of fifteen till her death at eighty-five. In quality, not merely in volume, this establishes her as perhaps the finest diarist of her time. It is a detailed chronicle of her life, intellectual development, moral dilemmas, spiritual searches, responses to people and places, and above all a record of her extraordinary partnership with Sidney as well as the range of their achievements and acquaintanceship.

The diary began partly as a kind of intellectual log book containing summaries and assessments of books recently read, hardly surprising in that even a girl with a lively intellectual curiosity was, in Beatrice's time, denied access to formal education. More particularly, the diary became a mode of conversation with an other self, an emotional vent for this second youngest of nine daughters who went through childhood feeling lonely and neglected.

Martha Beatrice was born on 22 January 1858, the daughter of Richard and Laurenciana Potter, at the Potter home in Standish, near Gloucester. Both her parents came from radical affluent industrial families of the north, with the puritanical values and moral discipline typical of their class. Richard Potter was in his own right an industrial magnate and Chairman of the Great Western Railway. Theirs was a household visited not only by the captains of industry but also by politicians, pastors and philosophers: possibly the earliest, and certainly the strongest, intellectual influence in the life of the young Beatrice was that of Herbert Spencer, the Potters' 'philosopher on the hearth'. While Beatrice went through the ritual motions of a Victorian girlhood, including several London Seasons and a formal 'coming out', she was always restless with the vapidity of upper-class London life and, having wheedled passes out of her sisters' suitors, frequently slipped out of parties to spend long evenings at Westminster, listening to debates in the Commons. As reflected in her diary, however, her youth was mostly spent in agonizing moral struggles (such as overcoming personal vanity!) and a serious and intense search for a 'craft' and a vocation. An incognito visit to the simple homes of her mothers' relations in Bacup (a small manufacturing town in Lancashire) went some way in influencing her choice: '*Laisser-faire* breaks down when one watches these things from the inside'. So also did the mid-Victorian zeitgeist: the belief in the scientific method on the one hand, and in 'the transference of the emotion of self-sacrificing service from God to man' on the other.

And so Beatrice was led into the homes of the poor, inspired not by the spirit of charity but by the ideal of 'enlightened philanthropy', advocating State intervention in a way that unknowingly prefigured her later socialist commitment. While the emotional trigger for Beatrice's decision was the 'collective consciousness of sin' which troubled many upper-class socialist consciences of the time, its intellectual equivalent was the desire, inspired by Herbert Spencer, to become an investigator into social institutions. This was her chosen craft and her first opportunity to practise it came in the form of an invitation to join Charles Booth, her cousin by marriage, on his monumental and eventually authoritative survey, the *Life and Labour of the People of London* (1891–1903). This study of the 'arithmetic of woe', based on detailed observation, established that thirty per cent of the people of London lived below the level of bare subsistence. The conclusions were, if not socialist, certainly an invalidation of the prevalent philosophy of economic individualism. In the following years Beatrice worked as a rent collector in the

East End of London, managing working-class housing, while using her spare time for study and writing. She turned out several articles in this period, including 'The Economic Theory of Karl Marx' and 'Dock Life in the East End of London'. By 1887, she noted with satisfaction, 'I was transformed into . . . a professed brain worker'. In the winter of that year she undertook to investigate the phenomenon of 'sweating' or sub-contracting—a system by which middlemen distributed work to women in their own homes, thereby circumventing the regulations of the Factory Act—and decided to gain first-hand experience by getting a job disguised as a trouser-hand. Despite the disguise her employer soon discovered that her sewing was 'too good for the trade', but this sociological adventure culminated in a well-received paper, an invitation to give evidence before a House of Lords committee on sweating, and to the conclusion—dramatic for the times—that 'The sweater is, in fact, the whole nation'. Beatrice's work had already prepared her, it would seem quite inevitably, for a conversion to socialism. 'At last I am a Socialist', she declared in January 1890, and it was not long before she threw in her lot with the Fabian Socialists and, more intimately, with one of their most dedicated workers, Sidney Webb.

Fabian Socialism was committed equally to an organic view of society and to the moral value of the human person and his rights. It frequently claimed to be merely an extension of liberal individualism and the fulfilment of the economic dimension of the democratic ideal. In this it clearly reflected a disillusionment with the more than manifest breakdown of the promise of *laissez-faire* economics and private enterprise. Thus, the Fabian philosophical premise that 'the individual is now created by the social organism of which he forms a part: his life is born of the larger life', found its practical realization in the conviction that social ownership, through a graduated programme of the nationalization of 'utilities' (which, incidentally, earned Fabians the pejorative title of 'gas-and-water' socialists) was the only solution to the inequality and poverty generated by the capitalist system. They proposed that all rent, i.e. 'unearned increment' on land and capital, be transferred to society as a whole and administered by a group of experts trained in science and statistics, thereby ensuring its use for the benefit of the entire community instead of a few. In 1911, in a Fabian tract entitled *The Necessary Basis of Society*, Sidney Webb propo: :d for every member of society a 'National Minimum of Health, Wages, Education, Leisure and Sanitation'—a goal that was later incorporated in the Labour Party's constitution, *Labour and the New Social Order* (1918). It was Sidney Webb, again, who was responsible for enunciating the principle of 'the inevitability of gradualness', which won this brand of socialism a common metaphorical usage synonymous with the word 'delay'. The Fabians deliberately eschewed direct participation in politics, preferring the more insidious strategy of 'permeation'—which amounted to locating the most susceptible political party (in this case, the Liberals) and persuading its influential leaders, largely through social contact. Throughout, the Fabians—unlike some other socialist groups in Britain, notably the Marxist-inspired Social-Democratic Federation—steered clear of revolution, trade-union action and even workers' control, prejudices which stemmed from their rejection of the ideas of class war and the irreconcilable opposition between classes and class interests. They were, in other words, the intellectual heirs not of Karl Marx but of Bentham, Mill and T. H. Green.

Beatrice was attracted to the work of the Fabian Society with the publication, in 1889, of its first volume, *Fabian Essays in Socialism*, edited by George Bernard Shaw. She wrote to a friend that Sidney Webb's was 'by far the most interesting essay'. Coincidentally, Sidney also, around the same time, reviewed her contribution to Booth's first volume, saying that 'The only contributor with any literary talent is Miss Beatrice Potter'. In the mean while Beatrice had constantly been trying to resolve an inner conflict between what she described as 'the Ego that affirms' and 'the Ego that denies'

Can there be a science of social organisation in the sense in which
we have a science of mechanics or a science of chemistry, enabling
us to forecast what will happen, and perhaps to alter the event by
taking appropriate action or persuading others to take it? And
secondly, assuming that there be, or will be, such a science of society, is man's capacity for scientific discovery the only faculty
required for the reorganisation of society according to an ideal? Or
do we need religion as well as science, emotional faith as well as
intellectual curiosity?

Throughout her life she found herself drawn towards mysticism and religion, and at all times acknowledged her personal
need for prayer and faith: 'it is impossible for a woman to live
in agnosticism'. At nineteen she had even experimented with
Hinduism and Buddhism, finding the latter 'logically and
ethically superior' to Christianity. She considered the doctrine of *karma* in harmony with science in so far as it suggested the universality of causation, and was captivated by
the idea of *nirvana*. Ultimately, however, it did not make a
convert of her, but only distanced her further from Christianity. It was 'charming', she wrote; it had 'a lovely morality', but it was 'based on falsehood' because its aim was
selfish—exhorting man to be passive, forbidding the exercise
of his faculties and thereby the growth and regeneration of
mankind. It is surprising indeed that there is no echo of this
youthful dalliance with Buddhism and Hinduism in Beatrice's Indian diary, not even in the description of her visit to
Bodh Gaya. *Vis-à-vis* Christianity, however, her relationship
was always troubled and complicated: she struggled constantly with what she perceived to be her own lack of morality. She resolved 'to make a faith for myself, and I must
work, work, until I have', concluding that were she to live
her life all over again she would probably have been 'a con-
forming member of the National Church'. Her flirtations
with Spencer's Religion of Science and the Religion of
Humanity of Auguste Comte and Frederic Harrison also belong to this phase of her life. It was only the direct exposure

to poverty and the resolve to make its alleviation her life's work that provided a fulfilling substitute.

The Partnership

The heartbreak occasioned by Beatrice's unrequited passion for the dashing Liberal politician Joseph Chamberlain made it difficult for her to accept Sidney's repeated proposals of marriage. When she did, in 1892, it was avowedly to start 'a working comradeship':

We are both of us second-rate minds; but we are curiously combined. I am the investigator and he the executant; between us we have a wide and varied experience of men and affairs. We have also an unearned salary. These are unique circumstances. A considerable work should be the result if we use our combined talents with a deliberate and persistent purpose.

Marriage to Sidney entailed many breaks with the past. Herbert Spencer had appointed her his literary executor, but her new connection with a socialist impelled him to withdraw the privilege, though their intimate association ended only with his death. Charles and Mary Booth also grew increasingly aloof, while Beatrice's family accepted the event with resignation—as a step only to be expected from the most eccentric of their number. Inevitably, the honeymoon ended at the Trades Union Congress at Glasgow, and the next six years (upto 1898) were a period of very hard work—researching, writing, proselytizing and, for Sidney, administrative work on the London County Council. The Webbs set up house at their later famous 41 Grosvenor Road residence, immortalized as 'a hard little house . . . a centre for quite an astonishing amount of political and social activity' by H. G. Wells in *The New Machiavelli*. They proceeded to divide their time between London (when the County Council was in session) and the country, where they were generally accompanied by the other two members of the Fabian junta, George Bernard Shaw and Graham Wallas.

The first major joint enterprise of the Webbs (Beatrice was already one book old when she married Sidney, having published *The Co-operative Movement in Great Britain* in 1891) was the *History of Trade Unionism* (1894), 'a scientific analysis of the structure and function of British Trade Unions . . . the relation of manual-working trade unionism to other forms of social organisation: notably, to profit-making enterprise, to political democracy, and to the consumer's co-operative movement'. It was well-received, widely translated and acknowledged as the most authoritative work on the subject. At the same time, Sidney busied himself with helping trade-union officials to draft a minority report to the findings of the Royal Commission on Labour, which Beatrice described as 'a gigantic fraud'.

Sidney served on the London County Council for eighteen years, starting with the second election to the LCC in 1892. Over time, the Progressives in this body overtook the Moderates (identified with the Liberals and the Conservatives respectively) in gaining a majority, which enabled them to push through far-reaching reforms, particularly in the sphere of educational administration. Sidney Webb, the ideal committee-man, was, virtually single-handedly, the author of these. The first step was the establishment of the Technical Education Board, to cover elementary, secondary and university education through grants-in-aid and an elaborate scheme of scholarships and bursaries. A comprehensive, co-ordinated and unified system of education for London as a whole was gradually brought into existence, covering every level, every geographical area and almost every field of study except, as Sidney remarked with satisfaction, ancient Greek and theology.

In 1894, as the result of an unexpectedly large bequest from an eccentric old Fabian, Henry Hutchinson, the Webbs enthusiastically embarked on 'the biggest single enterprise in

Our Partnership'—the establishment of the London School of Economics and Political Science. A young Oxford economist, W.A.S. Hewins, was recruited as Director, and the school—'at first a sickly infant, of doubtful parentage, born into an indifferent if not hostile world'—began functioning from a small London flat. Meanwhile, the search for a political science lecturer was proving disheartening and was eventually abandoned. 'It struck us always as a trifle difficult', wrote Beatrice, 'to teach a science which does not yet exist'! However, the London School of Economics went on to grow, quite in conformity with Sidney's promise that it would be an ideologically neutral institution for teaching and research. He was scrupulously careful to recruit faculty members who were known for their establishment scholarship rather than for radical or dissenting opinions. At the same time, the School could and did accommodate many scholars who also made a mark as socialists—notably Harold J. Laski, R. H. Tawney and G. D. H. Cole.

In the following years, alongside their other work, Sidney's involvement with London education continued and he acquired a well-deserved reputation as the chief expert on public education. In collaboration with R. B. Haldane, he was instrumental in the reorganization of London University from a body which only awarded degrees into one that undertook active teaching. Despite Sidney's preoccupation with education, in general, and the London School of Economics in particular, the Webbs continued to work on their study of English local government.

Meanwhile, Beatrice was invited by the Liberal Prime Minister Arthur Balfour to join the Royal Commission on the Poor Law in 1905. The Commission had only two other members of a socialist persuasion, both old friends of Beatrice—Octavia Hill (of the Charity Organisation Society) and George Lansbury. Amidst disagreements over procedure, methods, substance and even the very terms of reference of the Commission, Beatrice struck out on her own.

With Sidney and other fellow-Fabians, she conducted independent research into the question and eventually drafted a dissenting Minority Report.

The existing Poor Law of 1834 had claimed that 'public relief of destitution out of funds raised by taxation . . . devitalised the receipients, degraded their character and induced in them general bad behaviour' as well as created 'a wider pool of destitution'. The policy consequence of this analysis was the principle of 'less eligibility', according to which no able-bodied person could be helped to a level comparable to the independent labourer of the lowest class. To do this, it was maintained, would be to make the latter less industrious and induce them to enter 'the more eligible class of paupers'. The 1905 Commission was constituted to consider the suitability of the policy of 1834 for changed twentieth-century conditions. In its own self-image it was a commission designed to find the best means of relief for destitute persons. Beatrice had a larger and more radical vision of its proper task: she wanted it to investigate the *causes* of destitution, so that the state could, in answer to specific needs in particular areas, provide specialized relief. This was obviously too innovative for the bulk of the Commission, whom Beatrice then proceeded to ignore. With financial aid from Charlotte, Shaw's wealthy wife, the Webbs began to explore particular dimensions of the problem. Beatrice was politic enough to make friends with the Chairman of the Commission, Lord George Hamilton, while endeavouring to remain politely distant from the other members. Frequently, her resolve would give way to impatient intervention and earn a reproof from Lord George: 'you did not behave nicely yesterday'. 'However', confided Beatrice to her diary, 'I really will try. Dignified silence I will set before me, except when the public good requires me to come forward. Ah! how hard it is for the quick-witted and somewhat vain woman to be discreet and accurate'. She independently made special inquiries into the questions of medical relief, homeless children and unemployment. The '300 pages of reasoned stuff with a scheme of reform at the end' that was the Minority Report was completed in a spirit of great exultation, even though it carried only three signatures besides her own. Beatrice wrote superciliously in her diary that she hoped she would have colleagues of a higher calibre the next time she sat on a commission because it was 'shockingly bad for one's character to be with such folk—it makes me feel intolerably superior'.

The Minority Report recommended, among other things, that uniform treatment not be accorded to all sections of the destitute, for that category included the poor, the sick, the disabled, the old, the unemployed and many others; and that specialized departments of local authorities should deal with particular needs rather than wait for these needs to develop into technical 'destitution' or 'pauperism'. For the able-bodied unemployed and underemployed she envisaged the creation of a Ministry of Labour, functioning through an extensive network of labour exchanges, arranging training programmes and co-ordinating regional imbalances. Beatrice's confidence in the success of her report was, however, misplaced. The Majority Report proved to be well-received and popular with the Press, while the Minority Report was largely ignored. The chief reason was that, contrary to the Webbs's estimate, the Majority Report had turned out to be a fairly enlightened document which had, in any case, abandoned the 'less eligibility' principle and left relief to both voluntary bodies and statutory authorities.

After riding the crest of popularity, and even in some sense power, for a few years, the Webbs found themselves, suddenly and unhappily, dropped by their Liberal friends. Work on the Poor Law campaign, however, continued, with the establishment of the National Committee for the Prevention of Destitution, which was in fact a National Committee for the Break-Up of the Poor Law, for it saw destitution as 'a disease of society itself', as a 'moral malaria' which degraded people physically and spiritually. In a very short time the Committee managed to enrol 16,000 members, but the Liberal victory in the general election of 1911 rather stole their thunder, for Lloyd George's new government enacted a compulsory insurance scheme for unemployment and sickness, financed by taxation, wage deduction, employers' contributions and a grant from the Treasury. In 1916 a Ministry of Labour, too, was created, though it could not, as Beatrice later noted sadly, prevent the destitution of the able-bodied during the Great Depression. Towards the end of her life she continued to be disturbed by the phenomena of long unemployment and mass unemployment, finally looking for hope and direction to the Soviet solution.

Nevertheless, her work on the Poor Law remains and is widely acknowledged as the earliest statement of the principles of the Welfare State, which came into being some years after her death. It is no accident that William Beveridge, author of the Beveridge Report which constituted the basis of the Welfare State in the Labour regime of 1945, had worked as an assistant investigator on Beatrice's enquiry into the question of able-bodied unemployment in relation to the Poor Law.

Exhausted by the effort of this campaign and disheartened by the reception of the Minority Report, the Webbs set off in 1911 on a tour of the Far East, including Japan, China, Burma and India. On their return they threw themselves once more into intensely hard work, this time abstaining from active attempts at political permeation. Beatrice launched and organized the Fabian Research Department with a team of young volunteers, including G.D.H. Cole and several other Guild Socialists. The Research Department became 'a general enquiry bureau of the left . . . to collect for study a reference library of books, journals, and press-cuttings dealing with current Trade Union and Labour questions.' In 1913 the Webbs founded the *New Statesman* which was designed to perform a complementary function. They had in fact planned to call it *The Statesman* but were told by a fellow Fabian, S. K. Ratcliffe, that there already existed in India a paper of that name which Ratcliffe himself had edited until 1907. The *New Statesman* was planned as an essentially Fabian organ, and its famous Supplements, researched and written by members of the Fabian Research Department, became important sources of material for left-wing intellectuals. It outgrew its Fabian origins eventually, but the impress remains.

Meanwhile World War I intervened and British socialists found themselves in a quandary as to whether they ought to support the war effort or, like their Continental counterparts, assume a pacifist position. The precedent had already been set at the time of the Boer War: now, as then, the Fabians rallied behind King and Country. Sidney, with Ramsay MacDonald and Arthur Henderson, joined the War Emergency Committee, which also included representatives of seventeen left-wing organizations in Britain. The Committee was aimed at protecting the interests of workers in wartime, through price regulations in food, securing allowances for the families of servicemen, freezing rents and exposing wartime profiteering. In 1916 Sidney found himself on the National Executive of the Labour Party, so that when towards the end of the war the Party began to think in terms of drafting a constitution for itself he was in large measure its author. Beatrice had suffered loneliness, depression, neurosis and illness throughout the war but revived when the drafting of the constitution began.

In 1922 Sidney was invited to stand for parliament from Seaham Harbour, a predominantly miners' constituency in Durham. He was a successful candidate, though a less than successful Member of Parliament. While Beatrice's political ambitions for him had at last been realized, flamboyant Commons debating was not at all his style. Beatrice, however, was the ideal Member's wife, revelling in the admiration of the Seaham miners' wives and launching the Half-Circle Club to provide a less upper-class and overawing social alternative for the wives of Labour MPs who came from trade-union backgrounds. In Labour's first government in 1924 Ramsay MacDonald asked Sidney to take charge of the

Board of Trade, an invitation that Sidney accepted even as he described it as 'an unexpected and slightly ludicrous adventure for a man of sixty-four to become, first a Member of Parliament, and within a year, a Cabinet Minister'. Beatrice busied herself with the first volume of her autobiography, *My Apprenticeship*, which was published in 1926. Though Sidney was clearly unsympathetic to this venture, Beatrice hoped—and how right she proved to be—that the book would be more than the 'sentimental scribblings of a woman' and would be valued as 'a description of "Victorianism" '. The book draws largely upon her diaries and is valuable not merely for the insights it provides into Beatrice's personality and work but also as historical source material.

By this time the Webbs had acquired Passfield Corner, their eight-acre country residence, and began devoting much of their spare time to their garden. Just as they were beginning to settle down to a politically inactive retirement—to write books in the country—Labour came back into office and Sidney found himself once again in the Cabinet, as a Labour peer and Minister for the Colonies. Beatrice firmly refused to become Lady Passfield, making only the one concession of curtseying to royalty. With Sidney at Westminster, struggling with his portfolio, Beatrice began writing *Our Partnership* at Passfield Corner, the second and last volume of her autobiography which takes their story upto 1911.

It was at about this time that the Webbs met the Russian ambassador in London, G. J. Sokolnikov, and his wife. Conversation with their Russian friends inspired them to plan a visit to the Soviet Union and, after an extensive preparatory programme of reading, they set off for Moscow in 1932. The result of their three-week visit, spent chiefly in Moscow and Leningrad, was *Soviet Communism: A New Civilization*, an enthusiastic defence of the Soviet system, the new panacea for the capitalist malaise. Beatrice described their fascination for the Soviet Union thus: 'Old people often fall in love in extraordinary and ridiculous ways—with their chauffeurs for example: we feel it more dignified to have fallen in love with Soviet Communism'. Some of this affection inevitably abated as news of the horrors of Stalinist purges came through in the late thirties. By this time old age and disease had begun to take their toll. In 1938 Sidney suffered a stroke; he was completely recovered only by 1940. Beatrice, who had been preparing to 'pack up' from life for the last thirty years, was now truly tired of the business of living and hoped that in the future the state would provide facilities for VWL—Voluntary Withdrawal from Life. On 30 April 1943 she succumbed to the kidney disease which had first afflicted her ten years earlier. In 1927 she had written: 'I doubt whether one would long survive the other one—we have grown together . . .', and within four years of her death Sidney followed her. His ashes were buried beside hers at the bottom of their garden. Later that year, in response to a plea from Shaw, a sympathetic Labour government arranged for the ashes of both to be re-interred at Westminster Abbey—the first time in 900 years that husband and wife had been buried together. Appropriately, even as Beatrice's sister Rosy asked the question, no one knew which casket of ashes was Sidney's and which Beatrice's.

In their life and work the Webbs were as indistinguishable as in death. It was true, as A. G. Gardiner wrote, that they were 'two typewriters clicking as one'. When apart, Beatrice once said, each of them lived only half a life; while together, each had a double life. She also wrote, self-deprecatingly, that she was only the figurehead of the Webb firm and Sidney its backbone. However, her description in a well-known and oft-quoted passage, of how they *thought* jointly, belies this distinction:

It is a curious process, this joint thinking: we throw the ball of thought one to the other, each one of us resting, judging, inventing in turn. And we are not satisfied until the conclusion satisfies completely and finally both minds.

Shaw, who was unquestionably Sidney's closest friend, confirmed this in his Introduction to an early edition of *My Apprenticeship*: 'The collaboration is so perfect that her part in it is inextricable. I, who have been behind the scenes of it, cannot lay my hand on a single sentence and say this is Sidney or that is Beatrice.' If there was, however, as Shaw went on to admit, a separate literary Beatrice, then that Beatrice was above all reflected in the Diary. Generally, while on their travels, as in the United States and in the Far East, the Diary was a joint effort, with Sidney frequently recording events and contributing observations. There were, on the other hand, times—as on a three month visit to Scotland in 1904— when the Diary was altogether ignored, for this period was

so completely a joint existence that there was neither the desire nor the opportunity to record it in this book. When Sidney is with me I cannot talk to the other self with whom I commune when I am alone—'it' ceases to be present and only reappears when he becomes absent.

Their travels in Japan, China and India in 1911–12 were, however, fairly minutely recorded. In the Indian fragment there are ponderous passages by Sidney and more picturesque and personalized ones by Beatrice; but together they constitute an integrated whole, as if Beatrice were once again saying—as was her wont—'We think . . .', leaving her hearers to marvel how 'two minds should have so many single thoughts'.

India in 1912

The Webbs arrived in an India of which three-fifths of the area and three-quarters of the population were directly under British rule. The remainder consisted of the so-called 'native states', traditionally ruled by hereditary princes who enjoyed a measure of internal sovereignty subject to varying degrees of interference from the self-styled and widely acknowledged supreme authority of the British government in India. Just a few days before the Webbs disembarked in Calcutta the King Emperor had announced, in the Delhi Durbar, the transfer of the capital of British India from Calcutta to Delhi. This decision had, in substantial measure, been provoked by the explosive political climate in Bengal following its partition by the Curzon administration in 1905. While that decision—also by the King's Durbar speech—stood revoked, things were not to remain peaceful for long. Politically, thus, India in 1911–12 presented a picture of the lull before *and* after the storm. For if the years to come were to be tumultuous—the Rowlatt Bill controversy, the Jallianwala Bagh massacre, the rise of Gandhi and the Non-Cooperation movement—the preceding years had seen intense agitation, and revolutionary and terrorist activity both within and without Bengal. This mode of nationalist politics was by no means abandoned with the revocation of the partition. Even within the Indian National Congress, some years previously, a split had occurred between the moderate and the extremist factions, a divide that was patched up only in 1916.

The Government of India, in its *Statement exhibiting the Moral and Material Progress of India* (1913), described famine and plague, the Durbar, and 'unrest' as the three most distinctive features of the decade past. As for unrest, the government perceived it to be of two kinds: one, the legitimate aspirations of the educated Indian classes becoming increasingly articulate on questions of public welfare (such as education and sanitation), which it was the government's duty to encourage and fulfil; and the other, the 'seditious and anarchical' outrages, assassinations and speeches, which demanded stern repressive action by government. As fulfilment of the first they flourished the Indian Councils Act of 1909, popularly known as the Morley-Minto reforms, so called after the previous team of Secretary of State and Viceroy. This temporary and eventually unsuccessful palliative established, among other things, what Morley had, expressing his preference for it, described as 'constitutional autocracy' through the partial introduction of the elective principle. It was partial because, of the sixty members of the Imperial Legislative Council, only twenty-seven were to be elected. For the first time, however, Indians were placed on the councils of the Governor-General and the governors. Special provisions were made to facilitate the representation of the professional, landholding and business classes (European and Indian) and, most significantly, separate, i.e. communal, electorates were introduced. In 1912, thus, the British government in India was overwhelmingly white in composition, especially if the legislative and executive councils of the Governor-General and the governors are considered. The same could be said of the Indian Civil Service: of its 1300 members only between sixty and seventy were Indian.

A united nationalist opposition was slowly coming into being. Twenty-seven years earlier the Indian National Congress had been founded, initially following what have been called 'mendicant techniques' of supplication and petition. At the end of the first decade of the twentieth century the still young national movement had already thrown up quite an impressive galaxy of leaders—Gopal Krishna Gokhale, Pherozeshah Mehta and Mahadeo Govind Ranade among the moderates, and Bipin Chandra Pal, Lala Lajpat Rai and Bal Gangadhar Tilak among the more radical extremists. The Webbs, flattered by the attention and importance they received from nationalist quarters—as opposed to the government, which treated them as inconsequential—met and talked at length with Gokhale and Lajpat Rai.

Even early Indian nationalism was informed by an awareness of the economic dimension of imperial rule. Dadabhai Naoroji had, as far back as 1867, expounded the 'drain theory' of the extraction and remittance of India's wealth and capital by the British to England. Not only several early nationalists (including Gokhale) but also British socialists like H. M. Hyndman of the Social-Democratic Federation, had been profoundly influenced by this analysis. It was this theory, more than anything else, which popularly highlighted the exploitative dimension of British imperialism, showing the necessity for self-government.

In the economic sphere, land-revenue systems introduced by the British (particularly the Permanent Settlement of Bengal in 1793 which, incidentally, the Webbs described as 'a wise measure') had contributed to the impoverishment of the peasantry in a variety of ways. To begin with, land was, for the first time, made transferable, converting revenue farmers into proprietors, at the cost of the cultivator who, from a position of *de facto* ownership, was suddenly reduced to the status of a tenant. Losing fixity of tenure, he lost also fixity of rents. These were now pushed up at will by the zamindar and his intermediaries as the pressure on land, and the competition for it, increased. This increase, in turn, had been due to the decline of the handicrafts industries, which necessitated the absorption in agriculture of new additions to the labour force. Extortionate revenue demands placed the peasant at the mercy of the government in areas of *ryotwari* and *mahalwari* revenue-settlement as well. The difficulty of meeting excessive demands, further, invariably pushed him into the hands of moneylenders and eventually into losing his land. Even where high revenue demands were met, the peasant got little by way of return, for the government invested in the improvement of agriculture only a fraction of what it spent on developing an extensive railway network.

Simultaneously, imperial rule had encouraged the commercialization of agriculture. The area under cash crops like cotton, jute and tea increased at the expense of food crops, a process that made the peasant more vulnerable to famine, particularly at the turn of the century. Thus, overcrowding, rural indebtedness, excessive revenue demands, and the backwardness of Indian agriculture in technological terms meant that while moneylenders, landlords and merchants flourished, the ordinary peasant sank deeper into poverty and debt.

In the course of their travels the Webbs became con-
versant with only a small part of this complex web of
economic facts. On the basis of their observations they
recommended fixity of tenure, fixed rents and free sale,
claiming that areas in which the government dealt directly
with the peasant were the worst off. It is surprising that one
finds no comment on the 'drain' theory, which had already
received an airing in England through H. M. Hyndman's
The Bankruptcy of India and which, despite their distaste for
Hyndman's brand of socialist politics, the Webbs could
hardly have failed to notice.

Industrial development in India had been slow, except in
the field of railways where by 1911 there were 32,839 sq.
miles of lines in the country (inclusive of those in the
princely states), making it the fourth largest railway system
in the world. It is a well-known fact that British commercial
interests profited greatly from this expansion. The Swadeshi
movement, which came in the wake of the anti-partition
agitation, had encouraged the establishment of indigenously
owned cotton mills, which had first been set up in the mid-
nineteenth century. Nevertheless the imperial climate was
not favourable for the growth of heavy industry, and the
manufacture of steel began only with the establishment of
the Tata Iron and Steel Company in 1911, while the Tata
Hydroelectric Power Supply Company was set up a year
earlier. Industrial workers numbered only one million out
of a population of 315 million people, and despite the fact
that the industrial sector represented an insignificant proportion of all economic activity in India, and the industrial
workforce only less than one per cent of the entire workforce, the years 1905–8 were marked by industrial unrest—
strikes in printing presses, jute mills, railway workshops
and tramways. It is hardly surprising, in these circumstances, that the industrial establishments the Webbs visited
were chiefly cotton mills. They remarked upon the long
working hours, the poor working conditions, the 'baffling'
irregularities of the workers, and the absence of provisions

for Workmen's Compensation and Employers Liability. Altogether, they concluded, these mills were 'not a pleasing development' except in so far as they proved that Indians could successfully manage large-scale business enterprises.

The Webbs in India

The Webbs started their world tour in June 1911, concluding it almost a whole year later. After eight days in Rangoon and Mandalay, approximately midway through their journey, they crossed over into Bengal. The transfer of the capital to Delhi had been announced but it was to be some time yet before it was executed. In the mean time Calcutta, the commercial capital of British India, remained also its administrative capital, and it was in Calcutta that the Webbs disembarked in December 1911. Almost on arrival, they attended the twenty-sixth annual session of the Indian National Congress, originally scheduled to have been presided over by Ramsay MacDonald who eventually did not come on account of the death of his wife. Appropriately, the Webbs enjoyed for this period the hospitality of Bhupendranath Basu, a prominent Calcutta lawyer and the chairman that year of the reception committee of the Congress. Surprisingly, however, the reports of the Congress session make no mention of the Webbs' presence. For their part the Webbs described the session as a 'frost', expressing surprise at the small attendance, the uncertainty about arrangements for lunch, and the element of 'listlessness and unreality about the eloquent speeches'. The Congress could not, they said, be reproached for being 'all talk', for that was precisely what it was designed to be. They feared, however, that it stood on the brink of extinction unless an effort was made to revive or reorganize it. Calcutta also gave the Webbs a unique introduction to a traditional Indian joint-family establishment, firmly patriarchal and heirarchical in every particular. Beatrice visited the women of the household, still in purdah,

investigated the questions of status, property and deci-
sion-making, and came away with the impression that the
household was marked by dignity and charm.

Not all the hosts of the Webbs were Indian. They were
the guests also of collectors, residents, political agents and
governors—although Beatrice noted, with the amusement
of one who has a trump in reserve, that these government
officials treated them as a pair of harmless tourists. The
government appears in fact to have been right, for the
Webbs created no mischief, as their socialist compatriot Keir
Hardie had done in 1907. In Government House circles they
found themselves unutterably bored by the endless chatter
about polo, tennis and the races. In contrast to the 'conversationally destitute' English they sought out, somewhat like
E. M. Forster's English protagonists in *A Passage to India*,
the company of educated Indians with whom they felt they
could discuss philosophy, religion and the arts. The attitude
of the Webbs towards Indians as a people is, however,
somewhat ambiguous. The Indian, they noted, was no
typical Oriental. While they had thoroughly disliked the
'inscrutable' Chinese, reservedly admired the practical and
executive Japanese, they appreciated Indians as intellectual,
spiritual and 'an essentially lovable race'. It is worthwhile
ignoring the apparently patronizing quality of this description for the diary is written with disarming candour,
preserving all the prejudices and limited liberalism of the
Edwardian mind.

That is one of the great difficulties in our Government of India—a
stupid people find themselves governing an intellectual
aristocracy—the explanation being, as Gokhale more than once remarked, that the *Average man of the British race* is far superior to
the *Average man* of the Indian peoples. Until the average has been
raised the aristocracy of India will be subject to the mediocrity of
Great Britain . . .

The Webbian view of race is also of interest and importance because the early Fabians were fascinated by contem-

porary developments in biological theory in the field of
eugenics. Shaw and the Webbs appear to have been enormously impressed by Karl Pearson's ideas, which Sidney
drew upon substantially in his tract *The Decline of the Birth
Rate*, where he noted with fear and dismay that the 'abler'
classes were diminishing in number and that England might
gradually be 'falling to the Irish and the Jews'. Alongside
this fear of race deterioration, if not 'race suicide' as he
theatrically described it, was the openly warm approval of
the Fabians for the plans of Rosebery and Milner to breed an
imperial race, an aim the *New Statesman* in 1913 described as
socialist. Clearly, there is an incongruity here between their
creed and their assumptions of inequality, which is reflected
also in the Indian Diary. Throughout this document the
Webbs speak of Hindus and Muslims, of Brahmins, Kayas-
thas and Untouchables, implicitly recognizing distinctions
which they believed were reflected in physical and intellectual qualities. In a letter home Beatrice wrote: 'Some of the
Brahmins are exactly like Raphael's picture of the famous
Cardinal, whilst others have the features of Beatrice Cenci.
It is only the low castes that look negroid or mongolian.'
The Indian 'aristocracy of intellect' was superior to the
Westerner, they wrote, and the stereotypical image of the
'native' as a child was inappropriate as a description of this
section of the people: it was true only of the great mass
of the population which, if treated 'persistently as Men . . .
would probably "grow up" to Manhood'. The upper class,
on the other hand, was potentially the governing class,
and the British would do well, the Webbs recommended,
to take them into confidence and thus earn for themselves
the pride and the satisfaction of 'having been the finest race of
schoolmasters as well as the most perfect builders of an
Empire'.

It is not untypical of the European traveller at the turn of
the century to assess a nation in terms of its dominant religious tradition. In Hinduism Beatrice saw her theory of the
relation between the spheres of science and religion con-

firmed: in the 'lowest' forms of Hindu practice, she observed, superstition was supreme and science at a discount. The worshippers at Benares were 'a perturbing and even a horrible sight', the temple at Gaya was furnished with 'the usual hideous images', while those of Khajuraho were 'most grossly indecent' in their repetitive representation of 'lascivious figures'. In the 'nobler' forms of Hinduism, however, reason and the development of the intellect found a place: 'an almost perfect relation between religious emotion and intellectual life'.

Above all, the Webbs were peculiarly attracted by the 'Vedic Protestantism' of the Arya Samaj, with its emphasis on social service. In his Preface to Lala Lajpat Rai's *The Arya Samaj* (1915), a history of the movement, Sidney Webb described it as 'what may possibly prove to be the most important religious movement in the whole of India'. The historical importance of the Samaj is unquestionable, even if somewhat exaggerated by Sidney Webb. The Arya Samaj was founded in 1875 by Swami Dayanand Saraswati, the author of *Satyarth Prakash* (Light of Truth) and a popular itinerant preacher. The Samaj sought to purge orthodox Hinduism of superstition, ritual, idol worship, caste prejudice and untouchability, appealing to the Vedas as infallible and authoritative to the exclusion of all other Hindu texts. More important than the religious reform initiated by the Samaj was the work of social change and educational transformation that it undertook with great success. In the former sphere it fought against child marriage, and advocated inter-caste marriage and widow remarriage. It particularly turned its attention to the relief of the distressed and the destitute—through plague- and famine-relief work, and by the care of orphans and widows. In the realm of education, while one section of the Samaj established a wide network of Dayanand Anglo-Vedic schools and colleges (incorporating elements of modern scientific knowledge), a rival faction worked for the promotion of *gurukulas* where boys were educated in accordance with the ancient system of Hindu education. The first and most well known of these was set up at Hardwar. Beatrice and Sidney visited this institution in 1912 and appear to have been completely captivated, for in his Preface it drove Sidney to prose that is decidedly more picturesque than his usual ponderous style: 'Here, amid the beautiful scenery of the Upper Ganges', he wrote, 'within sight of the snow-clad Himalayas, there has been growing up, during the past twenty [*sic*] years, a new type of monasticism.' Since the boys were allowed to meet no women—apart from, occasionally, their mothers—Beatrice was kept out till the little scholars had been put out of sight. The curriculum, the library and the laboratories also impressed the Webbs. Despite their enthusiasm, however, they chose to reserve judgement on an institution only fifteen years old, preferring to wait and see what this eighteen-year monasticism would eventually achieve. There is no evidence that they did eventually pass any judgement.

All along their travels the Webbs met Arya Samajists. At Agra they attended a meeting of the Samaj, with a 'Havan', prayers and an essay read aloud on 'Is God a Reality?' At Lahore—and indeed throughout their journeyings in the Punjab—they were almost entirely in the company of the prominent Samajists of the region; at Gujranwala they actually stopped off to attend the Arya Samaj conference at the local gurukula. The Webbs did not miss the vital connection between Arya Samajist beliefs and nationalism in the Punjab. On the whole, so impressed were they by the Samaj's organization, achievements and purposes, that in Delhi Beatrice picked a furious argument with C. F. Andrews who tried to prick her admiration for the Samaj with stories of its seditious activities. By the time they reached Ajmer the Webbs appear to have become so popular with the Arya Samaj that 'when the train arrived . . . we tumbled out into a crowd of a dozen Hindu gentlemen, bowing and salaaming'. These turned out to be Arya Samajists, come to escort them around Ajmer to 'inspect' Arya Samaj institutions.

The Webbs's initial impressions of Lala Lajpat Rai were decidedly unfavourable: 'he has not an attractive personality—though he is pleasant tempered and open minded—but he has, at times, an unpleasant expression of successful intrigue. He looks a *Bunya*!' But Lajpat Rai quickly convinced them of the repressive policies of the government and the injustice of its land legislation, and, soon enough, 'the more we have seen of him, the more we like him. He is certainly not "loyal" to the British connection—but why should he be!' Eventually this grew into a warm friendship, much valued by Lajpat Rai. When in 1914 he visited England he was invited by the Webbs to a Fabian summer school in the Lake district. Those ten days, he recorded, were spent in delightful conversation, providing him at once with 'relaxation and instruction'.

Towards Gokhale—whom they saw much of, first at Poona and later in Bombay—the Webbs's response was altogether warmer: 'a man of singular sweetness of disposition, full of charm . . . political sagacity and calm statesmanship.' The Diary has many pages discussing Gokhale's political convictions and ideals, his Servants of India Society, and the Fergusson College at Poona with which he was so closely associated. The selfless dedication of the teachers at the college, who worked entirely gratis in the cause of nationalist education, impressed the Webbs as much as did the idea of training men for dedicated public service through the Servants of India Society. Not surprisingly, they were sympathetic to Gokhale's ideal of working slowly and incrementally—through social and educational reform, self-education and self-discipline—towards the goal of independence. Above all they were pleasantly surprised by the fact that Gokhale could speak equally admiringly of Tilak (with whom he disagreed politically) and of the spirit and work of the Arya Samaj; and so kindly about English officials, blaming the nature of alien rule rather than the individuals who represented it. They concluded, with typically Webb matter-of-factness and an element of relief, that Gokhale and his fellow workers recognized 'that a certain measure of alien rule is necessary at present'.

The Webbs's observations on the countless educational institutions they visited make this Diary quite singular in its unusual focus. It is a fair assumption to make that the recommendations on educational policy are largely the work of Sidney, who was already London's acknowledged authority in the field. They are based upon detailed observations of a wide variety of educational institutions— government 'Normal' schools, chief's colleges, gurukulas, mosque schools, missionary colleges, and so forth— virtually at every place the Webbs visited. While a government report lists the total number of educational institutions in British India (and the less important princely states) at 176,604, making a distinction only between primary and secondary schools on the one hand, and training schools, colleges and 'private institutions' on the other, the Webbs generally used a classification based on religious differences. The total number of scholars on the rolls in 1911 was 6,795,971. It is significant that it was only in 1910, just a year before the Webbs's visit, that the Education Department acquired an independent existence, with the addition of a sixth member to the Governor-General's Council to look after education: this had until that time been a part of the Home Department.

The Webbs appear to have been quite impressed by the experiments in 'national education' at Mrs Besant's Hindu Central College, Banaras, and at the Fergusson College, Poona. The latter is described as 'one of the greatest colleges in India', a community of equals with all teachers collectively administering the institution and dedicating themselves to it by voluntary vows of twenty years' service in return for meagre compensation. The Webbs noted, with the merest hint of *schadenfreude*, that it was the government's own policy of 'administrative Nihilism', of not taking the initiative in secondary and university education and leaving the field to private enterprise—that had resulted in the

growth of these colleges, entirely in the hands of nationalists, giving them an influence that was manifestly undesirable from the government's point of view. Much the same
could be said of the Arya Samaj colleges where nationalist
ideas were extremely popular. Both these types of institutions were characterized by a spirit of service and devotion
amongst their teachers which the Webbs found conspi-
cuously absent in the mosque schools they visited in the
United Provinces and the North West Frontier province.
Here, in their opinion, the maulvis were 'narrow-minded
and feeble', the curriculum limited to the Urdu language
and Islamic theology, with a distressing absence of any
Western scientific elements. Since these schools, they wrote,
could neither be ignored because thousands of boys attended
them, nor suppressed because the Koran made them obligatory, the Webbs offered a solution. It was an unoriginal
solution, borrowed from the report of the Director of Public Instruction in Sind, where the government had provided
substántial grants to such schools, enabling the purchase of
books, maps and other equipment, as also visits by peripatetic teachers for 'secular' subjects.

Sidney and Beatrice were equally dismissive of the Islamic
College, Lahore ('poor in spirit with inferior Moslem professors'), and of the Aligarh College. Disliking the principal
of the latter, they strongly recommended to a trustee in
Lahore that Hope Simpson, their favourite administrator,
be appointed his successor. They were at best willing to
concede that the mosque schools were 'extraordinarily picturesque', but no more; indeed throughout the Indian Diary
one detects an inexplicably negative strain *vis-à-vis* the
Muslim community. 'The Moslems are a slower and duller
race', Beatrice wrote home. 'They hate democracy and really
dislike Education and all that is modern.'

She also condemned the educational institutions run by
Christian orders as a failure from the missionary standpoint,
finding here a betrayal of their subscribers in England be-

cause 'the theological representatives of England in India' were incapable of an attitude of 'reciprocal superiority', of that genuine admiration for the Indian people which must be the basis of their missionary work. St Stephen's College—'practically the only University College in Delhi', (in fact there were four) had, they noted, made few converts. Nevertheless it had more to offer, in their opinion, than 'a feeble Hindoo College, of inferior grade'. The descriptions seem hardly to fit these two selfconsciously venerable institutions today. Equally unrecognizable are the Mayo College (Ajmer) and the Aitchison (then Chief's) College (Lahore) of their description, where, they remarked with obvious distaste, the sons of chiefs came accompanied by twenty-five servants, several horses, cooks, coachmen and chowkidars. Why, they asked, were these young men not taught 'personal habits' such as the use of knife and fork (instead of eating 'native style' with their fingers) that they might learn to associate with the English later?

On the basis of this varied experience the Webbs recommended—though only to Beatrice's diary—training programmes for teachers, grants-in-aid from municipal and district authorities and independent post-graduate institutions in the fields of economics, public administration, law, science and technology. They suggested also the conversion of the Educational Service into a 'covenanted' service, with some ICS recruits specializing in educational administration. However, 'the very best policy would be . . . to train clever well-bred Indians for the educational service'; in the same breath they admitted that the government would not do so for fear of sedition, the fear that had also prompted it to discourage a Boy Scouts movement for India.

The Webbs could not resist, having seldom passed up, an opportunity to influence or alter the course of events at the practical level. Armed with their observations of education in British India they arrived in Baroda state, where they found a very high percentage of children at schools which

were easily accessible to most of the population. They visited a high school in which classes were conducted in a
post office—because the headmaster in that village had to
double as the postmaster, too! Sidney lost no time in advis-
ing the Gaikwar to employ Arya Samajists in all educational
posts, nonchalantly waving aside the latter's anxious queries
as to whether he ought to seek the permission of the British
government first.

The administration of the princely states excited the
Webbs's attention and interest as much as their educational
achievements did. They visited Udaipur and Jaipur in Rajputana, Chhatarpur, Bhopal and Gwalior in Central India,
and Baroda in the west. In the two Rajput states they did not
meet the rulers but came away from the British residency in
Jaipur with the impression that political agents in the native
states hardly ever, and increasingly less so, interfered in the
affairs of these states. In Udaipur they were entertained by
the wife of the British resident at 'a rather "terrible" party',
snobbish and Anglo-Indian, describing which Beatrice severely concluded that 'these English in such Native States as
this have nothing to do, and it is just as well that those who
are fit for nothing better should be sent there'.

At Chhatarpur there took place a meeting between the
Webbs and the maharaja, of whom we find such a sad and
moving portrait in J. R. Ackerley's *Hindoo Holiday*, though
he appears in the latter work disguised as the Maharaja of
Chhokrapur. 'Poor Prince', wrote Beatrice, 'he has no one
to talk to, no one to confide in', and, while Sidney exhorted
him to 'live by admiration, hope and love', Beatrice 'captivated him by explaining the difference between science and
religion'. They proceeded thence to Bhopal, having left the
lonely monarch with a reading list consisting of the works
of Bergson, Father Tyrrell and William James, themselves
reflecting: 'It is a terrible problem how to bring up these native Rulers . . . We wonder whether a determined man
might not make a Weimar out of a little Indian State . . .'.
There is more than a hint here of avidity, and one can easily

imagine the practical streak in the Webb temperament secretly longing for some such field in which, unfettered, might be created the Fabian utopia.

In contrast to the weak and pathetic figure of the Maharaja of Chhatarpur, the Begum of Bhopal and the Gaikwar of Baroda quite overwhelmed the Webbs. If Beatrice had captivated the maharaja, in Bhopal it was her turn to be captivated by the 'energetic and enlightened' Nawab Sultan Jehan Begum who had founded a girls' school, organized a Purdah Club for lectures and talks, allowed only diploma holders to practise midwifery, and, while opposed to the movement for women's suffrage, believed that all rulers should be women. 'Not merely in education but also in Public health', wrote Beatrice, 'the dear old Begum' had proved to be more progressive than the Government of India. By the time they arrived in Gwalior the Webbs were quite emphatic that 'one can hardly say that Indians show themselves incapable of the art of government'.

This opinion was in sharp contrast to the conclusion they had arrived at in the first week or so of their travels, when they had claimed to sense among 'the Hindus' a dislike for administrative organization and 'no real interest in the problem of Government apart from the sentiment of National Home Rule.' But it was not merely their observations of the administration of the native states that had caused them to modify their earlier views: the change was as much a function of their assessment of the British administrators in India, few of whom possessed a capacity for sympathetic administration. The one exception in this respect was John Hope Simpson, collector in the Gorakhpur district, with whom the Webbs spent several days 'in camp'. Hope Simpson impressed his guests as 'almost ideal as an administrator over an alien race', and Sidney later, as Colonial Secretary, appointed him to a special post in Palestine. Simpson possessed all the physical, spiritual and human qualities that the Webbs valued. He was flexible and did not let rules and laws constrict his independent judgement as an administrator, was intimately acquainted with his subordinates, and with Indian lawyers and landowners in the district. But this intimacy, Beatrice wrote approvingly, kept within bounds by his firmness of will and energetic pace of work, never degenerated into looseness. Hardly any other civil servant the Webbs met measured up to Hope Simpson. The residents and governors were arrogant and saw the Indians only as seditious rebels, while the ex-officers from the army who had been inducted into the administration had no knowledge of or interest in administration as 'an art'. As for the middle-level Indian officials in the ICS, they were 'full of promise' for, though it was unlikely that Hope Simpsons would ever emerge from their ranks, or that they could take over the highest executive posts, they did at least help Englishmen in their enormous administrative tasks. Though they lacked the 'executive backbone', they made good judges for they were temperamentally better suited to 'the passive Act of judgement'. Sailing home in the summer of 1912 Sidney wrote:

as our acquaintance with the Indian bureaucracy has increased, and as we have more and more appreciated its alliance in the main with reactionary Imperialism and commercial selfishness in England we are less confident. Three months' acquaintance has greatly increased our estimate of the Indians, and greatly lessened our admiration for, and our trust in, this Government of officials.

Three years later, in his preface to John Matthai's *Village Government in British India*, he noted with interest and surprise that there existed in India an ancient, pre-British tradition of local village self-government which was clearly extra-legal but had survived the centuries. He remarked also that it was a system that worked efficiently on the basis of nothing more than consent and harmonious community life, transcending even caste barriers. Not surprisingly, for Sidney, the strong appeal of such a system lay in providing a 'higher alternative' ('like a Quaker meeting', he wrote) to conventional democratic procedures such as popular election and representation through the ballot-box. 'Decision by the General Sense of the Community', unlike 'Austinian pedantry', had the virtue of emphasizing the obligations of the individual to the public, thus weighting the process of justice in favour of the enforcement of duties rather than rights, as was common in Western liberal democracy. In typically Fabian fashion Sidney went on to argue that 'as a factor of effective social progress in India, the development of local government stands second in importance to scarcely any whatever'. He hinted in fact that it might be worthwhile to concentrate nationalist effort on this front because there were movements in contemporary France and England to show that government from above was 'dated':

It seems a pity that the aspirations of so many Indians for 'Indian self-government', and especially those of Indian students, should contemplate so exclusively that part of government which concerns India as a whole . . . It is the local government of Village or Municipality that touches most nearly the lives of the people. It is because they themselves run their local government, much more than in respect of any real share they have in the Dominion Governments, that these peoples are essentially 'self-governing' . . . There is here, as it seems to me, a greater and certainly a more accessible sphere for the exercise of autonomy.

The Webbs's reading of the economic situation in India led them to take what they curiously called 'the nationalist position' on the question of land revenue. They recommended the Permanent Settlement of 1793 as a wise measure, and protection for the individual small cultivator against exploitation by landlords on the one hand and excessive government demands on the other. This could be done by granting the farmer the three F's: 'Fixity of Tenure, Fair Rents and Free Sale'. They also advocated a scheme for co-operative credit societies which would use government capital for lending at low rates for 'legitimate purposes'. In fact, a fairly extensive network of co-operative credit societies had sprung up in the past eight years, most of these in the rural areas. In 1912 there were 8000 such societies, in addition to 120 central societies which lent only to other societies.

The 'fainthearted' economic policy of the government, the Webbs wrote, was due to its poverty and the small income from revenue. The sources of revenue were limited for several reasons, among them the Hindu joint family system, the low consumption of luxuries like alcohol and tobacco, and the difficulty of raising import duties on English goods for fear of offending English commercial opinion.

Under these circumstances we suggest a bold policy of government exploitation—taking into Government hands all the railways, developing the 240,000 square miles of forest by Government paper mills, match factories, timber trade, etc., and perhaps starting Government tobacco works and spirit distilleries. The I.C.S. is aghast at this, and even Gokhale does not approve, because to the Nationalists, the position is rather as it was to the *Laisser Faire* Liberals a century ago. To the Indians the Government is a hostile force, and they are loath to see it expand in any way. This cripples them in political programme, because they are always urging retrenchment.

Industrial policy and welfare were important Fabian concerns, and the Webbs visited some factories and textile mills in Agra, Bombay and Ahmedabad. They were appalled at the low levels of pay (usually on a daily-wage basis), the squalor of the living and working conditions of the workers, the long hours, the absence of basic amenities like ventilation and fire escapes, and insufficient factory inspection—hardly surprising when the entire country had just four factory inspectors. In the Indian-owned cotton mills of Bombay and Ahmedabad the Webbs noticed reasonable conditions of work, and benevolent and paternalistic managements which proved that 'the Indians . . . can successfully manage business enterprise on a large scale'. The factory they visited in Agra, on the other hand, was owned by two Europeans, the John brothers, who constantly complained of the idleness and the sulky and hostile attitudes of their workers. From this the Webbs concluded that the Europeans had not yet learnt

the art of managing the Indians. What is equally clear is that the Indian is sometimes an extraordinarily difficult worker *to sweat*. He does not care enough for his earnings. He prefers to waste away in semi-starvation rather than overwork himself. However low his standard of life, his standard of work is lower—at any rate when he is working for an employer whom he does not like. And his irregularities are baffling.

Fellow Travellers

The Webbs and their fellow Fabians have frequently been described as social-imperialists: seemingly an incongruity since, logically, socialism is antithetical to and incompatible with imperialism. Nevertheless it is not difficult to see how, in many respects, an imperialist position could in fact follow from a general Fabian one. The Fabian standard of civilization was unquestionably an ethnocentric and Eurocentric one, in the racial as well as the cultural sense. This motif is reflected in the Indian Diary. Similarly the question of nationalism vs. internationalism, which was to have a deep and divisive impact on European socialism in World War I, revealed the Fabians ranged staunchly on the side of a narrow nationalism. It was, however, the Boer War which was the first test not merely of the Fabian Society but also of the Webbs. Sidney, in particular, was reluctant to be drawn into the controversy (to the point where he stopped reading about it), having decided that his sympathies were with Asquith and Haldane. To Beatrice this war represented a blow to the 'ruling race' in so far as it demonstrated the superiority of the Boers.

On the institutional and administrative front, too, the Fabian ideals of a vast but centrally controlled government apparatus, of efficient large-scale enterprise, of a trained bureaucracy, and of the imperative need for conducting government by experts devoted to science and statistics, led them, it would seem irrevocably, towards a position not distant from an imperialist one. And certainly the Webbs's interest in Indian administration, in the recruitment and functioning of the bureaucracy, in the municipal allocations for education, in the education of princes and, finally, their concern for the absence of any conception of administration as 'an art', all reflect the essential Fabianness of their account. They were indifferent to the economic basis of British rule in India, hardly aware of a growing nationalist consciousness, and were completely ignorant of and even failed to raise structural questions.

In this, the difference between the Webbs and their fellow Fabians on the one hand, and their socialist contemporaries on the other, is one of degree rather than of kind. H. M. Hyndman of the Social-Democratic Federation and Keir Hardie of the Independent Labour Party had, like the Webbs, not questioned the basis of the British presence in India. None of them envisaged, or even considered desirable, the end of the Raj. Even Hyndman, whose attack on British rule in India was the most scathing, had a vision of a socialist Britain which, instead of dismantling the empire, would humanize and reform it. The Fabians—including the Webbs—saw the colonies in need of guidance for a long time to come, though their conception of guidance was essentially municipal, with education and sanitation at its very core. This inherent moderation of the early British socialist tradition on India finds reflection, in later years, in the moderation of the Labour party's India policy.

However, the Indian Diary of Sidney and Beatrice Webb is not only an account by two Fabians of society and politics in India in 1912, but also an immensely readable travelogue. Beatrice had often, particularly in her younger years, confided to her Diary her wish to be a novelist, and we find frequent references in the early entries to George Eliot (incidentally a friend of Herbert Spencer), and especially to the character of Maggie Tulliver in *The Mill on the Floss*:

This last month or so I have been haunted by a longing to create characters and to move them to and fro among fictitious circumstances—to put the matter plainly, by the vulgar wish to write a novel! In those early morning hours when one's half-awakened brain seems so strangely fruitful, I see before me persons and scenes; I weave plots, and clothe persons, scenes and plots with my own philosophy of all things, human and divine. There is intense attractiveness in the comparative ease of descriptive writing. Compare it with work in which movements of commodities, percentage, depreciations, averages and all the ugly horrors of commercial facts are in the dominant place, and *must remain so* if the work is to be worthful.

This fragment of her Diary particularly reflects Beatrice's talent for picturesque and evocative prose. In her very matter-of-factness lies an attractive singularity. Beatrice's observations were, at all times, sharp, witty and imaginative. But while in England the nuggets were tucked away in relatively obscure corners of largely dull accounts of trade-union conferences and committee meetings, on holiday the quality of writing became less restrained and more relaxed—perhaps also, to some extent, free from anxious glances at posterity. Fortunately, though, this last did not prevent the Diary from being meticulously and regularly maintained, with observations covering the minutest detail. The Indian Diary is also, in a sense, a more private work, for it does not appear to have been written for publication. This impression is reinforced by the fact that not a single paper or book emerged out of it. In subsequent years India was a problem that barely interested the Webbs. Despite stray references, such as an account of a visit by Rabindranath Tagore or of a party hosted by the Maharaja of Alwar in London, or even the occasional comment on Indian politics, there is nothing to suggest that a longer-term interest had been sparked off.

It is interesting to compare the Webb Diary with other,

more or less contemporary, accounts of travellers in India. Clearly, it lacks the narrative quality of J. R. Ackerley's *Hindoo Holiday*, a fictionalized account of a six-month visit to Chhatarpur as private secretary to the maharaja. Ackerley has given his book a novel-like quality by stringing together amusing descriptions of his encounters with the maharaja, the dewan, his Urdu teacher, and the servants at the state guest house. Primarily, however, it is the story of the rather pathetic dissipations of a minor ruler, his obsession for acquiring attractive young boys who, dressed like various gods of the Hindu pantheon, would participate in a nightly entertainment of music and dance. The maharaja's superstitions, his attempts at self-education, his ambition of building a Greek villa, are all objects of ridicule, albeit affectionate. In the Webb Diary, too, there is a certain pathos evoked by the spiritual longings and intellectual naivete of the same prince, but while Ackerley's is the more entertaining and charming account, the Webbs's is undoubtedly the more compassionate.

Ackerley came to Chhatarpur on the recommendation of E. M. Forster, who had made the acquaintance of the maharaja on his first visit to India in 1912–13. On this visit Forster, like the Webbs, had travelled widely, in the company of his friends Goldsworthy Lowes Dickinson and R. C. Trevelyan. His novel *A Passage to India* (which led Beatrice to describe the author as 'a genius, and not merely a man with an exquisite gift for words'), begun around this time, suggests that Forster was more receptive to India than were the Webbs. In comparison, his *Indian Journal* for this period, while absorbing, holds little attraction. It is less formally written up than the Webb Diary and reads rather like brief notes on the major—usually trivial—events of the day, including and especially 'atmospheric' details of food and drink, diarrhoea and discomfort, furniture, clothes, journeys, sounds and smells. There is an account of the Magh Mela at Allahabad, but it nowhere approaches the completeness and descriptive quality of the Webbs's.

However, from his letters home on a later visit (1921), Forster compiled and published *The Hill of Devi*, an account of his stay at Dewas in central India. Given their epistolary source the tone of these observations—on life in a princely state—is often light-hearted, and the possibilities for comparison with the Webbs's remarks on the same theme are therefore limited. Moreover, unlike the Webbs, Forster's view was that of a relative insider, for he came to Dewas as Temporary Private Secretary to the ruler, Sir Tukoji Rao Puar III. In the nine months or so he spent there, Forster formed a deep attachment to the maharaja and developed, by extension, a strong loyalty towards his state, with the affairs of which he seems to have identified himself quite completely. Thus, he speaks censoriously of the bad manners of the Political Department, and of how 'we made Adams [the political Agent] behave'. Indeed Forster saw himself as 'a resident Voltaire', immensely pleased by the thought that there was no European other than himself within a radius of twenty miles. He entered into the celebration of local festivals and marriages with considerable enthusiasm, enrobed in Indian raiment and squatting on the floor to eat. Clearly one cannot imagine the Webbs in such a spirit of self-abandon.

In an essay written in 1922 Forster asserted that in India, as all over the world, a new spirit was abroad—the democratic spirit of protest and questioning. He recognized that the princes in India now received more civil treatment from the British because they were being cultivated as counterweights to nationalist aspirations—forcefully expressed through the Non-Co-operation movement of the previous year—of the peoples of British India. In this recognition of nationalism as the most significant new political force Forster has the advantage of the Webbs, though it is important to remember that he enjoys also the advantage of time: a decade had elapsed between their visits in which political developments had taken a new turn, especially with the emergence of Gandhi.

Count Hermann Keyserling's *Indian Travel Diary of a Philosopher* (1925), a diary of travels in India in 1911–14, stands in sharp contrast to Forster's purely descriptive journal. This is an attempt to explore an unknown land on an altogether different plane and uses geographical locations— Rameswaram, Adyar, Chittor, Agra, Calcutta and Benares, among others—as springboards for reflections on metaphysics and religion. Keyserling himself recommended that his book be read as a novel, as 'an inwardly conceived and inwardly coherent work of fiction'. He came to India not out of tourist curiosity but impelled by a desire for self-realization, to allow 'the Indian mode of consciousness' to work its 'spell' on him. Thus, in Benares, sunrise on the river Ganges makes of him a sun worshipper, for in this manifestation of 'Divine creative power' he can feel 'the grace of supreme revelation'. There are observations on yoga, 'the culture of concentration'; on the concept of a pilgrimage, now forgotten in Europe; on the problem of realization in the Hindu metaphysic; and on the importance of faith, devotion and piety in religion. The Webbs's is not, like Keyserling's, a reflective diary, but it similarly eschews the exotic and the trivial, managing successfully to tread the very narrow path between the dull and serious on the one hand and the inconsequentially frivolous on the other.

The Webbs responded to institutions more than to people or places, and to people more than to places. Thus, they were happiest at gurukulas, colleges, famine-relief works and factories. The people they liked best, too, were those whose lives and personalities were closely bound up with ideals and institutions—as, for example, Gokhale and the Fergusson College; Lajpat Rai and the Arya Samaj; and Hope Simpson and enlightened administration. For the rest, Beatrice was entertainingly dismisive: the Afghans to her resembled 'our idea of Abraham, Isaac and Jacob', and were 'a people . . . which breaks nearly every Commandment, and is apparently of no earthly use in the universe'.

The Taj Mahal, the temples at Khajuraho and Mount Abu, and the Qutub Minar at Delhi are among the few places of historical interest that the Webbs visited, but none of these monuments are honoured with more than a few casual lines. A notable exception is the description of the Ardh Kumbh Mela at Allahabad, probably one of the most picturesque period accounts available. Strangely, though, no city impressed them as did Gwalior.

Gwalior is the most wonderful *Indian* city that we have seen. In all the cities of British India the 'native city' is always 'slummy' in character—narrow alleys, dirty and ill-paved, such fine houses as there are tumbling into decay or degraded by being used as warehouses or tenement houses. But at Bhopal, and still more at Gwalior, one finds broad streets, beautifully carved balconies, doors and latticed windows, mosques and temples, old and new Palaces, all telling of the Indians in possession of their own country, making for a civilised India 'without the English'.

Above all, there is an admirable intrepidity about the Webbs's travels—a journey on an elephant to the Nepalese border; a visit to the North West Frontier Province; and several days 'in camp' with a district collector. And all this at the ages of fifty-three and fifty-four.

The Indian Diary reflects most of the significant traits, personal and intellectual, of this remarkable pair of individuals. Despite the fact that it was Beatrice's diary, Sidney frequently contributed to this fragment, and, as with all their other joint works, it is hard to distinguish between their individual contributions.

The Webbs were accustomed to rewarding themselves with a holiday once every two or three years, usually upon completion of a book. Their Eastern holiday came in the wake of a particularly exacting campaign against the Poor Law. And yet one is struck by the fact that this Diary is so rarely self-indulgent, and so characteristically severe. The Webbs were probably incapable of being simply holidaymakers. Wherever they happened to be their intelligent curiosity would fasten upon something that was sociologically significant, and then focus on it to the exclusion of almost everything else. They were fairly impervious to what would have been for the average English traveller an onslaught upon the Anglo-Saxon senses, of unusual peoples, cultures and places, or, at the very least, of novelty. All this the Webbs took more or less in their stride. There is no excited squealing here over maharajas: on the contrary their brisk matter-of-factness promptly converts such an encounter into an opportunity for dispensing advice on how to govern in accordance with Fabian principles of public administration.

While Norman Mackenzie has appropriately expressed surprise at the 'curious detachment' of the Webbs who 'seldom afterwards referred to their experiences or made any serious effort to evaluate them', it is equally surprising that a travel journal not intended for any specific academic or political purpose should be maintained on this scale. How much easier it might have been for two such constant and prolific workers to give the pen and the mind a much-needed holiday. But that would have been out of character for the firm of Webb: and happily so, else we would not have available to us these pages of such an unusual and enjoyable diary.

Calcutta, 4 January 1912

We were met on our arrival in Calcutta by Mr. Minet, representative of Messrs. Longmans, Green & Co. (who brought with him a personal servant for us), and by the Hon. Bhupendra Nath Basu[1]—the Chairman of the reception committee of the Indian National Congress which we had come to Calcutta to attend. For the next week we lived in the patriarchal establishment of this distinguished Hindu gentleman. For the whole time I was ill, and I am still in a somewhat miserable condition. But before I forget I should like to record the impressions of a Hindu Household.

There were three separate houses joined together by covered passages—a large handsome guest house of the ordinary European style of these parts, a house for women and children (somewhat like a respectable tenement house with balcony outside and another balcony running round an interior court), and a smaller and shabbier edition for the servants. The family consisted of our host and his wife, two widowed sisters and some thirty or forty young people of

[1] Bhupendra Nath Basu (1859–1924), a prominent lawyer and nationalist, was President of the Indian National Congress in 1914. A member, successively, of the Bengal Legislative Council, the Imperial Legislative Council, and the Council of the Secretary of State for India (1917–23), he was also, for a time, Vice-Chancellor of Calcutta University.

two generations—sons and nephews and their wives and
their children. The ladies were 'Purdah', and lived in seclusion, and never left their establishments except on pilgrimages, or in the case of the married ladies to visit their own
mothers.

To this establishment I was taken by our host on the
afternoon of our arrival and I paid three or four other visits
during our stay. There was one decently furnished room—
the library and office of our host—bare of all furniture but a
writing table, some bookcases, two ordinary office
armchairs, and a couch prepared for sleeping. All the rest of
the house was made of dark and dingy bedrooms—one or
two with little ante-chambers—each provided with a four
post bed or a couple of single beds and with little other
furniture. There was a singular absence of any little belongings and the place might have been inhabited by quite poor
persons. It perhaps resembled most a conventual establishment—but a convent would have had Images and Altars
and books and pictures. The internal court, which was the
only place in which the Purdah ladies could take exercise,
was a bare dull yard, with no scrap of vegetation, and with
iron netting over the top of it to prevent birds from descending into it. The sounds of children's voices gave a
touch of humanity, but I have rarely seen such depressing
surroundings outside grinding poverty.

But there was no sign of depression among the ladies
themselves. Our host's wife was a woman of singular
charm, with the expression of the Mother Superior of a
Catholic Convent—gentle, peaceful but with a look of command and with a certain shrewd humour. Among the
young wives was a lively young person, who spoke perfect
English and, either as interpreter of her aunt-in-law, or on
her own account, carried on a lively conversation with me.
Her aunt approved of 'Purdah'—'only by this institution
could the woman's energy be reserved for her family'—they
were too busy with the children to be dull, and had they not
the companionship of their own and each other's hus-

bands—besides the pilgrimages to Holy Places, when they were 'out of Purdah'. I am not sure that my clever little friend was quite of the same opinion and she signified that if her husband were 'to command her' she would go to England with him and thereby break for good and all, her caste. Still, she would not like any of her husband's younger brothers to marry a 'Brahmo'[2] lady—they would not receive her into the family. They had many friends who came to see them who were "Brahmo", but they would not like one of their own men to marry an outcast. They were not permitted to appear before their husband's eldest brother except completely veiled, and they might not address him, but they laughed and talked as much as they liked with all the other brothers-in-law and with their cousins and nephews. The hardest part of the system was the life of the widows— they were debarred from seeing anyone outside the family, they could only eat rice and they had to fast both from food and water for twenty-four hours on the 11th of each month. Also she disapproved of the child marriages—the eldest girl of her uncle had been married at seven, and sent to her husband at nine years old. Sometimes the poor children cried so much that they had to be sent back home. Now her cousins were being married at 13 or 14. She herself had married very late—17 years old she was when she left the Convent School where she learnt her English. (Our host told us that he had selected her because his nephew had been many years in England taking his medical degrees and that therefore he wanted a companion as a wife). The other ladies were speechless—one or two had not only the inevitable bangles but Anklets and Nose Rings which gave their pretty faces an unpleasantly barbarous look. All these ladies were light skinned Hindoos with graceful figures; clothed in white

[2] Adherents of the Brahmo Samaj, a theistic society founded by Raja Rammohun Roy in Calcutta in 1828. The Samaj questioned the infallibility of the scriptures and undertook social reform in the areas of widow remarriage; the spread of education, particularly for women; and the abolition of caste distinctions.

muslin with coloured borders and with bare feet. In spite of the curiously disorderly bareness and gloom of the rooms—the absence of any personal belongings showing character and taste—the Purdah establishment had a charm of its own—the charm of love of parent, mate, and child, and the capacity of subordinating all personal desires for the good of the family. The discipline seems absolute. The male Head of the family—our host—was obeyed in his lightest word or wish by all the grown up men and women. The grave and handsome men who every now and again appeared in the Guest House always opened up communication with us with "My Uncle" or "My father" "told me to take you here or there". These men never ate with us, but if our host was absent or late for a meal they always accompanied us to the table and sat and talked to us. Directly he came they either sat silent or left the room. Apparently they and their wives never spoke to each other in the presence of one of the Elders—of their father or uncle, of their mother or aunt, or even in that of the widowed sisters of our host. Indeed these widows of the first generation are joint directress with the wife of the reigning Male, and are even given precedence on account of the sanctity of their widowhood.

There were about thirty or forty servants—15 women (all widows of low caste)—and about as many men—two Brahmins as cooks.

All the property is held in common and cannot be alienated except with the consent of all the Elders—both men and women. Where exactly this joint ownership ends, and what is the degree of relationship that entitles a person to support, no one quite knows. Probably every Hindu is entitled to be supported by his nearest relation having the means to do it.

With our host we had long conversations. He is a serious minded moderate man—tall and large and somewhat heavy featured. He is a Pleader in a large practice and has been a lifelong reformer of moderate views. He professed enlightened opinions on Purdah, the seclusion of widows, and child marriages. He had married his first little girl at an early age because his mother insisted on it and he could not disobey her. He had asked his wife to come to England with him, but she had begged to be excused, and he had not liked to insist on her breaking caste and violating her religious feelings. Any of his womenkind were at liberty to give up Purdah directly they desired to do so—he put no restrictions on their actions—they settled everything among themselves. The family system was too deeply rooted in the Hindu thought and feeling to make it possible to break through it. And it was clear that our host really approved of it. As for the widows, their life was hard, but then they were treated with the utmost reverence in high caste families and those of the older generation were always given precedence in authority even to the wife of the Male Head—while even the younger widows were consulted and deferred to when the young wives would be expected to obey without discussion. The absoluteness of the authority of the Head of the family prevented quarrels or troubles among the younger folk.

My general impression of this household was one of great happiness and considerable dignity and personal charm. Both men and women were tall, good looking and intelligent with grave and graceful manners. The servants were far more efficient than the Eastern servants of European households, and the Steward was a sort of friend of the family, who seemed on terms of equality with the sons and the nephews.

The Indian National Congress, which we had come to attend (in order to have the opportunity of making acquaintance with Hindoos and Mohammedans from all parts of India), proved rather a 'frost'. There were only between four and five hundred delegates, instead of twice or thrice that number; the great 'Pandal' or temporary Congress hall—a vast tent—constructed for 6000 spectators, was seldom more than half full, and there was an element of listlessness and unreality about the eloquent speeches. The decline of the Congress was admitted by its managers, and it was (by one or other of them) attributed to a combination of causes, some transient but others lasting; viz., (a) the competition of the Delhi Durbar, which many delegates had attended, and were unable to afford another trip; (b) a feeling that by securing partially elective legislative Councils[3] the Congress had both done all that it could practically accomplish and rendered its own continuance as the only exponent of native Indian opinion largely unnecessary; (c) the loss of energy and 'driving power' consequent on the secession of the 'extremists' at the Surat Congress some four years ago, which had never been made up; and (d) the growth, especially among the younger men, of discontent at the oligarchical management of the Congress by a little knot of 'old gang' who (for fear lest things should be said that would discredit them as being 'extreme' or 'seditious') always kept everything 'cut and dried'.

Certainly the Congress differed vitally in this respect from a great English popular conference, such as those of the Co-operators or Trade Unionists. All the resolutions were chosen and formulated by the 'Subjects Committee' (meeting in private, and having really no time); all the speakers were chosen beforehand by that Committee, and their names printed and announced beforehand; there was no room for any amendment (I doubt whether one would have been allowed), nor any chance for a mere delegate to rise to speak. Under these circumstances, although fifty or sixty eloquent speeches, by as many different Indians from all parts of the country, of all races, all three religions, all shades of brownness, and all possible varieties of dress and headdress, had some interest in themselves, they did not

[3] In 1909 the Indian Councils Act (frequently referred to as the Morley-Minto reforms) was passed, which raised the number of members in the Legislative Council to 60, of whom 27 were to be elected. However, the official majority was retained, the elections were mostly indirect, and, for the first time, the principle of separate—i.e. communal—electorates was recognized.

amount to a 'congress' or conference of opinions. It was impossible to gather anything of the real feelings of the rank and file of the delegates, or of those of the delegates, or of those of the thousand spectators. Nor was there any attempt to put more than one side of a question—practically no more than a single section of a side—or to debate difficulties or objections.

There was a curious uncertainty as to the hours of beginning, adjourning for lunch and concluding; a curious vagueness as to the arrangements for lunch etc; and a curious lack of explicit instructions to the delegates as to details. But the actual organisation of the meeting and the crowd was well done; and the vast tent, or, rather awning on countless pillars, open at all the sides, was quite free from the 'stuffiness' of an English meeting.

Our impression is that unless something is done to revive and reorganise the Congress it will 'peter out'. This would be a pity, as it does represent the only approach to a national opinion in India, and the very fact of men from all parts, all races, all religions, all castes, and all professions meeting together is a useful thing. It is no reproach to the Congress that it is 'all talk'—that is what it is intended to be, nor is it any reproach to say that these five hundred highly educated, widely cultured and usually travelled gentlemen—predominantly lawyers and editors, with a sprinkling of landlords and business capitalists, and such lecturers and teachers and medical men as not forbidden as government servants to take part—are not 'representative' of the 250,000,000 of peasant cultivators, petty retailers, jobbing craftsmen, artisans and labourers of India. They do not claim to 'resemble' them, any more than an elected Legislature of rich men and bourgeoisie resembles the millions of wage earning labourers in whose name it legislates. The Congress is a very useful means of exposition of the real and growing discontent of the educated class of Indians at being virtually excluded from deciding on the policy of the Government of their country. It is an absurd calumny, as regards the vast majority of them, to say that they individually want Government posts. They are, nearly all of them, too old for first appointment to any branch of the Civil Service; many of them are too wealthy or have too good occupations of their own to be tempted by official salaries.

At Basu's house and that of some other members of the Congress we met a good number of these cultivated Hindoos—also we steamed up and down the River Ganges for five or six hours, with some hundreds of them. Our impression is one of good looks, good manners, a quiet intelligence—a race that is, at any rate superficially, more attractive to Europeans than any other Orientals whom we have seen. They are, in fact, more like South Italians than they are like the Japanese or the Chinese. They are brought nearer to us by their training in English History and English literature—by the fact that they are to a large extent accepting the Public School University Englishmen as the model upon which to mould themselves. On the other hand, you can perceive in them almost a contempt for organisation and a dislike for administration—no real interest in the problems of government apart from the sentiment of National Home Rule. They are, I imagine, all individualists at heart, and think our craving after governmental efficiency wholly disproportionate to its value. Their family, their caste, and their religion, these are still the threefold centre of their life in spite of a perpetual striving to take their part in European sports and European political life.

Among the most interesting and attractive Hindoos are the Brahmo Samaj ladies—ladies who have chosen to abandon caste and break with Purdah. These are sometimes the wives of wealthy Brahmins and other high castes; they are frequently cultivated and able; and nearly always pretty and well-dressed. They have started a Girls High School, and an educational movement among the Purdah ladies. And, curiously enough, they are not treated even by orthodox Hindoos as outcast or in any way objectionable—they are merely accepted as *another caste*. Indeed the breakings of caste usually make a new caste, which soon passes from the first stage of opposition into an orthodoxy of its own. The Brahmo Samaj, however, seems more likely to become like the Unitarians, a general liberalising influence, and to lose its separate existence. These Brahmo ladies were all ardent Nationalists—more out-spoken than their husbands.

One of the most distinguished of the Hindus we met was Professor J. C. Bose.[4] He had made some remarkable discoveries in the nervous system of plants; and explained to us his experiments with interesting lucidity. He had an eager, graceful mind (more like an Italian than any other nationality); he was a moderate Nationalist, with a settled feeling that sooner or later the Hindu must govern his own country.

His wife was a bitter nationalist—did not believe that the English would ever relinquish their hold as a governing race until they were forced to by the growth of militant Hinduism. We thought we recognised among all these Hindus a certain pessimism with regard to the practicability of their ideals—the fear that we had driven a wedge between the Hindu and the Mohammedan, that would divide the Indian world; and that, even within Hinduism, caste was too strong to make popular government possible. 'How can you have democracy', sighed Gokhale, 'with fifty millions of untouchables?'

The Unification of Bengal was received with real enthusiasm, but our Bengalee friends were for the most part

[4] Jagdish Chandra Bose (1858–1937) was Professor of Physics at Calcutta University when the Webbs visited India. After many years of research in electrical radiation, he returned to the study of plant and animal life through the use of sensitive instruments for establishing the effects of sleep, air, light, food, fatigue, etc. on plants, in order to show a parallel between plant and animal responses. Bose was knighted in 1916 and made a Fellow of the Royal Society in 1920. In 1917 he founded the Bose Research Institute, Calcutta, and was its Director till 1937. He was the author of *Response in the Living and Non-Living* and *Plant Responses as a Means of Physiological Investigation*.

downcast about the removal of the capital.[5] Some of the younger men professed to rejoice even at that, because so long as the Viceroy of India was at Calcutta, real autonomy for Bengal was impossible. But the elder men shook their heads over the removal of the Government of India from all popular influences. The higher the official the more sympathetic; and the Central Government was more sympathetic than the Local Government. They feared not having access to the Viceroy and the Heads of Departments.

So far as we could judge from the look of the crowds at all the great shows of the King's visit,[6] the Emperor King was really popular and the people appreciated his coming to India and his free and easy way of going about. A Bengalee crowd is an attractive crowd—eager, gentle, responsive, and brimming over with enjoyment of the outing. The enormous number of 'Gharries' (the native carriage), holding women and children inside, and boys and men outside, that crowded on to the Maidan gave one the feeling of a great National celebration. Of course, the cultivated Hindu professed to be bored with the whole thing, or to deprecate the expense; but I think he was a little bit 'put out' by the obvious enthusiasm of the crowd.

Throughout our stay in Calcutta I was invalided with chronic catarrh which is still clinging to me. We saw little or nothing of the Government of India—which naturally enough was absorbed in the Royal visit. They have given us a bevy of formal introductions to officials on our route, and have arranged for us 'to camp out' with a collector. But they have showed no sign of wishing to see us. And we

[5] The unrest in Bengal following its partition in 1905, the more central geographical location of Delhi, as also its symbolic significance as the capital of many earlier kingdoms, were among the reasons that prompted the government to transfer the capital of British India from Calcutta to Delhi. The decision was announced by the King-Emperor at the Durbar in December 1911.

[6] The visit of King George and Queen Mary to India, to attend the Coronation Durbar of 1911.

were not sent an invitation to the Government House Garden Party! But even such invitations as we got from the Europeans, I was unable to accept; except a lunch with Sir Harcourt Butler[7] (member for Education in the Viceroy's Council) and Sir Richard Carlyle[8] (member for Agriculture, Viceroy's Council, and brother of Rev. A. J. Carlyle of Oxford)—both able, and broad minded men. They professed to agree that more Hindus must be taken into the higher branches of the Civil Service; that the Army must be opened to them; but they were not keen on it, and they objected to any particular way of doing it.

We saw something of an attractive wealthy Hindoo family—that of the Bonnerjees, who own land in Bengal. Bonnerjee is the son of the Chairman of the First National Congress 26 years ago;[9] he was himself educated at Rugby and went to Balliol; he is married to a highly cultivated Hindoo lady who is a member of the Brahmo Somaj; and they live in a large house in Calcutta which (unlike that of Bhupendra Nath Basu) had all the charm and drawing room comfort of an English home, coupled with the openness and magnitude of the Oriental home. Bonnerjee's position exemplified strikingly the practical exclusion of the Indians from public affairs. This wealthy young landlord, a man of local position and influence, cultivated and travelled, thoroughly equipped for public life, and apparently anxious to be of use

[7] Sir Spencer Harcourt Butler (1869–1938) of the Indian Civil Service was a member of the Governor-General's Executive Council from 1910 to 1915. In 1915 he was appointed Lieutenant-Governor of Burma, and in 1918 of the United Provinces of Agra & Oudh.

[8] Richard Carlyle is actually Robert Carlyle (1859–1934) of the Indian Civil Service. He was Chief Secretary, Bengal Government; Secretary, Revenue and Agriculture Departments, Government of India; and ordinary member of the Governor-General's Council (1910–15).

[9] W. C. Bonnerjee (1884–1906), a prominent Calcutta lawyer and one of the founders of the Indian National Congress. He presided over the first session at Bombay in 1885.

in the world, had not been made of any use by the Government of India. In England he would have been a member of his County Council, an active J.P., possibly a Poor Law Guardian in his own parish, and probably also an M.P. In India he had no sort of public function to work at. It does not seem ever to have occurred to a Governor General, or a Lieutenant Governor, that one of his many Private Secretaries and A.D.C.'s might well be an Indian gentleman of education and position such as Bonnerjee. Of course, there are now District Boards and Municipal Councils in India, having elected members, and there are even elected members of Legislative Councils, to which Bonnerjee might aspire. But the former are still extremely unimportant, uninfluential and, indeed, 'unreal' creations; and the latter (where the Indian members have no real power) have been so hedged about by qualification requirements as to make ineligible for election, not only Bonnerjee, but also such leaders as Bhupendra Nath Basu (whom the Government thereupon nominated) and S. P. Sinha[10] (who has the distinction of being the first unofficial Indian to be nominated a member of the Viceroy's Executive Council—he resigned shortly afterwards, finding it interfered too much with his law practice, and was replaced by Imam Ali).[11]

[10] Satyendra Prasanna Sinha (Lord Sinha) (1864–1928) was the first Indian to become Advocate-General of Bengal, and legal member of the Viceroy's Executive Council (1909–10). Later, he was Under-Secretary of State for India (1919), and Governor of Bihar and Orissa (1920). He also presided over the 1915 session of the Indian National Congress.

[11] Sir Syed Ali Imam (1869–1932) succeeded Lord Sinha as legal member of the Viceroy's Executive Council in 1910. In 1919 he was appointed the first President of the Executive Council of the Nizam of Hyderabad. He served on the bench of the Patna High Court and played an important part in the creation of Bihar as a separate province. He was also President of the Amritsar Session (1908) of the All India Muslim League.

Benares, 10 January 1912

We were glad to leave Calcutta after twelve days stay, as the distractions and crowds consequent on the Royal Visit made things extremely uncomfortable, and gave us few opportunities of talking with representative people. We accordingly left on the evening of the Pageant (5 January) for Gaya, in order to see Buddhgaya, the scene of Sakya Muni's meditations under the Bo tree, and now a renowned centre of pilgrimage for the Buddhist world. After a night in the train, we turned out on the platform in the cold grey dawn at six o'clock, intending to drive to the Dak Bungalow (there being no hotel). But a young official whom we had met at dinner at Calcutta had been telegraphing to the Collector (to whom we had no introduction); with the result that we found ourselves accosted by a quite unintelligible 'Chuprassee', or Government Messenger, and found a smart carriage and pair waiting, for whom there were no other possible occupants than ourselves. None of the servants could explain clearly who it was they were to carry off; but at last we decided to risk it; we were whirled away to the Collector's house; received by obviously expectant servants; invited to bedroom and bath; and urged to begin breakfast—all without being quite sure who was our host or whether we were really his guests. He presently emerged from bed, and made himself extremely hospitable—a man (Whitty) of about 36, with 12 years service, whose wife was in England. He sent us to Buddhgaya (8 miles) in state in his carriage, with a large tiffin basket; brought the local Civil Surgeon (Conor) to meet us at dinner; and sent us to the station next morning in time to pick up the train at six o'clock for Benares.

Buddhgaya was not particularly interesting in itself, and cannot be recommended for architectural beauty. But this lofty pyramidal shrine, enclosing various images of Buddha, and protecting the original Bo tree under which he sat (or rather a tree descending by continuous 'shoots' and reproductions from that original of 2500 years ago) had a real historical attraction. The remnants of the stone railing erected by Asoka 1600[1] years ago are certainly authentic. We saw pilgrims from Bhutan and Burma worshipping; and we made an attempt to see the Mahant or Abbot of the (Hindu) monastery in whose charge the shrine is. But all the monks were absent (the Abbot at Calcutta!); and all we saw of interest were two elephants in the monastery compound; and a Shan Raja (Burma), who was a pilgrim, distributing farthings in alms to each member of a vast crowd.

On our way back we drove to the native town of Gaya (70,000 population) and walked through its narrow streets to the 'Vishnupad' Temple (Hindoo), with the usual hideous images, and grossly superstitious observances by the crowds of Hindoo pilgrims, on whom the Brahmans were levying toll.

In the afternoon we found a young official (Paterson) who was 'Assistant Magistrate', temporarily living with the Collector and *who was in the first month of his service*, and was accordingly trying his 'prentice hand' at the administration of justice, imposing fines up to 50 Rupees and imprisonment up to a month. We were interested to see the I.C.S. thus in the making—the bright young Oxford youth, with

---

[1] Asoka reigned from 273 to 232 BC. Beatrice is obviously calculating on the basis of AD rather than BC.

the public school manner, just beginning to develop into the bureaucrat. It is certainly a remarkable thing, this annual export of sixty or seventy young men to be posted to all parts of India, nearly all of identical school and university training, all cast in the same mould as to dress, manners, language and habits and (to a great extent) also opinions and prejudices. India itself may be as diverse as Europe; but its administration and its governing bureaucracy can hardly fail to be, from Cape Comorin to the Himalayas, 'all of a piece', with infinitely greater similarity or uniformity than exists in England alone.

We spent five days in Benares, having tea with the Commissioner (Moloney), and dining with the Collector (Streatfield), the latter turning out to be a brother of the supporter of National Committee[2] who has just married Miss Lucy Deane. But our chief interests in Benares were unofficial. We had an introduction to a wealthy old Hindoo gentleman (Raja Madhava Lal),[3] who had been given the title of Raja and made C.S.I. because of his wealth, loyalty, public spirit and past service on the Legislative Council. He sent his grandson and carriage to meet us, and called at our hotel, but by accident we failed to see him that day, and then he had to go to Lucknow. So he sent in his stead his son-in-law (Baldeo Das Vyasa), himself a landlord, who on two separate days devoted himself to showing us how the Hindoos live. We first went over (a) his house in the midst of the city, where his wife had just been confined, and then (b) the Raja's country mansion some four miles off, on the Grand

[2] Probably a reference to the National Committee for the Prevention of Destitution, the campaign led by Beatrice Webb against the Poor Law.

[3] Raja Madhava Lal (b. 1840), lawyer, landholder and banker, acted as a subordinate judge in Agra and as a judge in the Small Cause Court at Allahabad. He was elected to the Legislative Council of the United Provinces in 1900, and in 1906 to the Imperial Legislative Council. He was also Chairman of the Reception Committee at the twenty-first session of the Indian National Congress held at Benares in 1905.

Trunk Road. These houses had the same sort of combination of spaciousness and narrow dark rooms, of splendour and squalor, of elaborate native ornamentation and the most childishly bad English oleographs and pictures out from the illustrated papers, that we noticed at Basu's in Calcutta.

Another day he took us to see one of his own villages, where he went to settle some estate business. After an eight mile drive, we descended from his carriage, and were conducted by devious field paths for half a mile to the little two storied house built for his accommodation on such visits. We were shown the working of the well, and the primitive crushing of the sugar cane; we walked round the garden which he kept up, and noted the mango and guava trees, the pepper plants, and a tuber resembling a sweet potato (which subsequently proved to be very good fried). But much more interesting was the group of peasants which collected to interview their landlord. There was no common grievance, but sundry individual applications and controversies, which the landlord listened to, asked questions about, discussed with his resident agent, and, with all kindliness and friendliness, peremptorily decided. One aged man, of at least eighty (he said) who had been a tenant on an eleven years lease begged to be reinstated. It appears that no application for renewal of tenancy was made, because his brother (a junior of some sixty-five years) thought it clever not to apply, believing that the landlord would be driven to ask the tenant to remain at a lower rent. But after a long wait, another applicant had applied, offering five per cent *more rent*, and had accordingly been promised the tenancy. Now the aged man wanted this undone. The landlord (who said he liked the aged man, who was an old tenant) eventually said he would try to get the new applicant to take another piece of land, and then reinstate the aged man. In another case a tenant had taken into cultivation a piece of waste land, and wanted his rent for that piece settled. This was decided, after some discussion, to be three rupees per acre per year. The third case was the most interesting. It concerned the desire of one tenant to extend his mud house in order to take in a nephew whom another uncle had turned out. The proposed extension would, however, bring the new household into closer contiguity with the open space surrounding a neighbouring mud hovel tenanted by another cultivator. Now, this latter was of the Brahmin caste, whilst the former belonged to a lower caste, described as that of the 'Ascetics' (Gosein?).[4] Hence the Brahmin, a tall, spare, handsome man, vehemently objected, pleading most vivaciously that the ladies of the two households would quarrel, that they would interfere with each other's cooking, and so on. So we all went to view the premises, in the village a quarter of a mile off. There seemed to us to be plenty of room round the mud hovels; and the 'ascetics', who did not look quite so ascetic as the Brahmin, pleaded equally vehemently that any other way of extending their mud hovel would be inconvenient, owing to trees, access, etc. Eventually the landlord said he would reserve judgment, and we came away amid the respectful and quite friendly salutations of the crowd of some thirty men—the women and children peeping timidly round the corners, and taking to flight when Beatrice walked towards them.

After tea, biscuits and fruit, with fried potatoes as specimens, we walked back to the carriages escorted by men with sticks from another village, belonging, it was said, to a caste of warriors, who had come merely to greet their landlord, Baldeo Das Vyasa. Vyasa, with whom we thus had long conversations, is a gentlemanly young man of about thirty-five, educated at the Queen's College, Benares; travelled all over India, but not beyond; a loyal subject of the King and unhesitatingly preferring British rule to any native administration, but also patriotic in his Hindooism, and complaining that the Government was not favourable enough to persons of proved loyalty among the Hindoos, and that it was unduly partial to Mohammedans. He had

[4] Religious mendicant; also a caste of Hindus in northern India.

applied for a commission in the Army, but had been refused (no natives of India are eligible)—he felt deeply this exclusion, and also the universal prohibition to any Indian to possess arms, and their exclusion from all the higher posts. He complained also of the lack of facilities for the education of the cultivators—some hundreds of schools had actually been closed by Government for lack of funds. He disliked the native Christians and the Government patronage of them. They were mostly of low caste—some "untouchables"—and yet they would be given posts in the Railways or the Post Office! He did not like the Bengalees, and rather sneered at them and at the "talk" of the National Congress; which he said did harm to silly boy-students, who had cast off respect for their parents and who hated the British Government as part of old established authority inconsistent with liberal ideas.

The vision of village life yielded us today brings into relief the dominance of caste as a distintegrating force, even of the village community. The little group of mudhuts which constitutes a "village", and which we visited with our landlord to settle the disputes described above, was divided sharply into the Brahmins and the Ascetics; and it was clear that if the dispute was not settled there would be a village fight and a Police Court case. Another village was made up of the Fighting caste; and others of that caste were assembled together in the yard of our landlord and came with us to the said village evidently to talk over matters with members of their caste. Between these different castes there was no community of action; there was even hostility which had to be perpetually smoothed down by the landlord. Our friend himself, when discussing a proposed journey to Europe, mentioned incidentally that he would bring the matter before his community, promise to remain strictly vegetarian, and not touch alcohol, and get their permission before he dared to leave the country.

Another impression of village life was that of the grinding poverty of the people. There is no amenity and no comfort in the little groups of mud huts used indiscriminately for man and beast—all the appliances are of the most primitive and inefficient type; and there seems to be an indefinite number of human beings only half occupied, and all in a state of semi-starvation; a vicious circle—a low standard of nutrition and a low standard of effort. The Brahmins and other High Castes are distinguished by the fact that they bathe daily in the village pool and that they do "Puja" (i.e. religious observances) either at the village shrine, or, in the case of the better off, at the family shrines in their own habitations. They are all particular about their food and the cooking of it. The lower castes have no daily observances, though probably they go on Pilgrimages when they can afford it. From the Western standpoint, the Indian Village, as we saw it yesterday, is a most depressing aspect of Humanity—listlessness and discord being its two outstanding features—a listlessness curbed only by fear of starvation, and a discord checked only by the village "choukidar".

It would be a waste of words to describe the beauty of the Benares Ghats and the extraordinary picturesqueness of the narrow irregular streets with their half hidden Temples and shrines, their Palaces and their infinitely varied life of booth and market place. Compare Benares with Canton, and Benares shines out as intensely human, and, in a sense, spiritual—fantastically and weirdly spiritual, as against the hideous insect-like uniformity of the narrow streets' of the Chinese town. The Hindus are a lovable race, with their indifference to this world, and their emotional and lively care for the next. But their religion is, in itself, a perturbing and even a horrible sight to the Western observer—the hysteria of the worshippers of Evil Gods, demanding the sacrifice of life, the anarchic choice of gods to propitiate, the absence of any conception of Right and Wrong, either in the conduct of the God or that of his devotee—the strange combination of meditation, indolence and fraud in the ascetic, and the mercenary dealings of the Professional Priest. Above all, the intensely egotistic Purpose of all religious rites—the "Acquiring of Merit" and consequent advancement to a more enjoyable existence, and hence the complete unconcern for the common good. The cultivated Christian missionary—a Rugby and Oxford man (Rev. Frank Lenwood)—who took us over the Ghats, said that "Christianity was the only hope for India"(!). But those who have watched the effect of Christianity in its converts say that it loosens the obligations of family and caste, without substituting the obligations towards the Kingdom of the Christlike God, or towards a Commonwealth of Fellow Human Beings.

We visited the Hindu Central College, affiliated to Allahabad University; and had an hour's talk with Mrs. Besant.[5] She is the centre of the "New Hinduism", i.e., the attempt to appeal to the religious patriotism of the Hindu in favour of combining a maintenance of Hindu tradition and mysticism, with the Power of Conduct and a Power of Knowledge of Western Civilisation. Owing to her personal magnetism she has established a successful educational institution with 1000 students (500 boys and 500 Undergraduates), which has attracted the praise and the money of Maharajahs and Rajahs, and latterly the approval of the British Government. She has 50 professors, only three or four European—(I think all women for the younger boys) all the others Hindu men. Many of these Hindu Professors

---

[5] Annie Besant (1847–1933) was one of the original seven Fabian Essayists. In 1889, drawn towards theosophy, she abandoned socialism and the Fabian Society. From 1907 to 1933 she was President of the Theosophical Society. In 1893 Mrs Besant arrived in India, eventually establishing her home in Benares where, in 1898, she founded the Central Hindu College, an experiment in National Education, and the nucleus of the Benares Hindu University. In 1916 she succeeded in establishing the Home Rule League and, in the following year, she set up the Indian Boy Scouts Association and the Women's Indian Association. She was closely associated with the Indian National Congress and was its President in 1917. Mrs Besant's efforts were aimed at the development, through education, of a national spirit, founded on Indian tradition but enriched by Western ideas.

work for love—out of enthusiasm for the New Hinduism—
and it is clear that there is an intimate relationship between
the Professor and the pupil, which is lacking in Government
institutions. Added to this peculiar atmosphere of Hindoo
patriotism and educational enthusiasm, Mrs. Besant has,
owing to the support of wealthy Indians, been able to give a
good education at half the fees of Queen's College—the local Government institution.

This latter University College, also affiliated to Allahabad, is presided over by Mr. Venis,[6] a well known Sanscrit
scholar who took us over Sarnath and was delightfully lucid
in his explanations of these wonderful relics of Buddhism.
But he showed no inclination to show us over his college
and quite clearly did not care for his job. He was of the
same intellectual type as Sir Charles Eliot of Sheffield University—an iconoclastic secularist who combined a great
technical knowledge of Sanscrit literature with the most
thorough-going contempt of Hindu philosophy, or as he
would call it, Hindu mythology. He poured out bitter ridicule on the proposed Hindu University—how could you
have a University without men of learning and how could
you have a man of learning who believed in any of the childish barbarisms of the Hindu or Buddhist Scriptures? How
could *he* work with a colleague who tried to discover the
doctrine of evolution in the Vedas! (I should have thought
the difficulty would have come in, if his Hindu colleague
had tried to *disprove* Evolution by quoting passages from the
Vedas). No exposition of the sacred books of the Indians
was worthy of a University or was to be *tolerated* in a University which did not proceed on to assumptions of modern
physical science and modern historical criticism. He refused
to express his opinion of the Central Hindu College, which

[6] Arthur Venis of the Indian Educational Service was appointed
Principal of Queen's College, Benares in 1897. He was also a Fellow of the Asiatic Society of Bengal; Professor of Post-Vedic Sanskrit at Allahabad University; and a member of the Legislative
Council in the United Provinces.

would I think have been beyond polite words. With high fees and an unsympathetic Principal, the Queen's College is rapidly declining. We saw something of C. S. Streatfield, the Collector. He is a talkative, prejudiced, middle-aged Englishman, eager to go home directly his time is up. He has no standards of administration, and is a passive resister to any liberal inspiration from the Government of India. He showed us a "Municipal Free School"—a dark little mud shanty, supposed to accommodate eighty-five pupils, with an illiterate Brahmin as teacher, and no time table or fixed time for coming or going: he showed it to us with no sense of the absurd inadequacy of this "popular instruction". He glowed with pride over the magnificent new police quarters, and was quite complacent over the neglected and squalid gaol. He talked, talked, talked. Doubtless he is honest and impartial in character and gets through the routine of his duty without failure. But he represents the low-water mark of administrative aim, if not of administrative execution. "Damn the educated Native and the liberal Government", would, I think, represent his state of mind.

Over every three or four Collectors there is a Commissioner, who naturally lives in the largest town (and therefore in the same town as one of the Collectors). On asking whether this was not an extravagant duplication of the exiguous European staff, we were told by the Commissioner (Molony) that the work was quite distinct. But except that the Commissioner hears legal appeals from the Collectors— which perhaps ought to be done by a Judge—we still enquire whether the Commissioner might not also be the Collector for the district in which he resides, having a quite junior man under him. It is a question of principle of administrative organisation whether it is possible to get the best out of a District Officer if his immediate superior lives in the same District. In the Madras Presidency there is no such grade as Commissioner.

Allahabad, 11–16 January 1912

In this great 'station' (the Club has 250 members), we have been fortunate enough to see a "Magh Mela",[1] a great Hindoo religious gathering or fair. The junction of the Jumna with the Ganges is a specially sacred place for ceremonial bathing, and once a year at this season there is a great

[1] The month of Magh (mid January to mid February) opens with Makara Sankranti, signifying the sun's entrance into Capricorn, and ends with Shivratri. The entire month is consecrated to Vishnu, to whom and to the sun prayers are addressed and offerings made. A bath at the confluence of the rivers Ganga, Yamuna and the subterranean mythical Saraswati at Prayaga (modern-day Allahabad) is prescribed before sunrise on every day of this month. Around this ritual (the *magh snana*) a fair (the Magh Mela) springs up. While the Magh Mela is an annual occurrence, the Purna Kumbh Mela is held once every twelve years. It is a celebration of the myth of Jayanta who wrested, from the hands of the demons, the pitcher (*kumbha*) of nectar which guaranteed immortality and, transforming himself into a rook, brought the pitcher to paradise where the gods anxiously awaited his return. The journey took twelve days to complete, with four stops at Nasik, Ujjain, Allahabad and Hardwar. Since one divine day is traditionally considered equal to one mortal year, the event is observed once every twelve years. Every three years, however, it is held by rotation at each of the four places at which, according to the myth, it rested. The Ardh Kumbh Mela, which the Webbs visited at Allahabad, is, as its name suggests (*ardh* means half), held once every six years.

gathering of pilgrims; once every twelve or fourteen years a huge concourse (the Kumh); and once every six or seven years an intermediate sized crowd, the AdKumh. This year it is the latter, and it is computed that a million people will attend in the course of the six weeks. We were lucky enough to see the sight on one of the greatest days, when eight separate processions of "Saddhus", or men who have devoted themselves to the religious life, made their way to the spit of sand where the two streams meet.

This point is some miles from the city, and is not approachable by carriage, so we were fortunate in getting from the Collector (at the Club the night before) an order addressed any officer entitling us to annex any Government boat. We started at 8 a.m., got to the riverside at 9, found a boat there (a paddle-boat worked by six men), and were taken thus down the Jumna to the junction with the Ganges. There, on the sandy river-bed left uncovered, was a gaily dressed crowd of many tens of thousands, amid hundreds of tall flags, each denoting the little wooden stage of the "Pragwal" or Brahmin having the prescriptive right to the attendance on the pilgrims of a particular district. There were to be eight processions—of which we saw three—an almost indescribable sight. Each procession included one or more native bands; half-a-dozen acrobatic performers who danced about to music with swords and sticks and sometimes did tumbling tricks; gorgeous silk banners borne aloft, by men naked or clothed; camels with drums; capering horses; gaily dressed abbots and monks in litters; idols carried in palanquins; and from 50 to 200 "saddhus". These latter were mostly stark naked, smeared with ashes, and often bedizened with yellow ochre. Others were clothed in various degrees from the loincloth up to flowing robes. Some of the naked men sat on gaily caparisoned horses. Others walked hand in hand by twos, or in irregular groups. Some played weird sorts of "serpent" instruments: but most of them chanted some invocation to the Ganges and the God Ram. With them were scores of (fully dressed) little boys, who we were told were their pupils and apprentices; and some dozens of (clothed) female anchorites or nuns. These "Saddhus" were sometimes grossly fat, but usually emaciated; some were aged, and some quite young men, but the bulk were in the prime of life. A few looked really pious and contemplative; but for the most part their countenances gave them no good character for spirituality. After each procession had passed, the crowd prostrated itself in the dust on which the "holy men" had trod; or took it up and put it on their foreheads. In front of the procession usually rode a young English officer in khaki, followed by two Hindoo mounted policemen; the procession was escorted by foot police; and the road was kept clear, and elaborate precautions were taken by the police to prevent the several processions jostling each other, or being hindered by the crowd. All day long there rode up and down these young English Assistant Superintendents of Police, in khaki, with the Collector and the Doctor specially charged with the sanitation of the fair. Five hundred police were on the ground, all carefully picked out as being Hindoos; and inside the Fort squadrons of cavalry and companies of infantry stood ready but concealed, to come out the moment they were signalled for from the look-out platforms erected near the tent of the officer in charge. Inside that tent, his wife dispensed a scratch "breakfast" to English friends, including ourselves; and discussed the incidents of the day.

It is impossible to convey any idea of the sights and scenes and sounds of the huge crowd of families among which we walked. The elaborate "houseboats" from which the 'purdah' ladies bathed without entering the crowd or exposing tnemselves to the vulgar view; we saw, in one case (that of the household of the Maharaja of Bettiah) the ladies descend from a carriage into a sort of movable square tent held up from the outside by retainers; and this moving tent enveloped them as they descended the sloping path down to the river, and as they entered the "houseboat" which was to take them to the bathing place. The ceremonial shaving of the head of men and women, squatting on the ground, without cover or screen, the barber receiving a fee high or low according as the operation was performed exactly at the confluence of the two rivers, or merely on the banks of the Jumna—the hundreds of "Pragwals", sordid and mercenary looking Brahmins receiving rice and money from the pilgrims, and reading aloud the sacred books, or "blessing" in this way or that—the voluminous books of family records carried by the servants of these "Pragwals", in which the names of their particular pilgrims are recorded, together with various items of family "happenings" told on this occasion for record in these books—the cows and calves tethered here and there among the crowd, partly because holding the tail of one of these sacred animals, with due Brahminical incantations, has the same advantageous effects on a lately deceased relative as if he himself held the tail and thereby got carried safely across the Styx; partly because the gift of a cow to a Brahmin is the most "merit-acquiring" of gifts, and if you cannot afford a cow, you can at least buy a cow for four annas off the Brahmin, and then present him with the animal thus purchased, and so for fourpence acquire the merit of presenting a whole cow—the images of gods set up on the sands for reverence, and to induce the gift of a handful of rice or a copper coin to the Brahmin keeping the idol; or sometimes it would be a little boy dressed up to represent the god—the beggars everywhere asking for alms—the family groups of pilgrims, before bathing and after, squatting down to eat or to restore their toilets—the individual fakir or Saddhu carefully performing his toilet with grey ashes, with a little mirror which he repeatedly consulted so as to get the "make-up" as artistic as possible.

We have seen three leading Mahomedans, Sayid Ali Imam,[2] the legal member of the Viceroy's Executive Council at Calcutta; Karamet Hussein,[3] Judge of High Court at

[2] See footnote 11 on p. 12.
[3] Saiyid Karamat Husain (1852–1917) was a judge of the Allahabad High Court (1908–12) and a member of the Legislative Council

Allahabad; and an able young lawyer, Ibn-i-Ahmed, who is local secretary of the All India Moslem League. The two first named personages were of the heavy, dull type. Ali Imam professed himself in sympathy with the aims of the National Congress—they wanted more Indians in the administration; but he objected to simultaneous examinations, he wanted a certain number of places reserved for Indians (Hindus and Mahomedans getting them in proper proportion) and these nominated boys to be sent over to England to be educated specially for the competition—either sons of wealthy men, or on provincial scholarships. The elderly judge at Allahabad was wholly mute; but asked us to dinner at his house; and he arranged for us to see the young and energetic secretary of the All India Moslem League, with whom we have spent the better part of two mornings. He is a rather bitter opponent of the Hindu—does not want any relaxation of British rule, as this would inevitably mean, if peace were maintained, that the Hindu would govern the country and oppress the Mohamedans. He professes to think that if Great Britain withdrew her troops the Mohamedans would re-establish their Empire over the Hindus.

He did not care to associate with Hindus; and their caste rules prevented any friendly intercourse. He wanted equal representation on all local bodies, even where the Mohamedans were in the minority—if this was not accorded, he wanted the British Government to be the Arbitrator in all matters of dispute. He admitted that among the lower orders there was a good deal of amalgamation—in the villages the Mohamedans and Hindus would worship at the same temple. But in the higher ranks of society there was no sympathy and no possibility of joint action.

---

of the United Provinces. He attended the inaugural session of the All India Muslim League at Dacca and started an organization to protect Urdu. He was a Fellow of Allahabad University and the author of several books in Arabic.

He took us to see three or four Moslem Schools. One for the early training of Moulvis was rather a pitiable affair—some fifty little boys learning the Koran (in Arabic) by heart under the rule of some aged Moulvis—honest and pious men no doubt, but obviously of the most narrow minded and feeble type; only one or two would become Moulvis; the others drifting into teaching! The other schools showed a little pretence at teaching arithmetic and Urdu reading and writing, but the education given to little boys, who came and went when they or their parents chose, was obviously that of an uncivilised race. None of these Moslem schools received government money. (Some elder pupils were learning elementary Persian and Arabic.) All that could be said for them was that they were extraordinarily picturesque, these gatherings of gaily dressed youngsters, swaying their bodies to and fro, droning out the sacred words, in the open verandah of the mosques, with the grave old Moulvis wandering up and down amongst them. But these young citizens of the Oriental Empire were not learning anything that could be useful to them as independent members of a self governing State. Every mosque has its school, at which children attend free, and are taught by the Moulvis as above. The question arises (as these thousands of Mosque schools cannot be suppressed, and will in the aggregate be attended by thousands of children) whether Government might not make them a little more efficient by some simple form of aid. We suggested to our young lawyer (i) the free grant of suitable school books, maps, etc., (ii) the free service on one or two hours a week, or more, of a trained visiting teacher, a Moslem, whom the Government might appoint and pay to go round from school to school, teaching English, arithmetic, geography, etc. We had also been taken by a young Hindoo lawyer to see Hindoo schools. In the queer picturesque houses in the narrow lanes in the recesses of the native city we found four schools, set going by committees of leading Hindoos, getting fees and subscriptions and some minute Government grant; and teaching several hundred boys and girls Hindi reading and writing, and some arithmetic. The first (Lower Primary) consisted of some 40 little boys, with half a dozen elders, taught by a wild looking Brahmin with dishevelled hair, not speaking a word of English, or possessing any examination qualification. The girls school was far better, and in fact, had elements of real efficiency. About a hundred girls, from 5 to 14, were being taught by half a dozen women (all married but one, and that one a widow). The headmistress had been through a Normal School; there were maps, physiological diagrams of the internal organs of a man, a globe, a sewing machine, a shifting frame like a giant abacus for teaching the letters and numerals, etc; and some showy needlework was exhibited. Two other boys schools were under a single committee, the lower and the upper standards being for convenience in different buildings. The headmaster was a graduate of Muir College and his half-a-dozen assistants had all passed lower examinations. He himself spoke English well, and seemed a capable man. This school was an 'Anglo-Vernacular Middle School' and sent pupils to the Government High School, some of whom went on to Muir College.

This Muir College we also saw, the principal Government University College (with Queen's College, Benares, and Canning College, Lucknow) in the Allahabad University. It has 450 students, excellent buildings and scientific laboratory equipment, but a very poor library. There are four hostels—Hindoo, Mohamedan and Christian, and one Government. The Principal (Jennings)[4] had risen through the Indian Educational Service—Sub-Inspector, Inspector, Professor, Principal—and was a competent official, but not an inspiring personality. He said that what they had done

---

[4] J. G. Jennings of the Indian Educational Service was appointed Principal of the Muir Central College, Allahabad in 1895. In 1917 he was appointed an Additional Member of the Governor-General's Legislative Council. He edited a collection of English poems and a translation of Kalidasa's *Shakuntala*.

hitherto was to "turn out graduates": he hoped they might now do a little for learning! This College, nearly fifty years old, struck us as "wooden", but efficient in a rather poor way. The Professors were partly English—chosen in England by the India Office and appointed as Professors at large—and partly Indian, paid at a lower rate, with good qualifications, sometimes from English Universities. The students paid about 10 rupees a month (£5 to £6 a year) for tuition, and about 2½ rupees a month in the Hostels for board and lodging (30/- a year!); or about £7 for the school year altogether.

We had some talk with the Director of Education for this Province (De la Fosse)[5], an able and openminded official under forty, who was alive to all the shortcomings, but said he had been unable to get the Government to improve things, partly from lack of funds, and partly because the Education Service was put in a second place, its head having no direct access to the Lieutenant Governor but being subordinate to the Chief Secretary. All depended on whether the Chief Secretary was or was not favourable to education (and of course in the end the Lieutenant Governor). The Public Works Department and indeed all other Departments, had direct access to the Lieutenant Governor, but the Education Department not. But ultimately all turned on the amount of money that the Government chose to make available. The Municipalities and District Boards were naturally loth to levy local rates; and the small funds allocated to them by Government were largely spent in roads, etc., by the influence of Collectors unappreciative of schools. They were bound to spend five per cent of their income on schools, but one big city had got it reduced to three and a half per cent.

[5] Claude Fraser de la Fosse was appointed Director of Public Instruction in the United Provinces in 1906. Earlier he was Professor of English Literature and Logic at Queen's College, Benares. He was also a member of the Lieutenant Governor's Legislative Council.

Altogether De la Fosse impressed us as more keen about his job, and more definitely thinking about how to overcome obstacles, than any of the civilians we have so far met. He had a great admiration for Orange, who had been head educational official for India, and who retired, he said, largely because he could not get the Government to give any attention to his proposals.

At Lucknow we were taken to see two Moslem schools—one a large Mosque school of a hundred or so boys and young men, picturesquely squatting on the floor in half-a-dozen circles, in a series of open rooms next to the Mosque in the great Imambarah; taught, by half-a-dozen Moulvis who understood no English and had apparently no academic qualifications, Persian, Arabic, and the Koran, and Logic (by a Moulvi renowned for learning). (This latter seemed to be simple, the difference between genus and species, etc.) This school got no Government aid, and charged no fees. Here, however, it seemed that some real education was going on. The second school had higher pretentions (Nadvatullama);[6] it had been established by the leaders of the Faith as a boarding school for all India in which English teaching should be added to the usual religious and linguistic Moslem curriculum. It was in temporary buildings, but we were taken to see the large new building under erection on an extensive site (central hall and 32 rooms). This school had a hundred or so boys and young men present, from 10 to 25, with half-a-dozen very able and thoughtful looking Moulvis, some of whom had small academic qualifications (the English teacher was a studious looking Muhammedan who was a B.A. of Allahabad University). Here we saw real teaching going on (to judge from the faces and gestures and tones of the teachers), in Muhammedan law, philosophy, logic, literature, mathematics and English. To teach philosophy in Arabic they had got a man from Arabia. (Per-

[6] Established at Lucknow in 1894, the object of the Nadwah-ul-'Ulama was to reform the Muslim educational system and resolve theological controversies within Islam.

sian, the boys knew when they entered, it was stated). This school attracted boys from all over India, and was said to be unique. It got about £400 a year, Government grant, and the Lieutenant Governor had laid the foundation stone of the new buildings.

We lunched with the Principal (Rees) and English Assistant of the Colvin Taluqdars School (Lucknow)—with them Prof. A. W. Ward (Science, Canning College) brother of Prof. James Ward of Cambridge. The Taluqdars School is established and run nominally by the Taluqdars or 'Barons' of Oude, great landowners of from £500 to £5000 a year income, part Hindus, part Mohammedans, for the education of their own sons and no one else. Really, we gather, it is a Government nurseling, the Commissioner being Chairman of the Committee. These boys—there were only 40 or 30, between 10 and 25—half Hindus, half Mohammedans, are treated as plutocrats; each bringing his own three or four servants, and having his own set of rooms, his own kitchen, stables and his own horses, and providing and having cooked his own food, to be eaten alone in his own apartments. (They are forbidden to visit each others rooms). The school of only 40 odd had to be divided into ten classes, of different ages, etc., which were taught by as many Indian teachers. (Such small classes were said to have the drawback of providing no stimulus and evoking no emulation). The English Principal and his Assistant seemed entirely occupied with administration and games (to which great attention is given). English is the medium of instruction and apparently the only language taught. It seemed an attempt to create an English boarding school for wealthy boys without infringing their caste or religious customs. But the atmosphere was necessarily disintegrating to Hindu or Muhammedan religion; and it is not altogether to be wondered at that Taluqdars (and especially their pious women kind) are not very eager to send their sons. We were told of one lady who broke her Purdah to come and kneel before the (late) Principal, begging him to 'let her son go'.

It is to be noted that though the idea is to give an English education, and the "public school training", the boys' rooms were lacking in all amenity and charm, and were even squalid. Nothing in the way of personal habits seemed to be taught. The boys ate with their fingers in native style, and were not taught to use knife and fork, or to sit at table, so that they might associate with the English later on. No doubt the idea has been to avoid scrupulously anything that would be hostile to caste or custom. The boys paid some £20 a year each for tuition and lodging alone, all food and service being provided by themselves in addition.

This vision of educational organisation in the United Provinces (which we shall supplement by seeing village schools, and also Aligarh College) joined with a perusal of the educational reports and statistics both for the U.P. and for India, gives rise to disquieting reflections. We have been at it for half a century (Muir College itself was founded in 1857); and only a tiny proportion of boys, and a handful of girls are, even now, getting any decent education in the primary grade, let alone anything in the higher. The Government's efforts seem to have been (and still to be) quite absurdly "amateur" and spasmodic in their character. There has been no deliberately thought out policy, and no intelligently devised adjustment of means to ends. This has been aggravated (as it is also explained)—as we infer and believe—by a curious half-hearted indecision of the Civil Service as to whether they want to educate the Indians or not, and how they want to educate them. An instinctive dislike for the education of the Indian reveals itself in the frequent oscillations of policy which successive administrations inspire or impose, in the alternation of preference between English and vernacular teaching, and between the higher education of the few and the elementary education of the masses. It is less easy to suggest the remedy. If a strong Viceroy would definitely mark out a definite policy, clearing up all ambiguity and explaining what was negatived as well as what was approved, and insist on substantial action being immediately taken to begin to put it in force, a great deal would be done. Lord Curzon, however, tried this with only moderate success. The Education Department ought clearly to be put on as high a position as any other Department, with equal facilities for explaining its own needs, and developing its own policy. The whole method of organisation and recruitment of the educational service seems calculated to ensure and perpetuate its subordination to the older Departments of administration. It would almost seem desirable to make it from the start an integral part of the "Covenanted" service, recruited at the same time and by the same examination, without distinction of pay or title—in fact, simply assigning some of the successful men to educational work (sub-inspector, inspector, director of public instruction, etc.) instead of making them Assistant Magistrates, Settlement Officers or Collectors; and letting them specialise from the outset in educational administration just as some others do (though at a later stage) in judicial work. The same principle might be followed in other (at present) subordinate services, whose technique is really not any more "expert" or difficult than that of the mere administrator. It is clearly impossible to get as good men for education as for civil administration unless they are given the same pay and prospects.

Coming to details, there ought to be (a) a much more determined effort to train teachers, female as well as male, Muhammedan as well as Hindoo, supplying, in the main, secondary schooling, with only a comparatively small veneer of pedagogy; (b) a widely advertised and influentially pushed system of Grants-in-Aid of Municipal and district board educational expenditure, based on the principle of "pound for pound"; (c) whilst there need be no objection to giving similar grants to "private venture" schools, this should only be done where there is a highly organised, extensive institution, and the present plan of (practically) subsidising the individual "hedge schoolmaster" living by his fees should be wholly abandoned; and there should be ingenuity in devising forms of aid acceptable to the Mosque and other religious schools not adopting Government code or rules; (d) the Government should be equally liberal in aiding vernacular schools and English schools, letting either be established according to the demand, and certainly setting no limit to either; (e) the secondary schools should be differentiated and varied, so as to allow room for greater attention to science, manual work, art, economics, etc; (f) the Universities should be supplemented by Schools of Economics and Public Administration, Law, Medicine, Engineering and Technology, which might in some cases be run as post graduate institutes for all India.

There seems no reason why Mr. Gokhale's Bill[7] for universal and compulsory education for boys should not be passed, safeguarded as it is by the provision that compulsory powers are not to be put in force except at the request of a Municipal or District Board, and only when it can be shown that 30 per cent of the boys of school age are already on the rolls. Such enterprising and advanced places should be given greatly increased Grants-in-Aid. The law should be enforced in these—for a long time to come—exceptional places by School Attendance Officers, not the police. This omits consideration of certain obvious difficulties (such as diversity of language, and the struggle between the Urdu (Muhammedan) and the Hindi (Hindoo) forms of Hindustanee), and also the standing obstacle of lack of funds. We cannot, however, believe these difficulties to be insuperable.

[7] The Elementary Education Bill introduced in the Imperial Legislative Council by Gopal Krishna Gokhale in March 1911, seeking to gradually make elementary education compulsory, financed partially by local municipal authorities through the levy of an education tax. The bill had to be re-introduced a year later, during which interval, in the face of consistent opposition from British officials, Gokhale worked hard to mobilize public opinion and the press in support of it. In March 1912, however, the official majority helped to defeat the Bill, and it was only in 1917 that a similar measure was successfully enacted for Bombay.

But the educational problem needs both inventiveness and public discussion, for neither of which there seems at present adequate provision. We cannot discover who is "doing the thinking"—certainly not the Collectors or Commissioners, hardly the Secretariat—we doubt whether the Inspectors of Schools and Directors of Public Instruction have time to think, or ability to make their voices heard if they do think—and Sir Harcourt Butler, able administrator as he is, brings only an amateur and very imperfectly informed mind to bear, and that distracted by Viceregal functions and Imperial Council duties. And there seems no machinery for discussing problems and projects with the native leaders of thought in the different provinces, with a view, on the one hand, to gaining their consent, and on the other, to promulgating to the public the views that it is desirable the public should adopt, if there is to be the indispensable unofficial co-operation. One would imagine that it would be most valuable if the Viceroy could preside at public conferences all over India, at which all educational questions could be freely discussed; or, as the Viceroy has too much to do, the Minister for Education might take his place. The suggestion is doubtless revolutionary. Lord Curzon's educational conference at Simla consisted only of a small group of English Government officials with one aged head of a Christian College in Calcutta, and absolutely no Hindoo or Muhammedan! The result was that he raised a hurricane of opposition, and his schemes have made little headway. An interesting episode at Lucknow was our visit, by way of the Chowk Bazaar, a long narrow street of Indian shops that picturesquely recalled to us Canton, to a renowned Muhamedan "Hakim", or medical practitioner, qualified only in Muhamedan medicine. In a ramshackle, extensive ground floor, up a narrow lane in the native city, we found him (11.30 a.m.) squatting down just inside the open window, dealing with a succession of patients. One by one they came up to be questioned as to symptoms, to have the pulse felt at both wrists, to have the abdomen fingered (for liver or spleen enlargement?) (there was no use of stethoscope, or clinical thermometer), and then to receive a prescription which was dictated rapidly in a loud singsong drawl for the benefit of the kneeling students. For inside the room there knelt in two rows about a score of young men listening to the interrogations and noting down in a kind of shorthand the prescriptions given. Among the patients was one purdah lady, who was brought in an orange-coloured curtained chair or palanquin, out of which she protruded her pulse to be felt, and even peeped round the curtain at the physician or perhaps at us. Our Moslem companion remarked that a Moslem lady would not have lifted the curtain at all! The cases, we were told, were mostly cough and fever; and the prescriptions were nearly all herbal (though one contained sparrow brains, and quinine was said to be prescribed by a few native doctors, also mercury for syphilis). It is interesting that all that we saw was gratuitous, the physician taking no fees either from patients coming to him or from the students. He was said to charge a fee when he was called to visit a patient (5 rupees, plus carriage hire). In Delhi, the native doctors do not charge even for visiting within the city; but only when called to patients outside the City. The Muhamedan tradition is that healing, like instruction, should be gratuitous; done in the performance of duty by those who have the gift. When we asked how the doctors could live, we were told that they often had received old grants of land, or had inherited family property, on the understanding that they were to practise; but also that they got the fees for visiting patients. The Hakim whom we visited, who looked a man of ability and strength of character, and might well be a magnetic personality, was said to make as much as £400 a year. He took us to see (a) his medicine shop, where herbs were being chopped and emeralds were being ground to powder, whilst various messes were being boiled and steeped; (b) his little distilling place, where three or four rude stills were on the fires, the vapour from which was being condensed slowly into glass vessels; and (c) the

free dispensary, where the medicines were given gratuitously to the poor—all indescribably picturesque and primitive,
with no attempt at cleanliness or accuracy. The practice was
usually for the patient to take the prescription to a native
medicine shop (the apothecary in *Romeo and Juliet*) which
we saw close by, where the prescribed ingredients were
simply sold to him, and he made up the medicine in his
own home! The whole thing was singularly interesting as an
unaltered survival from the Middle Ages. On the other
hand, the Muhamedan community was becoming alive to
the advantages of Western Science, and had extracted an
incautious promise from the Government that, in the
gorgeous new Medical College just erected, there should be
courses of instruction for Hakims in Muhamedan medicine.
Against this, some of the Civil Service were revolting, on
the ground that the Government ought not to encourage
error! It does not seem to have occurred to anyone that,
even accepting that view (which we do not, for a Government which does not endow "error" can never endow
"truth" since all truth is error to someone), there are heaps
of things in chemistry, physiology, and hygiene which the
Hakims would be the better for knowing, and which good
and qualified Muhamedans might be hired to teach, without
venturing on the dangerous ground of Muhamedan therapeutics. The difficulty in which the Government finds itself
on this point, and the lack of ingenuity displayed by the
Civil Service in finding alternatives, seem characteristic and
typical of India.

We dined at Lucknow with the Commissioner (Lovett)
and lunched with two members of the Secretariat (Stuart
and Burn)—all men of good though not striking ability,
with real good will and desire to do the best possible, all
working very hard, but all giving the impression of
amateurishness and lack of ingenuity in devising or remembering alternatives; all unspecialised, doing a hard day's
work at a succession of different subjects about none of
which they had expert knowledge or professional skill, and

about some of which (e.g. education and sanitation) they had only a half belief.

More interesting were our successive interviews with groups of Muhammedan and Hindoo gentlemen. We went first to the house of Aziz Mirza,[8] a wise, shrewd, well-informed, and even humorous Secretary of the All India Moslem League. There we met the Raja of Jehangirbad (a landlord worth some tens of thousands pounds a year), his dissolute nephew, and a dozen Muhamedan barristers and vakils, with the Secretary of the Nadvatullama School above described). These specially enlightened Muhamedans deplored to us the backwardness of their own community, the general lack of wealth among them, so that they had still not got the money together for the new University, their unwillingness to spend money on education even of their own sons (A Moulvi at 10 rupees a month seemed to many a Taluqdar enough for his sons and neighbours sons): the special unwillingness of the wives to let their sons be educated properly; the absolute inability to get the women educated. They insisted on the necessity for separate representation, and for their having equality with the Hindoos (lest they should be outvoted), in spite of the fact that they numbered only 14 per cent of this Province. They said that only in this way could they have assurance of fair treatment in schools, language, etc., at the hands of the Municipalities and District Boards. They were insistent on Urdu being taught, not Hindi, because Persian had been the Court Language of Delhi and Oudh, and Urdu was the real popular language (the imported words being from the Persian); whereas the literary Hindi desired by the Hindoos was really made up from Sanskrit. They resented, quite as much as

[8] Maulvi Muhammad Aziz Mirza (1865–1912), Hyderabad judge and politician, who lived in Aligarh after his retirement. He was the Honorary Secretary of the third (1910) session of the All India Muslim League, the office of which he shifted from Aligarh to Lucknow. He particularly helped to organize support for the League in the Central Provinces (now Madhya Pradesh).

the Hindoos, the social exclusiveness of the English and their occasional rudeness to Indians; and it was they who complained that the Collector did not return the calls even of most distinguished Muhamedans, and that they had to take off their shoes on entering his presence. On the other hand they wanted the British Raj; and they strongly objected to Bengalees being put in authority over them. Ruling was their hereditary business: they had left trade and even education to the Hindoos; and now that they had been ousted by the English from ruling, they felt very much their backwardness in the professions and business. But they were striving now to improve Muhamedan education. The next day we went to tea with a young Moslem barrister (a Cambridge graduate), Naziruddin Hassin, whose father was a retired member of the Statutory (or Provincial) Civil Service, a District Judge in Central Provinces. There we met a dozen young Muhamedans, mostly Vakils; and B.W. went to see the Purdah ladies. She found a dozen or fifteen collected to meet her; extraordinarily backward and unintelligent, only two or three speaking a few words of English. One very clever girl of 14, not in purdah, was the daughter (pure blood) of a Muhamedan mathematical coach at Cambridge, and spoke English well. The Hindoo group we met through the Hindoo Editor of *The Advocate*, a leading member of the Municipality and a man of great ability and public spirit (Ganga Prasad Varma), who was an advanced Nationalist and had been a friend of Tilak. We met apparently in the rooms of the 'People's League' or some such society; and found a dozen or so of Hindoos (with one Moslem Nationalist). The best way to describe them is to say that they seemed to us in tone and temper and grievances and opinions to be almost identical with the Muhammedans; except that they wanted Hindi and not Urdu, and that they bitterly resented the undue representation conceded to and claimed by the Muhamedans. The Hindoo community as a whole was apparently wealthier, more successful in trade and at the bar, and more eager for English education than the Muhammedan community as a whole. But between these two groups of enlightened leaders, there was no discernible difference.

In Camp at Ganrer,[1] District of Gorakhpur, United Provinces, 24 January 1912

We have now been three days "in Camp" with a Collector, on his progress through his district, which is the largest and most populous in all India, having over three millions of people, and covering some 4,500 square miles. The 'Camp' is a collection of four principal tents and an indefinite number of minor erections for kitchen, stores, clerks, servants, etc, pitched usually in a grove of mango trees. We "break camp" at about 8 a.m. each morning, and go on by carriage and on horseback to the next halting place 10 or 13 miles off. There we find a duplicate set of tents etc. already erected, with our trunks, which have gone on in advance. Our beds and rugs and toilet requisites arrive by the afternoon. On the way we inspect a vernacular school or visit some particular village. In camp, there is an assemblage of village headmen, to the number of a hundred or a hundred and fifty, whom the Collector harangues in fluent Urdu, about the necessity of reporting crime, the advantage of anti-plague inoculation and the state of the crops. We inspect the local police station and the village school. Yesterday we had a grand inoculation, the (native) Assistant Civil

[1] Probably Gaura in Gorakhpur district.

Surgeon being on his own progress round the district, and, with the help of the presence of the Collector and his Assistant (who was inoculated to encourage the others) actually induced over 200 natives to be done. It must be added that they were most of them policemen, or servants of officials, or else boys at the school (whose willingness to undergo the operation was encouraged by a bribe of two pence each from a local Hindoo landowner). The Collector hears appeals in civil suits from the decisions of the Assistant Magistrates; mostly 'partition cases', where the land of a Joint Hindoo Family is being divided up among the participating members one of whom is dissatisfied with the allotment. His "Court" is of course the large tent which is our common dining room. He is attended by three clerks, and the litigants appear in person without formality, and argue their own case one against the other, of course in the vernacular Urdu. The Collector listens, interjects questions, explains to us in English what it is about and then questions them again, and finally abruptly declares that the appeal is dismissed, or else remits it back for some alteration to be made. The litigants seem on the best of terms with each other, and their lawsuit, often about a matter of trifling pecuniary value, partakes of the nature of the excitement of mill gambling. Various people come to see the Collector— minor officials of the locality, a small landlord on horseback followed by an armed retainer on horseback carrying a quaint sword, a cultivator with some grievance against the Government, and so on—everyone having perfect freedom of access. During the day trays of presents arrive, in the form of beautiful flowers, fruit, vegetables, locally made sweetmeats, and even the fresh fish from the local rivers— all of small pecuniary value, and, as such, difficult to refuse without rudeness (the regulations strictly prohibit all other presents whatever).

We continue our progress "in camp" with unfailing interest, so unceasing indeed, that we find but little time to read or write. At night the camp is guarded by half-a-dozen or more "goraits", or village watchmen (holding land rent-free on condition of performing service; practically an hereditary office, although if there is no fit son, the Zemindar nominates and the Government appoints some other successor). These village watchmen, armed with long staves, squat about the outskirts of the Camp at night, but in the early morning they gather together round a fire, and carry on endless conversation.

The gathering of the Mouktars or village headmen at each stopping place is really most remarkable. These one or two hundred men (there are over 7000 villages in the District) gather by ones and twos during the day, to sit about and gossip until summoned to the meeting. Then they squat down in a semi-circle close around the Collector's chair, an outer circle standing up, flanked by a few other men and boys from the adjacent village, and a policeman or two in khaki uniforms and red puggaree. The Collector speaks familiarly to them, with gestures, jokes and smiles. They interject freely, make comments and criticisms one against the other without the slightest fear. When the Collector talks about the nuisance of the multitude of Brahmini bulls, and asks whether compulsory registration would not be a good device, there is a hum of satisfaction although they will not commit themselves to approval. One intelligent looking young man, with suggestions of fanaticism about his eyes, objects to any interference with these bulls, on the ground that the cow is the salvation of Hindustan, and must not be hindered. The Collector turns the laugh against him by instancing a village in which no fewer than 130 of these bulls are at large, feeding on the crops; and asking whether it was really suggested that the cows of that village required so many bulls. The Collector tells the meeting to take the suggestion of registration home to their villages, and talk it over with their neighbours, so as to report to him at his next meeting what the people think. He talks to them about the plague, and explains the rat-flea theory of its transmission, and the benefits of inoculation. As soon as the latter point is reached, there is a comical movement of the crowd. Those who are standing up, especially those on the outside of the circle, edge away—apparently by an involuntary movement of fear lest the Collector should suddenly inoculate them on the spot! The Collector notices this with a laugh, and comforts the crowd by the assurance that no inoculating doctor is present, and that in any case the matter is entirely optional. The collector concludes with friendly enquiries about the crops, whereupon several persons assure him that things are very bad in their villages. The Collector laughs at them, and calls on the others to witness that this year they have simply bumper crops; which the crowd smilingly assents to, whereupon the Collector rises and with frequently renewed salutation dismisses the meeting in great good humour. These extraordinarily picturesque meetings seem to us of the greatest possible usefulness, in all sorts of ways. We wonder whether all Collectors hold them, or hold them with the "verve" and "bonhomie" of our Collector.

The 'Brahmini Bull' is becoming a very serious pest in many parts of the District. It is a great act of piety to dedicate a bull to the gods; and it has long been customary for leading families of Brahmins to make this sacrifice on special occasions, in memory of some deceased member, or some thing of the sort. But now the practice has become common, and it is being adopted by families of inferior castes, who think by that to improve their status. The bull so dedicated is turned loose to wander at will. He is so sacred that he must not be killed, or even struck, and as the fields have no fences, he practically eats his fill of the growing crops. To have 130 of these depredators loose in one village seems pretty serious! But what is even worse is that as these bulls are naturally the worst and most defective that the owner possesses—for any bull will do for the gods—and as these wandering bulls serve the cows of the village, there is a tendency for the breed to deteriorate steadily. Yet neither the villagers nor the Government ventures to put a stop to the practice, out of fear of stirring up a religious fanaticism, fomented by the Brahmins. The suggestion of requiring registration (which we made) seems a possible way out. Registration, it is said, would in itself probably greatly diminish the number of bulls dedicated, because the people would have a nervous fear that it might involve some dreadful unknown consequences.

On Sunday we borrow a motor car from a friendly Raja—a wealthy Hindoo landlord, who has also a sugar factory and much money out at 12 per cent interest—in order to pay him a visit at his "palace" some 20 miles off. On the way we go to breakfast with the Assistant Magistrate (who is in semi-independent charge of the further end of this huge District). We find him living temporarily in the "Inspection Bungalow", at one corner of his territory—this being a one-storied brick erection available for any Government officer coming to the place. He is a quiet, refined Ulsterman of about 30; an Ll. B. of Trinity College Dublin (Bennet) who impresses us as a competent and careful executive officer, conscientious and plodding. There come in to breakfast two Railway officials who are building a new line close by, a young engineer and an inspector. We breakfast extensively on five or six courses at 11 o'clock; and the Collector afterwards goes into an inner room to discuss the affairs of the district with his deputy—apparently, principally, movements of the subordinate staff, whether this man had not better be sent there, and so on. Eventually, we go on to our Raja of Padrona[1]—he is in siesta until 3 p.m.—and we find him waiting to meet us on the outskirts of his "palace", in the midst of extensive outbuildings of one sort or another. He takes us to see his "hospital", a free dispensary maintained by him; and his "agricultural bank", which is not co-operative but is run by him as a sort of benevolent money-lending place, to keep his tenantry out of the grip of the usurer. He started it with a free gift of 20,000 rupees, which forms the nucleus of its loan fund; but whenever it needs more capital, the Raja himself supplies it at 12 per cent, which is the rate that the Bank charges to its borrowers. Then we inspected the coachhouse, with his second motor car and several stately landaus and barouches; his formal gardens, which were really rather attractive though bare to our eyes; his collection of animals, two magnificent cranes (whom the servant with an umbrella as weapon, had to keep from attacking us), a whole array of birds in cages, and of rabbits in a large barred hutch; and his sugar-factory where he had installed a steam engine to crush the cane in a steel mill, and a centrifugal sugar-crystalising machine of which he was very proud. It is perhaps characteristic that this centrifugal machine was set going for our edification without bearings, so that three men with giant bamboos had to hold it in position; and with an imperfectly mended driving belt, which threatened to slip off the wheel, and presently broke with a loud report that made us all scatter in alarm. However, some sugar was made and presented to us. The Raja was making, he said, £2 a day from this sugar mill, which represented a queer intermediate stage between the hand and the machine industry. Finally we came to the "palace", a rather attractive

---

[1] The Rai of Padrauna (a *tehsil* in Gorakhpur district) was a landholder with a large estate in the north of the district, where he also maintained the dispensary to which the Webbs refer.

two-storied, battlemented, white-painted building, which
we entered by one of those strangely narrow winding stone
staircases characteristic of Hindoo houses—like going up a
cottage ladder to get to Windsor Castle—and arrived at a
drawing room full of carpets, furniture, ornaments and pictures in "Early Victorian" English style! We were presented
with perfume and cigarettes, B.W. with half-a-dozen excellent photographs and S.W. with a silver cardcase. Then we
went to see the carpenter's workshop, where the Raja's artisans were building a new "howdah" for use on his elephants,
and also new chairs. Finally we visited the temple built by his
father, at which he prostrated himself; built of costly marble,
surrounded by a grove of trees grown in three feet of earth
brought by his father from Muttra, a sacred place on the
Ganges, and containing images of Krishna, and Radhika, his
wife. Our Raja is said to have an income of £20,000 a year
clear, half derived from the rent of 400 villages (on which
he pays some £6000 a year Land Tax) and half from money
out at interest. But the Raja in spite of his wealth and his
Government title, has a skeleton in his cupboard: he is of low
caste—a circumstance which not one of his fellow country-
men—Rajas or peasants—ever forgets!

We finished our Sunday with a visit to an indigo planter,
whom we found living in great state in a charming house
with lawns in English style. The estate is an old jungle-grant,
which has been cleared and put under cultivation. The business is a very fluctuating one,[2] almost a gamble; and this

[2] In the mid nineteenth century indigo was a major export from
India, its cultivation having been encouraged by the East India
Company in response to the requirements of the European textile
industry. The cultivation of indigo was frequently forced upon the
peasantry as an alternative to more traditional crops. Indeed this
was very profitable for the planters as indigo was bought at very
low prices and sold at much higher rates. Repression and physical
torture were common in the plantations, as Dinabandhu Mitra's
celebrated novel *Nil Darpan* showed. Gradually, however, the introduction of synthetic dyes made indigo cultivation less profitable,
and planters began to use their estates for growing other crops. In

planter is gradually taking to other crops—is contemplating, indeed, starting an up-to-date sugar mill.

Altogether we have motored 55 miles, exclusively over country roads, unmetalled and sandy, with ruts and hollows and ridges and culverts; returning close upon sundown after a ten hours day, during which we have seen a great deal of the country.

There remains little for me to add to Sidney's description of our life in camp except a word or two about the Collector, his Assistants, and the little world that surrounds him at his station at Gorakhpur and in his four months in camp. Hope Simpson[3] is not a remarkable man: but he is remarkably fitted for his work—to us he seems almost ideal as an administrator over an alien race. Tall and muscular, with a strong but kindly face, splendid nerve and health, a genuine love of guiding and serving other people, he is the exact opposite of the bureaucrat. In fact, if he has a fault as an administrator, I should think it consists of too great an independence of, and indifference to, the common rules of law and administration—a determination to give full play to the human

---

1901–2 exports were less than half of what they had been only five years earlier, and by 1912–13 they were one-seventh of the 1901–2 figures. The area under indigo cultivation correspondingly shrank.

[3] John Hope Simpson (1868–1961) belonged to the Indian Civil Service, from which he retired in December 1916. Later he was a Liberal Member of Parliament (1922–4) and Vice-President, Refugee Settlement Commission, Athens (1926–30). In 1930 Sidney Webb, as Minister for the Colonies, appointed him to a special mission to Palestine. In a letter to Mildred Bulkley from India, Beatrice Webb described him in glowing terms: 'Our Collector—Mr. Hope Simpson—is an ideal one—perhaps he was chosen by the Government of India to take us around for that reason. He is a tall good-looking middle-aged man—the son of a Liverpool Bank Manager—educated in France and Germany and eventually going to Oxford—a good sportsman, and a Patriarchal Head of his district, speaking the various vernaculars with perfect fluency and associating almost exclusively with the natives.' Norman Mackenzie (ed.), *The Letters of Sidney and Beatrice Webb*, volume II (1892–1912) (Cambridge University Press, 1978), p. 383.

side in each particular case, without, perhaps, considering whether his decision was a safe precedent for other people. For instance, his intimacy with all his subordinate officials and with the Indian lawyers and landowners of his district, is one of the strong points of his administration, and results in a greater measure of "common consent" than is usual in the British administration. But this policy of intimate intercourse would be impracticable, and perhaps unsafe, for a man with less firmness of will and with less absolute straightness of purpose. He can afford to be good-natured with his subordinates because, owing to his energy and perfect health, he sets the pace so quick that they are kept up to the mark by having to work up to him. Also, being a man of genuine piety (he is a fervent Congregationalist) his easy and intimate manner are consistent with an almost puritanic hatred for looseness of life and conversation. And all this piety and integrity are prevented from appearing as prudishness and priggishness because they are tempered by his love of outdoor life and his devotion to sport.

It is interesting to note that Hope Simpson is the son of the General Manager of the Bank of Liverpool and that his family both in the past and the present are of "banking stock". He is himself par excellence a "General Manager", and not a specialised officer. I doubt whether he has either the patience or the intellectual curiosity to be a good Expert. Perhaps that is the reason that he is so fitted for the work of a Collector. The Collector of an Indian administrative district is essentially a General Manager. He is expected to make roads and bridges, to carry on works of drainage and irrigation, to start and manage schools, to decide on appeals both criminal and civil cases, to direct the education of great landlords who are minors, and if necessary, to manage their estates and settle their family quarrels, to detect sedition and prevent crime, to protect the religious life and stop the fanaticism of Mohammedans and Hindus, and to be the leader of society, white and coloured. And for all this multifarious work he has no responsible assistants more specialised than himself (though there are very subordinate—usually Indian—engineers, school inspectors and police). He has, moreover, to put up with and make the best of the assistants sent him by the Government of his Province and the Government of India—and he is handicapped by the tradition that no man, however incompetent, can (so long as he is decently conducted) be, in practice, dismissed from the Government service. He can only be "removed" either to another part of the district, or, if the Collector is fortunate, to another Collector's district.

In our rides together I had long talks with our host and learnt something of his personal and professional life. "Out of eleven years of married life I have spent five years with my wife and children." And the man adored his wife and children—idealised the one and idolised the others. His wife was a Girton graduate and has an income of her own. From her portrait and his description of her she seems to be a homely domestic woman whose whole existence is centred in her husband and children. With great naïveté he insisted on reading to us her long letter from Switzerland, whither she has taken her five children—four of whom had had the Plague!— and this letter, which the dear man glowed over, revealed a gentle and charming nature, absorbed in the little pleasures of the children, and eagerly awaiting his decision to come home, if possible for good. And clearly Hope Simpson is now being tempted, in the prime of life, to throw up his job. With his pension of £1000 a year, and his wife's income, he could just manage to retire (he entered the I.C.S. at nineteen and is still under forty-five); and yet send his boys to Rugby and Oxford. Should he retire this year; or should he remain on for another year, take two years furlough, and look about him in England before he settled not to return to India? When we arrived he had almost settled to go home this year, and to retire at the end of his one year's furlough. When we left he had finally settled to stay on another year, and thus take two years to consider whether or not he should break off his Indian career—and I think that change of mind was partly brought about by our immense interest in, and admiration for, his administrative work.

Part of his discontent was due to a sort of estrangement between him and the Lieutenant Governor (Sir John Hewitt), and the lack of any connection with or encouragement from, the Government of India. We had heard him spoken of as a first rate administrator, and quite clearly the Government of India, in selecting him to entertain us, had considered that he would be likely to give a good impression to two potential critics. And yet, in spite of this reputation Hope Simpson has been more or less left behind. Men who are less able than himself, and who are not senior to him, are Commissioners (a higher grade than Collector) or have got into the Board of Revenue or Secretariat or into other places from which promotion may be expected. Obviously Hope Simpson is not liked by the Lieutenant Governor, and has not secured any kind of recognition from the Government of India. We suspect it is largely due to his independence and to the fact that he is "pro-native", and to the homeliness and carelessness of society matters on the part of both himself and his wife. Indeed, the only time he showed any bitterness was in his description of the inanities of Simla, and the intrigues, reputable and disreputable, that went on at dinner, at balls, during games and sports, in the Government House sets of the Province and of India.

Hope Simpson had three Assistants in the Covenanted Indian Civil Service—one Englishman, one Hindu and one Mohammedan. The Englishman (Edye) was a bright, energetic, clean young man of 28—Public School (Harrow), and University (Oxford), the son of the Chief Accountant of the Bank of England and belonging to a family of Public Servants—naval constructors, army and civil service. He, too, had married a lady with an income, and did himself well. But he was not in the least slack—on the contrary, he seemed as successful in administration as he was in sport. He was, in fact, of the same sort as Hope Simpson—a first rate "General Manager" with a great capacity for "despatching business"—

though he lacked his chief's human interest and religious inspiration. The two Indian assistants were not so satisfactory. The Hindu (Mehta)—a Gujerat Brahmin, married to a pretty little Bombay Brahmin lady who was well-educated and out of Purdah—had been educated in India as a boy but had passed through Cambridge with distinction, and entered the Indian Civil Service by examination. He was a tall, pleasant-looking man with somewhat servile manners and fluent talk—in his heart a Nationalist but very discreet in Hope Simpson's presence. His Chief did not really like him—he said he worked for show, that he wrote reports which were patently inaccurate in their "white-washing" and defended them on the ground that they would impress public opinion. Also he was far too intimate with one of the subordinate officials. Worst of all, he lacked courage. When told to go round during the cholera epidemic he developed a lame leg—and this was typical of other small incidents. One felt in talking to him that it was almost inconceivable that he should step into Hope Simpson's place without a gradual deterioration of all branches of administration.

The Mohammedan assistant—Ameer Ali—was a raw recruit, just out from England. He was the grandson of a minister of the King of Oude, and a son of a celebrated Indian barrister and Judge of the Supreme Court in Calcutta, now the first Indian member of the Judicial Committee of the Privy Council in London. But his mother was an anglicised German (Konstam) with Indian connections and he had been brought up in England—Wellington College and Balliol—he therefore was technically a Eurasian. A delicate and somewhat pretty youth of 25, with dandified dress and manner, he did not impress us. Hope Simpson, in whose house he lived, treated him with kindly contempt. He was always talking of his father and his father's distinguished friends, and was always telling us rather stupid little stories, so as to show his knowledge of the great world. He professed to be an enthusiastic sportsman. But he lived in chronic funk of plague, cholera and enteric, and the poor boy was evidently destined to be in a state of perpetual terror about his health. He was very *slack*—showed no inclination to exert himself physically or mentally. When not talking about English Society, glorifying sport, he was abusing the Hindu or the Italians and the Russians for their hostility to Islam. He frankly confessed that he loathed India—regarded England as his home, and Islam as his faith. In this latter respect he compared unfavourably with Mehta—who, for all his nervelessness, was devoted to the country of his service. Altogether we prophesied that Ameer Ali would not last out over the rains—some pretext would be found for leaving India, and settling in London.

But Hope Simpson was more fortunate in his subordinate Indian officers. One of them, Ganga Prasad, an Assistant Magistrate in the Provincial Service and a member of the Arya Samaj, seemed to be a quite excellent person; and others impressed us favourably. Indeed, the intermediate class of Indian officials (the Provincial Service), native-born and mostly native-bred, with a high standard of work, and a low standard of expectation, well-educated in Indian Colleges but not spoilt by English University examination successes, seemed to us full of promise. They may not produce Hope Simpsons, or be able to take over the top executive posts. But their help already enables one Englishman to administer a district of one or two millions of people, and they will enable the number of English to be further diminished.

Hope Simpson was inclined to be pessimistic and despondent about the English administration. There had been a marked improvement in the past seven or ten years in such matters as roads, schools and sanitation; and Lord Curzon, in spite of his insolence, had done much good in stirring up a service which had become wooden and mechanical in its routine. But there was no definite purpose or plan about the Government of India. Were we really trying to enable the Indian people to dispense with our guidance, or did we intend to remain for ever in command? To pretend the one and secretly to mean the other crippled and nullified much of the practical work. The bulk of the officials who thought at all—

together with all who did not think and all the army officers—believed (and occasionally let it be known that they believed) that English rule would go on for ever, and that the Indians were inherently incapable of self-government. Hence the continued agitation, which could not fail to grow in strength. The Government would give way on one point after another as soon as it was demanded with sufficient agitation; but give way too ungraciously and too tardily for the boon to do anything but stimulate agitation for more. At length something would be demanded which could not or would not be conceded—and then he feared an outbreak, a popular rising, in which the smaller stations would be overwhelmed and the larger temporarily invested or paralysed, when we should find ourselves back at the position of Mutiny of 1857! This, however, he said in a moment of pessimism. For the most part he believed in his work, and went straight onward in faith and hope that somehow a definite policy would get itself adopted.

We have omitted to note that the whole expenditure on Local Government services in this huge Gorakhpur District, having 3¹/₂ millions of people, is £20,000 a year. With this sum, the 'District Board'—really, the Collector as its Chairman ex-officio, for the Indian members show no initiative or independence—has to provide roads and bridges, schools and sanitation. The Provincial Government has taken over the one High School, and provides school inspectors. It also supplies two or three doctors, and a supply of quinine for free issue. With regard to roads and bridges it maintains a few miles of main road and makes grants towards exceptionally big local works. With these inconsiderable exceptions, the £20,000 a year, which is the whole of the District Board's resources, has to provide schools, roads, medical attendance and sanitation for 3¹/₂ millions of people! And even this sum is something like twice as large as it was ten years ago. Though Gorakhpur has been British territory since 1803, its real administration in these matters does not seem to have begun until the twentieth century.

In Camp with P.H. Clutterbuck, Conservator of Forests, near Sonaripur (Kheri district), 3 February 1912

We left Gorakhpur with regret after an agreeable ten days, and travelled a day and night to this place, where we begin five days in camp with the officer in charge of half the forest area (Eastern Circle) of the United Provinces. The forest area of India is something like one-fifth to one-fourth of the whole, so that one ought not to leave it out of consideration, though apparently it has practically no visitors except those who come to shoot tigers or stags. We were met at the station by our host, the Conservator (who has supreme charge of seven forest districts) and by the officer in charge of this particular forest district. With them came two elephants, which took our luggage, and would have carried us, but after twenty-four hours on the train we preferred to walk. The "Camp" is around a Forest Bungalow, in the upper floor of which we sleep, and enjoy the comfort of a wood fire.

We began our experiences of the forest by an afternoon ride on our elephants through miles of high grass, and then miles of dense and trackless wood. The elephant stalks majestically at the rate of four or five miles an hour, picking his way skilfully, through the jungle, down into "nullahs" and up again on to steep banks, the "mahout" seated on his neck both guiding the beast so as to avoid tree trunks and branches too strong to be broken, and warding off other branches by his hands—occasionally slashing them off with a heavy and sharp knife (a most formidable weapon), or telling the elephant to break down a thin tree or a branch by his trunk or foot. It is astonishing how easily a huge elephant goes through what seems a thick wood.

The next morning we started out at 7 a.m. on foot, as it was cold and foggy and drenched with dew—the elephants following us—for the two Forest Officers to inspect two "coupes", or felling subdivisions of the forest, in which the contractor who had bid for the timber had found too large a proportion of unsound hollow trees, and claimed a rebate. After three miles walk along a forest road, we mounted our elephants and penetrated into the dense mass; finally returning on foot a couple of miles by road. Forestry in India means, it appears, the conservancy and wise exploitation of existing self-sown forests. With one small experimental exception, the Government of India does no planting or re-afforestation, having neither the requisite staff nor the pressing necessity. The huge area covered naturally with trees supplies all needs and demands all the available staff for mere preservation and management. The problem is therefore quite other than that in the U.K., and the position is also quite different from that of Germany and France, where scientifically planted forests are now in full and regular bearing. The Indian forests are only now beginning to recover from past neglect; and the older trees now being felled date from a time when no care was given. Even so, however, the forests yield to the Government between one and two millions sterling net annual revenue, besides large free concessions to the local inhabitants of fuel, grazing, etc. Our enthusiastic Forest Conservator declares that the net revenue could be largely increased merely by increasing the Forest Staff; and he gives statistics showing that the revenue per acre of forest area in the different provinces varies almost exactly according to the expenditure per acre on staff. The tall grass that here surrounds the wooden area in broad belts, and rising eight or ten feet high, is now burnt as useless, for the sake of protecting the forest from accidental fires. But our Conservator has long had the idea that it could be made into paper and has more than once tried in vain to induce the Government to experiment with it. Last year he was put in charge of the Forestry Exhibit at the Allahabad Exhibition, and allotted a lakh of rupees (£6666) for expenses. He promptly took the opportunity of engaging a paper making expert, and getting paper making machinery, with which he demonstrated at the exhibition that paper could be made of this valueless grass. The Government is now seriously considering how to turn to account this new forest product. The timber is sold by auction to Indian sawing contractors from Delhi, mostly Moslems, who come and camp in the forest for months, and fell the trees marked by the Forest Officer, which they saw by hand on the spot, and drag by bullock cart to the neighbouring railway, which was constructed mainly for this traffic. The payment is in two parts, one (the "monopoly" fee) a lump sum (say 4000 rupees) for the privilege of all the felling in a given "coupe" for one season; the other a fixed royalty charge per cubic foot for all that is taken away. But as no wisdom or care can estimate how many of the trees will be hollow and comparatively valueless, the bid used to be almost a gamble. Our Conservator introduced the idea of a Government guarantee that the sound timber in a coupe should be not less than a specified quantity. This abolished the gambling element to a great extent, and resulted in much larger biddings, as the contractor did not need to "make himself safe". But it involves the occasional allowance of a rebate when the proportion of sound timber turns out to be less than was anticipated; and then the Conservator finds some difficulty in explaining to a suspicious and unintelligent Finance Department at headquarters why any allowance should be made. There seems, in fact, to be no definite sanction for the arrangement, which the Conservator appears to have made on his own authority (though it has gone on for some ten years or so); and it has not been adopted elsewhere.

Perhaps for this reason our Conservator decided today to satisfy the two complaining contractors by letting them cut more trees, instead of returning the money!

Another day we sally out in the misty morning as before, but proceed to our next day's camp, making a long détour through high grass plains at the edge of dense wood, past swamps and bogs without end, in order to settle exactly where "His Excellency"[1] (who is coming in ten days to shoot stags) shall be placed. We see a score or two of graceful deer bounding away amid the tall grass, a herd of wild pigs rooting up the grass, monkeys now and then in the trees, a flight of wild peacocks and peahens, the jungle fowl from which all domestic poultry have been derived, beautiful white "egrets" or goose like birds, and in a swamp a black object which our keen sighted "mahouts" (elephant drivers) declared to be a crocodile. There are innumerable leopards, panthers and bears in the woods, and a tiger to every 100 square miles or so, but these do not reveal themselves in the daytime to the casual visitor.

[1] The first Baron Hardinge of Penshurst, Viceroy of India, 1910–16.

Chandan Chowki, 4 February 1912

This "day's" camp is on the very edge of the little river which separates India from Nepaul; or rather which used to be the boundary. As the river shifts its course constantly, the Nepaulese Government was induced to consent to the substitution of a demarcated land boundary a few hundred yards away. The foothills of the Himalayas rise rather abruptly a few miles to the North; and over them we catch peeps of snowclad mountain peaks which are the Himalayas proper. The scene is here graceful and charming, with the silent flowing stream amid woods and glades and tiny villages of aborigines. We go for our afternoon walk into Nepaul, across the new boundary, in order to consider whether the river can be prevented from cutting away the forest bungalow which is on its very brink.

We come to an idea, in our talks with our Forest Officer, which has been germinating in our minds for the past month. The Government of India is committing the sin of "faint-heartedness" in more departments than one. It is desperately in need of more revenue, to fill the void that is being left by the loss of its opium profits[1] as well as to meet the rapidly

[1] In the nineteenth century opium as a source of revenue was second in importance only to land. It was being grown chiefly in Bengal (where the government had an exclusive monopoly on its cultivation) and in the princely states of Central India (exports from

growing demand for popular education, etc. It cannot raise money by Death Duties (as the Joint Hindoo Family system stands in the way, and also intense feeling); its potentialities in Income Tax are limited by influential opposition and by the inability to discover Indian incomes; it cannot get much out of taxation on alcohol or tobacco, because the Indian takes relatively little of them, and no tea or coffee; it dare not increase the Land Revenue by more than the periodical increment corresponding to increased productiveness; it is precluded by English opposition from raising its import duties, and moreover, as the Indians purchase few imported commodities, even protective duties would yield very little; it fails to bring to its aid, with any effectiveness, either Local Government or Local Taxation, because of the invincible reluctance of the Local Authorities to impose local rates on house property. The result is that its revenue is inelastic, and insusceptible of increase. There remains the resource of profitable Government enterprise. Unfortunately the Government of India is averse from "competing with private enterprise"; the English commercial interests in India and in England are quick to raise objection; the Secretary of State for India is naturally disinclined to sanction any Government commercial adventures; and the civil servants in India, who *are* the Government of India, are intellectually "individualists", vaguely remembering the political economy textbooks that they crammed up twenty years before! Thus, the railways,

---

which were heavily taxed). Most of the trade in opium was designed to finance British purchases of silk and tea from China. Through most of the nineteenth century, thus, a significant volume of opium was exported—an euphemism for being smuggled out—in the face of strong opposition from the Chinese government, which was met by threats of war from the British. In 1907 and 1911 the Government of India concluded agreements with the Chinese to restrict the export of opium, so that by the time of the First World War the volume of trade was quite negligible. As a result the land area under opium decreased, as also the government's revenue from it.

though often owned by Government, are nearly all leased to companies; the gas and electricity supply in the large towns is in private hands; the employment of the prisoners in gaol is restricted to a few articles which do not compete with English enterprises; and there is no advance towards profitable Government monopolies. The exceptions are opium (now disappearing under treaty), and salt, an indefensible tax on the poor which has rightly been reduced to a low figure. Fortunately, the irrigation canals, have been kept as a Government service (because many of them are unremunerative) and these now yield a steadily increasing income. The 240,000 square miles of forests have also been kept in hand, and these now yield nearly two millions a year net, a sum which should steadily increase as the trees which have enjoyed a generation of scientific conservancy come to felling point, and as the means of communication enable the sale of fuel and other byproducts to develop. There is a small government factory of resin and turpentine, and another of quinine. Here, apparently, Government enterprise stops. It is not that profitable concessions have been granted to capitalists. Partly out of Treasury caution, partly out of past aversion to European exploitation of industries which might injuriously affect Indian agriculture, but mainly owing to the absence of desire on the part of European and American capitalists to embark in the difficult and unhealthy circumstances of India when more profitable fields lay open to them in Argentina, Canada, etc; and perhaps principally to the absolute indisposition of Indian capitalists to make industrial ventures, the field has (apart from jute and tea, the gold of Mysore, the coal needed by the railways and the Bombay cotton mills) remained as yet almost unworked. We cannot help thinking that it would be well for the Government of India to turn over a new leaf—to go in for tobacco and spirit Government monopolies, take over the railways and work them on a unified system for public ends, to put capital—perhaps attracting it out of native hoards by a "patriotic national loan"—into the more complete and more rapid development of its 240,000 square miles of forest, to start Government factories for matches, for paper, for rope and string and what not, if only for its own enormous consumption in the first instance. The Indians do better as minor Government officials than in any other capacity. They all desire Government appointments. The new movement might be made to appear essentially "Nationalist" in spirit, and might even be made to seem to be inspired and demanded by the Nationalists themselves. And the Government—like that of Japan—might in this way get large and growing new sources of revenue without appearing to tax the people, and indeed without really taxing them at all.

Our host Mr. Clutterbuck has not so attractive a personality as Hope Simpson. In physical appearance and voice he is a cross between Michael Sadler[2] and John Kemp. He comes from the landed gentry class—his mother became a catholic and his four sisters have all taken to the religious life—one a Roman Catholic nun and two Anglican nuns, and the other the Headmistress of the Catholic school, having been rejected by the convent because of her strong will! He is tall and muscular, a spare liver, and a good sportsman—or rather an ardent lover of the Forest and the wild animal—for killing seems to be with him a minor consideration. I must add to this that he is an enthusiast, almost a fanatic, about the value of his profession; regards the wise exploitation of the Forests as the central question of Indian administration. He has the reputation for being a hard and untiring worker at his jobs. He is, in fact, an excellent official within the narrow limits of the technique of his profession. But outside his profession he has no knowledge and no wisdom—his sayings are really rather absurd in their ignorance of facts and strange medley of prejudices. And even with regard to his own subject he is wholly incapable of seeing its relation to general administration, and his proposals of reform are not likely to recom-

[2] Sir Michael Ernest Sadler (1861–1943), Master of University College, Oxford; Director of Special Inquiries and Reports in the Education Department, 1895–1903; and President, Calcutta University Commission 1917–19.

mend themselves to his superiors because they combine good technical suggestions with foolish reflections on Indian Government in general. In explanation of this mixture of efficiency and unwisdom, one must remember that for the last twenty-one years—ever since he became a man—he has lived in remote districts—for months at a time wholly solitary except for the native coolie—at other times cooped up with an inferior European or Indian assistant. Also his work does not bring him into any responsible relationship with the inhabitants of the district—he is merely an employer like any other employer, or a trader dealing with native contractors on strictly business lines. Whether from circumstance or training, he lacks the broad humanity of Hope Simpson—and directly one leaves the forest and its development his company is tedious.

His assistant (John Tulloch, also of the Indian Forest Department, a few years junior to Clutterbuck) is, I think Eurasian—married to a buxom English woman of lower middle class origin. He is an unattractive but socially harmless person—silent and commonplace—suffering in health and activity from chronic over feeding. His wife eats the same five meals a day without apparently spoiling her digestion; her eyes and her skin are bright and clear and she is a pleasant creature of the fat, fair and forty type. Clutterbuck lives with the Tullochs—apparently he entertains them—while he is in their district—a relationship we should think undesirable between a chief and a working assistant—he treats Tulloch as something between an intimate and a foreman—the relationship lacks the dignity which qualifies all Hope Simpson's friendliness with his assistants.

Clutterbuck's great hero is Sir J. Hewett, the Lieut. Governor of the U.P. It is interesting to note that, though he has been 23 years in India, Hewett is the first Lieut. Governor he has ever known—and this acquaintanceship is due to Hewett's love of Forest sport. (Among all the other officials of the U.P. whom we have seen, Hewett is unpopular, regarded as a self-advertiser, and condemned as a devotee of

sport when he ought to be attending to business.) For the rest
of the Government of India, Clutterbuck has nothing but
abuse: the Viceroy is a useless Figure Head, the Secretary of
State a damnable nuisance, the Secretariat all selfish obstruc-
tionists, the Collectors amateurs who meddle with matters
they don't understand. And yet when S.W. or I make some
mild criticism of any part of the Government of India, our
host fires up as if we had attacked him personally! As to
England, it is going rapidly to the bad—Lloyd George is a
blackguard and Keir Hardie ought to be hung, drawn and
quartered. We cannot help suspecting that our host in spite
of his kindly hospitality and his eagerness to make us realise
the immensity of the Forest, as an asset to Indian finance, has
a somewhat unfavourable opinion of his present guests. Any-
way we perplex and irritate him—he cannot make out who
and what we are or what are our political intentions.

This morning S.W. visited on an elephant the two aboriginal villages close by the camp, in company with the Indian "Extra Assistant Forest Officer" who is permanently in this district under Mr. Tulloch. This Indian, a pleasant-speaking, efficient looking man of 45, had had 27 years service, and had been through the Government Forest College at Dehra Dun. He has reached the highest grade open to him, but as he has only just passed his last examinations, he is getting only £200 a year though he could go on further by increments up to 800 rupees per month (£600 a year). He lived all the year round at Sonaripur, with his wife, but sent his son to a boarding school at Naini Tal. The aboriginal villages, inhabited by "Tharus"[1], or dwellers in the Terai, the low-lying country on either side of the Nepaul frontier, differ ethnologically from the Hindoos of the Gangetic plain and it is said also from the hillmen of Nepaul, who are definitely Mongolian. But they struck me as being probably a result of intermixture between these races. They are now Hindoos by religion, of a sort; they burn their dead by the river, and they go on pilgrimage to Hindoo sacred places. But they kill and eat fish and game of all sorts, as well as domestic fowls and pigs,

[1] The Tharus, a tribe of the Himalayan Terai region in Uttar Pradesh (now a Scheduled Tribe), account for about one-third of the entire tribal population of that state.

and they make no use of Brahmins or other priestly personages, even on the most solemn occasions. They have no temples or obvious shrines or images; but on being questioned
they said they "did puja" in a recess of their hut. Their
habitations were in groups of half-a-dozen or so only, often
the households of relatives. They only marry one wife and
within the tribe, but they must choose outside their own little
village. One girl, who may have been 14 or 15, was described
by her mother as lately married, but not being sent to her
husband in the neighbouring hamlet for two or three years to
come. They are reported as being entirely chaste, honest,
truthful, industrious and almost completely free from crime
of any sort. They cultivate, each household, a few acres of
land, which the Forest Department lets them have at a
nominal fixed Land Tax, on the understanding that they will
labour at wages for the Forest Department when called upon
(e.g. outbreak of fire, etc.). They have oxen and various
tools; they crush their own mustard seed for oil and husk
their own rice by foot-lever and pounder; each house has a
"godown" or open shed in which grain, tools, etc. are
stored; their houses are elaborately constructed of white mud
walls, often worked into panels for ornament, surmounted
by a good roof of regularly cut beams and well constructed
grass thatch. They grow wheat, rice, dal, mustard, pepper,
potatoes, etc., and they make butter from the milk of their
cows. They were well and decently clothed; the women in
different coloured gowns and shawls, with many silver and
brass bangles, nose rings, ear-rings, necklaces, ankle ornaments and toe-rings. Altogether they seemed to be quite as
far advanced in "civilisation" as the Hindoos of the villages in
the Gangetic plain. But though they make their rude pottery
and their own carts, etc., and weave baskets and matting,
they have no handlooms for cotton cloth, which (with their
metal pots, etc.) they buy.

They were said to be apt to shift their habitations without
apparent cause—often on account of omens of one sort or
another—and the population on each side of the Nepaul fron-

tier was thus constantly fluctuating. The Government makes them report births and deaths month by month to a Forest Guard who visits for that purpose; and it sends periodically a Hindoo Vaccinator (whom S.W. saw with his pony laden with vaccine, etc.) to operate on all the children thus reported. These hamlets had just been done; and all the children had bad sores on their arms in consequence. The Forest Officer collects their Land Tax of a few pence per acre per annum; and allows them unlimited fuel free, whilst some of them are licensed to have guns of a rude sort to frighten away the deer. This sums up the whole of their contact with Government. There is no thought of a school for them, or of sanitation, or of medical attendance. They make no use of the police or post or civil courts and they are practically never in the criminal court.

Dudwa, 7 February 1912

We end our forest excursion today in an ideal "camp" in the very centre of this vast tract of wood, with seven straight roads radiating in all directions for ten or fifteen miles, with monkeys in the adjoining trees, and wild peafowl resting in the branches around us. Certainly it has been a most novel and interesting experience. And today come telegrams notifying that the Viceroy is, after all the preparations, unable to come owing to the serious illness of his brother-in-law Lord Alington. Fifty elephants are converging on this place from different directions and cannot easily be stopped or diverted, whilst preparations for feeding some five hundred persons of all ranks are in progress—all of which our host has now as far as possible to countermand.

Chhatarpur, Bundelkhund, Central India, 11 February 1912

We stayed a night at Lucknow and another at Jhansi on our way to a visit to the Maharajah of Chhatarpur. Professor A. W. Ward (brother of Prof. James Ward of Cambridge whose daughter married our friend, Lawson Dodd), with whom we stayed at Lucknow is the senior Professor at Canning College, and is bitterly disappointed at not being made Principal. He is an example of how men of capacity but without professional zeal go to seed in India—especially if they happen to be of the sensual type. From his appearance we infer that he has come down from a talented man to a lounger whose habits have brought him under a cloud. At his house we met a young fellow (McMahon, of Owens College, Manchester, and Oxford) just out from England, as Lecturer in Chemistry, who, if he stays in India, will certainly go the same way. From the slackness of these two men one would gather that there has not been a Principal of any personality at Canning College.

At Jhansi we were met by the Collector, the Judge and the Railway Engineer: we were eventually carried off to the house of the Railway Engineer. The brother and sister had a really well-appointed house—more luxurious and comfortable than that of Government officials. The sister (Miss Barnett) was a remarkably pleasant, able lady—much travelled—who deplored the futility of the lives of most Anglo-Indian women. "They give way to the climate and lounge all day, and then wonder that they lose their health". The brother was a hard-grained individualist—he seemed to be kept at work for long hours and had very little leave. They were the children of the General Manager of the Railway, and had been born in India, and were thoroughly acclimatised. But they knew nothing of the Indians, except as servants and subordinates, and were not interested in the Government of India or in any of its problems.

The Collector, Mr Silberrad (who dined with us and took us round the Fort in the morning) was a distinctly able, openminded man—said to be one of the ablest administrators—well thought of by the Government of the U.P. and of India. He was a harder and more reactionary person than Hope Simpson, and though pleasant and sympathetic in manner, did not really believe in raising the Indians to a higher level. His excuse for the negative policy was that English civilisation was doubtfully good—why then "impose it" on the Indians—why not keep them in a state of primitive bliss! He looked so efficient, so healthy, so agreeably self-complacent and so energetically happy that one could hardly believe that he was honestly doubtful of the civilisation that had produced him! In his attitude towards Indian unrest and Indian aspirations, he reminded one of Alfred Cripps[1] when he assures you that the labourers on his estate are, on the whole, more happily contented than his own class. In both cases the wish is father to the thought, and is a mere excuse for a sort of passive resistance to the upheaving forces.

Jhansi, normally a city of 36,000 inhabitants, was reduced in population by one half (and half the remainder only came in by day, and slept in rude shelters in the adjacent plain).

[1] Alfred Cripps was married to Beatrice's sister Theresa. Their son Stafford came to India in 1942, and again in 1946, to negotiate a settlement with Indian leaders.

The people have fled from the plague. The remainder were dying at the rate of forty per day! (forty-three was the statement for the day before we arrived). Nothing practical could be done, except watch the sanitation, remove the dead bodies of rats and men and inoculate the living. Some 3000 had been inoculated there within the last three months. At Cawnpore, where we stopped between trains, we drove to the Memorial Gardens, which surround the consecrated tomb, once the well into which the women and children were thrown at the Mutiny. This tomb, with its somewhat meretricious Marochetti statue, is quite properly fenced in and only opened by a soldier to visitors. But what is most objectionable, *no Indians* are allowed to enter the beautiful ornamental gardens, which are kept up out of public taxation. This dates from the Mutiny days, and is really an invidious piece of vengeful feeling. The soldier on duty defended the exclusion on the ground that if the Indians were admitted they would picnic all over the grounds, and make a mess—but this is a mere excuse. The clerk at the Bank of Bengal to whom we mentioned the matter said that he thought the continuance of an invidious race exclusion was a mistake.

14 February 1912

The journey from Cawnpore to Jhansi revealed a new India—an India of rocky fortresses and walled cities and villages—reminding one of the internecine warfare devastating the continent before the British Raj. The state of Chhatarpur[1] seems to be a place of Temples, the little capital where the Maharajah has his Palace and Guest House, being almost Burmese in the number of its temples in all stages of decay and smart newness. Very wonderful are the Temples of Khajuraho, whither we were motored by the Dewan on the second day of our visit to the Maharajah of Chhatarpur. Situated in a remote part of the state—52 miles from a railway station by a decent road and 30 miles by a bullock wagon track—they are seldom visited. They are reputed by Experts to be one of the finest groups in Northern India—some say in the whole of India. To antiquarians and art-dealers I suppose these temples have not only interest but also charm; but to the Philistine and Puritan mind they are spoilt by their incessant repetition of lascivious figures—

[1] A small state in the Bundelkhand region of Central India, with an area of 1169 square miles and a population of 1,73,148. Over this ruled H.H. Maharaja Vishwanath Singh Bahadur, immortalized as the Maharaja of Chhokrapur in J. R. Ackerley's *Hindoo Holiday*. The Maharaja was host not merely to Ackerley and the Webbs, but also to E. M. Forster and Goldsworthy Lowes Dickinson.

some being most grossly indecent in their representation of "unnatural" lust. Their beauty is confined to the attractiveness of a surface made up of innumerable carvings. But their location is also picturesque in its wild isolation.

We were motored out to them from Chhatarpur—doing the last mile or so in bullock carts for lack of a road—by the Dewan or Prime Minister of the State (salary £600 and house etc.), an able, attractive and outspoken Hindoo who had been Deputy Superintendent of Police and Deputy Collector in the United Provinces (provincial) service, and who was now "lent" to his present office (Misra). He was an "enlightened" Brahmin of Lucknow, whose nephews were being educated in America and England, and whose son (aged 8) was destined for England. He described to us how he had felt his career in the Provincial Service baulked by being denied promotion owing to the places being reserved for Englishmen, although they could not say he was unfit; and how he consequently accepted the Maharaja's offer to make him Dewan, although he would greatly prefer a Superintendentship of Police or a Collectorship in British India—notwithstanding his present great power of executing improvements, he did not like the attitude of servility to the Maharaja, nor the uncertainty caused by the absolute rule of a capricious person.

He described to us also in detail how his official career was once nearly wrecked—a warrant for his deportation without trial may perhaps have actually been out—because a subordinate whom he had reported got a venal informer, who had actually been convicted of forgery, to lay a secret charge against him of having subscribed his name (as a donor of 20 rupees) to a fund for upsetting British rule. Elaborate secret enquiry was made by the highest officials, and troops were even got ready. At last, one of the officers confronted him with the charge and produced the incriminating document, which he denounced as a clumsy forgery. He fortunately got the officer to order an instant search of the informer's house where they found all the apparatus of forgery, which led to the conviction of the informer. It is clear that the U.P. Government was in the most credulous mood, and prepared to swallow the most absurd delations.

He had, in his eighteen months of Dewanship, succeeded in greatly increasing the revenue, decreasing the waste and peculation, and doubling the number of village schools. The State had been suffering for a decade from bad and incompetent Dewans with the result that it had sunk near bankruptcy.

The Maharaja himself was rather a pathetic figure; a man of 45, sickly and weak, who had been married at 16 to the young daughter of a neighbouring little Maharaja like himself, who had borne him no children and who (like his own mother) was superstitiously religious in Hindoo fashion, and without education. He himself had had Theodore Morison[2] as tutor, and had taken to reading Comte and Herbert Spencer and G. H. Lewes (alternating with Marie Corelli). Without children, without anyone to talk philosophy to, without friends, without faith, he had (we were told and he almost confessed it to S.W.) taken to sexual malpractices, and was profoundly unhappy, and unable, as he said, to "find peace". He had found utterly useless the Anglican chaplain of the nearest Cantonment. He went every year on Hindoo pilgrimages (perhaps to please his ladies), but bathing in the sacred Ganges did not, he said, bring him peace of mind. "Where can I find God?" he asked us. "Where can I discover the ideal like Buddha or Jesus? How could Comte find this ideal in Clothilde de Vaux", he demanded at each of our three interviews. S.W. could only urge the way of work and duty and quote to him "We live by admiration, hope and love"; B.W. captivated him by explaining the

[2] Sir Theodore Morison (1863–1936) was appointed tutor to the Maharaja of Chhatarpur and Chharkari in 1855. In 1899 he became the Principal of the MAO College, Aligarh (having already taught there for ten years), and in 1903 Additional Member of the Imperial Legislative Council. He was also the author of *Imperial Rule in India* and *Industrial Organization of an Indian Province*.

difference between science and religion—the one demanding a perpetual striving after making our order of thought correspond with the order of things; the other supplying the purpose of life to be gained by aspiration or communion or prayer whereby our order of thought, in the realm of purpose, is brought into harmony with a higher order of thought, the great spiritual force that we hope and trust is above and behind all the worlds. He was familiar with translations of Plato and Hegel, and had been satisfied with Spencer, until G. H. Lewes's materialism had sapped his faith. We could only recommend Bergson and Father Tyrrell and William James (which books he instantly ordered from London), together with a sincere effort to do his duty by the 160,000 subjects in his charge.

Certainly it was an odd position—to be recommending Bergson and Father Tyrrell to a little Indian Kinglet, ruling over the area of an English county, in the most backward and secluded part of India, we the only white folk in the whole state. He was profusely grateful to us for coming to see him and childishly eager to detain us longer. Poor Prince: he has no one to talk to, no one to confide in. It is a terrible problem how to bring up these native Rulers. They must have some sort of education, and once educated, they can hardly escape an intolerable loneliness. We wonder whether a determined man might not make a Weimar out of a little Indian State; develop the best possible High School, graft on to the local hospital a miniature medical college, and on to a State Printing Press and Engineering Works, the nucleus of a Science Faculty and Technical Institute—calling to him the ablest men from all parts of India, and thus at the same time making his little principality a centre of intellect, and securing congenial society for himself. It might not cost more than dissipation or sport or building extravagant palaces. We accidentally met at the Guest House the "Political Agent" who has charge of all the twenty-two ruling chiefs of Bundelkhund, under the "Agent to the Governor General" at Indore, who has responsibility for all the States in the "Central India Agency". This "political", an ex-officer of the Indian Army (Colonel Impey) was touring round Bundelkhund with his sister; and we spent one evening together very pleasantly. He was much more of the polished and cultivated diplomatist than the typical Collector. It is interesting that when we tried on him the suggestion of the "Boy Scout" movement for India, as tending to give the boys manliness and vigour and discipline and manners, he instinctively objected lest it might lead to a demand for a volunteering movement in India, or at any rate, to a training which might one day be found dangerous to British rule! The question arises always, are these officers really desirous of improving the character and capacities of the people of India? Col. Impey (as we heard next day) is to be the new Resident at Baroda, a great promotion for him.

We gather that the relation between the Government of India and these Native States is a peculiar one. Practically nothing is published about their goings on. (Col. Impey said that Tupper's "Political Practice",[3] a secretly printed official book in four volumes, contained most interesting precedents, but that it was kept strictly confidential.) The relation varies with the size and importance of the State. Those big enough to have separate residents (like Hyderabad, Mysore, Cashmere, Baroda, etc.) were treated very carefully, and not interfered with except in extreme cases. The smaller states were more summarily dealt with. They did not all have the power to inflict death sentences; and most of them had to submit them for confirmation before they were carried out. The officer in charge of them was always open to receive petitions and complaints; and these were either simply filed (if frivolous), or forwarded to the Dewan for him to act on as

[3] *Indian Political Practice: A Collection of the Decisions of the Government of India in Political Cases* (1895), compiled by C. L. Tupper of the Indian Civil Service. Tupper's preface to the work describes it as a compilation of the 'leading cases showing the practice and policy of the Government of India in their dealings with the Native States'.

he chose (if unimportant), or else sent "for favor of a report" (if they disclosed any *prima facie* injustice or malpractice). The "political" would comment informally on anything bad in the way of administration that he noticed, and might make suggestions for improvement in an unofficial way. But mere inefficient administration, mere customary peculation or waste, mere ordinary cases of capricious favoritism or injustice, mere common extravagance in expenditure, would not be interfered with, any more than consistent lack of improvement, or personal immorality. On the other hand, any glaring and serious tyranny of a gross kind, and actual bankruptcy of the State, as well as serious, persistent, long-continued drunkenness in the Ruler, led to summary deposition; the seating of the next heir on the throne; and the deportation of the erring Ruler to some obscure corner of India, there to live on a fixed allowance, under the eye of a vigilant officer. The Maharaja of Datia, a neighbouring kinglet, had lately been deposed. He was addicted to drink, and used to extort money from his richest subjects. One unhappy victim went home and slew all his family, and then committed suicide, rather than comply with the tyrant's whims. This led to instant deposition.

The legal position is peculiar. These Native Rulers are in law independent sovereigns, and their people are not British subjects. But they are under a definite suzerainty, which deprives them of all foreign relations, defines and limits their criminal jurisdiction, prohibits wars and sets arbitrary bounds to the number and quality of their armed forces, receives complaints of their administration and actually entertains appeals against their action in internal affairs, keeps a tight hand on their raising loans, watches and to some extent controls visitors to their States and themselves, and makes them personally liable to trial and punishment, even to summary deposition at the hands of the British Government for gross maladministration, crime or grave misconduct.

In confirmation of our impression as to the idea of Boy Scouts for India, we have just learnt that one Chaplain did start a corps, but has been told by the Government of India *not* to recruit any further—the reason alleged being that it was not yet decided whether there should be an organisation for India, or a branch of the English organisation—or (as we suspect) any at all! (See further confirmation from Sir Louis Dane at Lahore, March 14th.)

We have been two days in this State—about seven times as large and five times as populous as Chhatarpur—on the invitation of the Begum,[1] an exceptionally energetic and enlightened ruler. In the luxurious "guesthouse" in which we were entertained we found an Anglican chaplain and his wife (Martin) who were touring round their extensive "parish" of many hundred square miles, in which he dealt only with the few Anglican Christians. He reflected the usual "army" prejudice against the "niggers", which he owned to sharing, though he was openminded enough to recognise it. He said that discontent with English rule was universal and increasing, and that there would be grave danger in the future. When it was put to him that the Government of India had no clear purpose, he said it seemed to him that their purpose was to develop the Indian to manhood and nevertheless keep him in leading strings after attaining manhood! He admitted and defended the English race-exclusiveness, whilst recognising its invidiousness. He approved of excluding Indians from the English clubs. The exclusion was occasionally relaxed for money. He related a case, which he admitted to be one of

[1] Her Highness Nawab Sultan Sir Jehan Begum of Bhopal (1858–1930) succeeded her mother in 1910. She was eighth in lineal descent from the founder of the dynasty, Dost Mohammed Khan, and the third woman to occupy the throne.

rather mean behaviour, as to the new club at Indore, which is the seat of the Agent to the Governor General for all these Central India Native States. As the new building cost money, the club committee actually asked all the Native Rulers for donations, which many of them gave, and these were then, with much heart-burning, personally and exceptionally, admitted as members. It did not seem to strike him that any such application for donations, under the very peculiar relations of the English officers with these Native Rulers, was quite unwarrantable.

We have seen the Jail, with a couple of hundred male and a dozen female prisoners, under the superintendence of the State Engineer, the son of a previous (Scotch) State Engineer . . . . A large proportion (a quarter?) were under life sentences for murder, and there were only five belonging to a criminal tribe. (We infer from these facts that mere petty theft does not usually lead to jail).

Under the guidance of the energetic lady doctor employed by the Begum (Mrs. Dissent Barnes) we inspected her own hospital for women and children, and also the men's hospital (under Dr. Sarabji, a parsee). Syphilis is said to be almost universal, and unnatural vice as well: there is, in fact, no idea of sexual morality, among either Hindoos or Musselmans. The most interesting feature was the attempt to regulate midwifery. The Begum had ordered the "Bais" or native midwives, who were to the last degree ignorant and superstitious, to attend classes held by the Lady Doctor; and the police were now stopping the practice, in Bhopal city, of any who had not received a diploma, or who, being qualified, had been suspended (by the Lady Doctor) for malpractice or carelessness. We have heard of no such attempt in British India. One thing we note about all these Central India States— Chhatarpur, Bhopal, Gwalior and the intervening British territory—is the very large proportion of land lying waste and unproductive. Vast stretches of sparse scrub and bushes, plains covered with a scanty natural herbage of the coarsest kind, little bits of self-sown woodland of no pecuniary value, acre upon acre of boulder-strewn rock surface, weathering into brickmaking clay—all indicate that there is, here at any rate, no pressure of population on the soil. In Chhatarpur, for instance, the Dewan was fully conscious of the need for more population, which would actually increase the yield per head. Wells and tanks—even more than irrigation canals—would apparently well repay their cost. The Begum of Bhopal is reported to be keenly alive to this need, but we did not learn what was being done. In Gwalior much is being spent on irrigation by the State.

We spent the afternoon with the Begum of Bhopal—at least we ladies did (the wife of the chaplain and two relations of officials and myself), Sidney and the other men being restricted to an hour's interview during which her Highness kept her veil down—just showing her eyes. The conversation was chiefly between the Begum and myself, as the other ladies were shy, and before the afternoon was ended, we were on very friendly terms.

The Begum of Bhopal is the one woman among the Native Rulers of India, and she is the third or fourth(?) woman in succession in the State of Bhopal (the eldest child, whether boy or girl, inheriting the Chieftainship). She is now an elderly woman with two grown up sons and another at school. She has a great reputation as perhaps the most dutiful and statesmanlike of the Indian Chiefs. And certainly her personality fully bears out her reputation. She is small and thick in stature, but when she threw back her veil, on the departure of the men, I was surprised and attracted by the strong fine features and humourous and kindly expression (somewhat like the portrait of George Eliot) and with the total absence of any self-consciousness either as a woman or as semi-royalty. A wise old mother and an able business woman—not a bit of the great lady—clad in austerely simple garments, far more simple than those of the Mahommedan dames we afterwards met at her Purdah club, she is obviously a masterful woman, who is her own Prime Minister, having direct relations with each head of department. Her officials are devoted to her, but they record that she checks every penny of expenditure and insists perhaps overmuch in getting full value for her money. We talked about women, their position and their education, about the education of Chief's sons, about the sphere of religion, about Turkey and Egypt and their reform movements, about European society. She has recently been on a tour beginning with the Coronation in England, and ending with her reception in Constantinople by the Sultan. She seemed to take the British Dominion for granted and to have an almost naive respect for the King Emperor and the British Raj. But she did not wish the Indians or the followers of Islam "Europeanised". "The English are very "habile"—Europeans know a great deal—when they are evil they are powerful for evil. If our young men go there, when they are young they may get into bad hands, they may learn to abuse India and their own religion. I go to a house of a duchess in England and see all the magnificence and though I am an old woman, when I come back here, I think my own Palace very plain and I am tempted to abuse it".

And certainly when one followed her eyes round the homely and almost bare room—more like the parlour of a very large farm house—one saw what she meant. So she was against Chiefs' sons being sent to England: she was dissatisfied with the Chiefs Colleges as too luxurious and not sufficiently advanced in learning—she wanted her sons to go to an Indian Public School where they would have to compete with boys who were going to be Pleaders and Medical Men and Civil Servants and Engineers. "I want my youngest son to go into business so that the race may become rich". About religion and its relations to the state she was depressed. "Our Mulvis are too Conservative, they are against English education and science, our clever young men despise them and throw off religion—that is not good. The young Turks abuse religion; we shall not prosper unless we are true followers of our Prophet". Apparently the old lady is a strong believer in Islam; what money she can spare from the temporal wants of her people she is lavishing on a new Mosque which is to be more magnificent than any at Delhi. But at the same time she refused to give to beggars, and is a sworn critic of the idle Mulvis. "My mother used to give to beggars: I always send them away saying that 'I pay teachers and doctors and nurses and not idle ones' ". Her main preoccupation is the education of women. She wants the Mohammedan woman to become highly trained before she leaves off Purdah. She even approves of Purdah as a permanent institution—at any rate the modified Purdah of never going unveiled among men. "The Turkish ladies are breaking Purdah, before they are fit for it. They are reading bad French novels and they do what is wrong". So she has started a first-rate girls' High School— said to be one of the best in India—and she is trying to educate the married ladies by a Purdah club, where they have lecturers and talks once a week. As to the position that women should occupy, her views are somewhat conflicting. She is dead against the Suffrage Movement,[2] but she thinks that *all*

---

[2] Beatrice Webb herself was but a recent convert to the suffragist cause. In 1889 she had been a signatory to a manifesto opposing the enfranchisement of women. Seventeen years later she wrote to Millicent Garrett Fawcett, the leader of the constitutional movement for women's suffrage, informing the latter of the change in her position on the issue. It is a measure of Beatrice Webb's importance that Fawcett immediately had the letter published in *The Times*. In the letter Beatrice claimed that her earlier opposition to the vote for women had been based in her conviction that women preferred 'to leave the rough and tumble of party politics to their mankind', while concentrating their own energies on the particular social obligations of women, namely the bearing of children, the advancement of learning, and the transmission and promotion of spiritual life. This division of labour, she claimed, was possible only because it was rooted in a feeling of consent to the actions of government. This she compared to the ready acquiescence of 'the more spiritually minded Eastern . . . in the material management of his native country by what he regards as the Anglo-Saxon "man of affairs". The time had come, however, Beatrice wrote in 1906, when the obligations of women had become the concerns of the entire community, and the objects of governmental action. Women, therefore, were now losing their 'consciousness of consent', and

Rulers should be women. "My mother and my grandmother were Rulers before me; I lost my two daughters and now a son will succeed me. It is a great misfortune. Men care for their pleasures; they must have sport and races. A woman Ruler is the mother of her people; her whole life is spent in thinking what is best for them". And she seems to have been as good as her wŏrd. Not merely in education but also in Public Health she has been more advanced than the Government of British India. Three English lady doctors, and one Parsee medical man and an assistant, are engaged in hospital and dispensary work at Bhopal. At present they are trying to educate the native midwife, and the Begum has practically adopted the English Midwifes Act for Bhopal city. Any energy she has left over from the supervision of her Government she spends in translating English textbooks and school books. "I want to start a department at Bhopal for translating and publishing good books for all India in the vernacular—I have tried to get a clever young man to come and live here and do that work, but I have not yet found one. What we want in India more than anything else are good books in Urdu and Hindi. You cannot teach children in a foreign language; they only pretend to understand what they read".

She took us to the Purdah Club held in one of the old Palaces. Here were some twenty Mahomedan, and two Parsee ladies—the Hindus had not joined the club. With their bright coloured and elaborately embroidered satin leggings and soft silk gauze veils they made the dear old Begum with her cotton leggings and knitted woollen shawl look more than ever the Wise Old Woman, too wise and careful about

---

were rightly claiming a share in directing the actions of state to more effectually fulfil their obligations. If, Beatrice added, the British government in India were to interfere with the religious obligations of Hindus and Muslims, British rule in that country would be similarly threatened. She did not, however, carry this strange analogy any further than this conjecture. Beatrice Webb, *Our Partnership* (Cambridge University Press/London School of Economics, 1975 edition), pp. 360–3.

the good of other people, to care how she looked herself. She was treated with great deference but with no kind of servility—more the deference shown to age and knowledge than that shown to social position. She chatted some half hour with them, and then, as the lecturer failed to come (a lady doctor who was to have lectured on "First Aid" but who was detained by the dangerous illness of an infant), she rose and left, saying that she must go back and do her gardening. For the Begum has one or two relaxations—gardening, "Sketching from Think" she calls it (i.e. driving out and seeing something and then trying to reproduce it), and playing on the piano with one finger, tunes she had heard played by the English teacher to her little grandsons. She has also adopted a handsome little grand-daughter. I doubt not she would like to make her the Begum—for quite clearly she adores her. The little girl is extraordinarily handsome and intelligent looking —more like a North Italian than a typical Hindu. Her youngest son's wife—a girl of 13—not yet allowed to live with her husband—was also under the care of the Begum and was being carefully educated.

Gwalior, 17/19 February 1912

We are staying here in the Hotel—we had no introduction to the Maharajah, and the Political Agent to whom we had a letter, was not "on-coming"; but the Mahomedan Minister of Gwalior (an old pupil of Theodore Morison) and the Hindu Physician to the Maharajah to whom we had a Nationalist introduction, have been most kind and helpful. Gwalior is the most wonderful *Indian* city that we have yet seen. In all the cities of British India the "native city" is always "slummy" in character—narrow alleys, dirty and ill-paved, such fine houses as there are tumbling into decay or degraded by being used as warehouses or tenement houses. But at Bhopal, and still more at Gwalior, one finds broad streets, beautifully carved balconies, doors and latticed windows, mosques and temples, old and new Palaces, all telling of the Indians in possession of their own country, making for a civilised India "without the English". And so far as one gets a glimpse of the actual administration one can hardly say that Indians show themselves incapable of the art of government. Of course the officials have often been educated in England, or taken from the ranks of Indians in the Government of India's service. But there is certainly no sign of these officials being inherently weak, or corrupt, or partial between creed and creed, or caste and caste. In fact, in all the three Native States that we have visited, there has been no kind of tension be-

tween Mahomedan and Hindu, and each ruler, Hindu or
Mahomedan, has officials of the other creed.

We were interested in talking to two energetic young Hindu business men, one of them having a workshop in Gwalior
and another in Bombay, and both of them being ardent
Nationalists, to learn that on the whole they preferred living
under British rule to that of a Native Chief. "We are more
free in British India", they both exclaimed, "we can say more
what we like and we know that there will be no arbitrary
government. Here we can be imprisoned without appeal and
tried in secret. We are not secure. Anything may happen".
The old physician, who was the uncle of one of them,
disagreed—but then he was a Court functionary. On the
other hand, the Englishman who was acting as Director of
Education preferred working in a native state as he had more
scope for initiative and was not tied down by rigid rules or limited by the necessity of elaborate reports to the Government of India.

We met at the Minister of Justice's house some half dozen
of the other Ministers (all Hindu or Muhammedan except
the Director of Education, though three out of the four chief
engineers are English also). One gathered from them that the
Maharajah,[1] an active man of thirty-five, is a good administrator and really concerned to make improvements. His

[1] H.H. Maharaja Madhav Rao Scindia of Gwalior (1876–1925)
was ruler of the largest Maratha state (26,637 sq. miles) and one of
the four Indian princes entitled to a 21-gun salute. He was also
among the most loyal supporters of the British government in India, going so far as to name his children George and Mary, after the
King and Queen. He was a member of an Imperial Service Unit to
China and a generous contributor to the war effort in World War I,
when he financed a hospital ship, appropriately named *Loyalty*. In
Central India he led the princely opposition to the Non-Co-
operation Movement, proscribing eight nationalist newspapers
within his state. He was particularly well-known for his fondness
for practical jokes and his interest in mechanical devices, the prime
example of which was a silver train which went around his banquet
table dispensing after-dinner port, mints, nuts and cigarettes.

Palace and beautiful gardens are open to every one, and from the tasteful and sober internal decorations of both the public and private rooms one would gather that he is a man of refinement. He pays great attention to the performance of religious rites, and keeps Mahomedan as well as Hindu festivals. Just now his domestic affairs are in a state of confusion. His present wife has borne him no children—his subjects desire his re-marriage and he himself is courting the daughter of the Gaikwar of Baroda.[2] But the young lady is making elaborate conditions—she refuses to keep Purdah, insists on six months in Europe, and even, so report says, demands the key of the treasury, besides a written guarantee that any boy of hers shall succeed to the throne. Meanwhile there is a left-handed lady who is doing her best to stop the marriage, though the legitimate wife—a pious and popular woman—has given her consent to the Maharajah's second marriage. Altogether one imagines that the Palaces of the Native Rulers are veritable hot-beds of intrigue—usually revolving round a woman.

As a contrast to the elaborately civilised palace and capital city of the Maharaja, there came a glimpse of his mental attitude towards his deceased father. That potentate, long since dead, is still treated as living. In a palatial tomb on the outskirts of the city, his life-sized statue in black marble sits on a couch, fully dressed in his royal habiliments. On either side is said to sit, similarly attired, a statue each of his two wives; but these were behind a purdah, so we did not see them. Before him twice a day is spread a varied repast, which is offered by attendant Brahmins with appropriate incantations. And every evening in the great hall below his raised chamber, there is performed from six to eight p.m. an entertainment for his delectation, of singing and music, and (we were told) dancing. The whole daily celebration is organised and performed by a hundred Brahmins. It was not the Minister of Justice

---

[2] The engagement broke, for the Princess Indira of Baroda was determined to marry Jitendra Narayan, the Maharaj Kumar of Cooch-Behar, which she did eventually, though in rather strange circumstances: at a Brahmo ceremony in Buckingham Palace.

who told us of this as he seemed a little ashamed of it, and refused to accompany us, though he kindly sent us in his carriage. Nor is it mentioned in the guide book. But the hotel
keeper put us on the track of it. Certainly the scene was
strange. Putting off our shoes, we ascended steps in the dark
to the great hall, which we found brilliantly lighted. Four
performers (three men and a gaily dressed girl) were singing
and playing, as if to the Maharaja, whose black figure one
saw in the raised inner chamber, before which a great sculp-
tured bull was kneeling. Inside, the Brahmins were offering
food, chanting sentences, and lighting incense. A score or so
of other persons, presumably Brahmins, sat around and listened to the weird music. Day by day this barbarous rite is
repeated.

Agra, 19/23 February 1912

The wonderfully beautiful buildings here—far more beautiful than we had ever imagined, of a charm and grace that no photograph gives any idea of—compel the reflection that, only 250 years ago, these people were capable of conceiving and executing work of quality unsurpassed by anything or any race in the world. Not only in conception and design, but also in craftsmanship, the Indians of the Mogul Court (1550–1650) stand unrivalled. In England at that date we were building St. John's College, Oxford, and the Banqueting Hall at Whitehall, and to this day, we have no building which in grace, and charm and beauty of design or workmanship, comes anywhere near the work of these "niggers", as the Army Officer calls them. It is clearly a case for the recognition of "reciprocal superiority" as the proper mental attitude between races. And from some of these beautiful creations of Indian art—the Mosques and Palaces inside the Fort—all "natives" are excluded, since the Mutiny, unless they procure a special pass though all Europeans—foreigners as well as the English—go in and out as they choose without let or hindrance. This is all the more detestable as Indians delight in visiting famous and beautiful places, and their behaviours at the Taj or at the ancient city of Fatehpur Sikri, where we graciously admit them without question, are most decorous and even reverential.

We spent a morning with the John Brothers,[1] Sir Edwin John and Mr. Ulysses John, the great capitalists of Agra, employing 7,000 workpeople, in cotton and corn mills, and miscellaneous works such as ice-factory, brick-fields, etc. This family is of Greek origin (some say Eurasian) and R.C. religion. It claims to have been settled here for over one hundred years, always marrying Europeans, usually British women. Sir Edwin John and his brother were real "bounders"—self-indulgent and commonplace—but apparently energetic and enterprising in investing their money to win. We saw most of the younger brother, who took us over the mills and after a sumptuous lunch in a luxurious bungalow drove us out to the Dowla tomb,[2] across the Jumna. He and his brother had the most unutterable contempt for the Indians—Hindu and Mohammedan—and quite clearly thought that their right position was that of slaves who could be beaten if they did not work. In the course of our conversation I hardly think there was one bad quality that they did not accuse them of. And—though their most acid criticism was reserved for the educated native ("a damnable mistake to educate the native") they were equally angry with the cultivator and the coolie: "We employ no natives in positions of responsibility—they all rob and lie and cheat. Come to the Mills and see for yourself how the native works—he never works more than 4 hours in the 24 and he is away every other day". And certainly the scene at the mills seemed to give colour to their statement. At some building operations not a single man had

[1] Sir Edwin John and A. Ulysses John were proprietors of Messrs. A. John & Co., Agra. They were the descendants of Anthony John, a Greek dealer in diamonds who came to India in 1801. His successors, particularly Edwin, were responsible for the expansion and success of the firm which, in the first decade of the twentieth century, boasted several spinning and weaving mills, a ginning factory, a flour mill and a factory for the manufacture of ice, all located on 80 acres of freehold property belonging to the John family.

[2] The tomb of Itmad-ud-Daulah, the father of the Mughal empress Noor Jehan.

turned up at 9.30: the unfortunate contractor saying that they had all absented themselves, without notice, he supposed to attend a wedding! In shed after shed half the mechanics were idle. We learnt afterwards that a quarter to a third of all the hands had not turned up during the whole day. In some cases the machines were running without an attendant and the output was littering the floor. For it was not only a case of absentees—the men and boys who were there, were in many cases, sitting outside the mill, or eating or sleeping near their machines. In one case a youth was fast asleep between two looms. After several kicks from Mr. John he started up and with the usual servile attitude of folded hands remarked that he "had not slept last night"—another way of saying that he had been amusing himself! Every room was dirty and the waste of material was amazing. All the hands seemed in fact to be deliberately skulking and even wasting the material, and their attitude was hostile and sulky. It must be added that John swore and cursed them and would have struck them, if he had not feared the consequences. "They put us into Court, if we try to punish them—and if we scold them they simply don't turn up the next day. Oh! it is cruel" he went on saying. "Look at them, they are eating all day, and when they are not eating, they are gambling or smoking or sleeping". When I asked which were the worst, the Mohammedan or the Hindu, he replied "that the Mahomedan could work if he chose—two Mohamedans would, any day, put an end to 20 Hindus. But then he was a real 'Budmash',[3] he stole and he lied. The Hindu had usually no brains—when he had brains, he was far *too* clever and cheated and lied". We tried to find out on what method these hands were paid—he told us they were all paid piece work; but the Scotch foreman told Sidney that only one man out of nine (the chief "minder" of the self-acting mule) was paid piece work, the rest (i.e., piecers) were on a daily wage. In fact, all John's statements were vague and inaccurate. He told us that 4000 out of the 6000 were boarded

[3] Wicked, a rogue or rascal.

and lodged in a compound, but when we went to inspect, it turned out that they were only given cheap rooms, paying 4 to 6 annas per month rent—he had apparently not understood our question. The families living in these houses or rather holes looked as sulky and hostile as the hands in the mill. They were all low castes, John Brothers refusing to employ Brahmins *in any capacity* "if they knew it" apparently because they thought Brahmins were centres of sedition against the John's Firm and the British Raj.

One interesting sidelight they gave us—Japan was becoming a formidable competitor in cotton piece goods in Calcutta because of the *first-rate quality* of her cloth.[4] They had a great admiration of the Japanese business man.

They were bitter critics of the liberal policy of the present administration, but curiously enough they talked just like Nationalists about "the drain";[5] and said that India was better off before railways made the export of corn easy. From the John Brothers' bad tempers, I should gather that their enterprises are not going well and that the rebuilding of Delhi[6] is

---

[4] After about the mid 1880s the cotton mills of Bombay—largely indigenously owned—had become a serious challenge to the export of British yarn in the Far East, especially China, forcing British producers to specialize in finer-count yarns. However, foreign demand for Indian cotton dropped as the Japanese market was lost to India in the early years of the twentieth century. This was followed by the loss of the Chinese market also, due partly to the emergence of Japan as a competitor and partly to the sudden development of the cotton spinning industry in China itself.

[5] The early Indian nationalists' critique of colonialism was based upon the 'drain theory' of Dadabhai Naoroji, which subsequently also found votaries in Justice Ranade, William Digby and R. C. Dutt. The chief claim of this theory was that a substantial portion of India's national wealth was being exported to England, and that economic exploitation by the British was thus the cause of the poverty of India, which paid this heavy price or 'tribute' in return for British rule. Dadabhai Naoroji, *Poverty and Un-British Rule in India* (1901).

[6] When the construction of the new capital commenced, the Public Works Department employed a veritable army—of 29,000

making their labour market even more unsatisfactory than usual. What is quite clear is that these old standing European inhabitants of India have not acquired the art of managing the Indians. What is equally clear is that the Indian is sometimes an extraordinarily difficult worker *to sweat*. He does not care enough for his earnings. He prefers to waste away in semi-starvation rather than overwork himself. However low his standard of life, his standard of work is lower—at any rate when he is working for an employer whom he does not like. And his irregularities are baffling. [At Gwalior the wages of highly skilled stone carvers and painters were 8 annas per day (15 Rupees per month). In Agra a Punkah coolie, who used to get only 3 to 4 Rupees a month, now got 6 Rupees a month, which is 3 annas a day].

We had, in Gorakhpur, jumped at the chance of attending a Hindoo wedding, which Gokal Prasad, an Assistant Magistrate of the Provincial Service was going to attend at Agra on 20th February. We heard no more of it, but on the morning of the 20th no fewer than six members of the family, introduced by Gokal Prasad himself, called upon us, and formally invited us to come at 8 p.m. There were various weddings going on—the season is the favourite one—and the Indian city was alight here and there with primitive illuminations. Avoiding with some difficulty a great Bunnia wedding, we at length reached the house to which we had been invited, the whole street being lit up with primitive oil lamps. Entering the courtyard we found it covered by a huge awning, and arranged with long tables for the two or three hundred guests. Presently the bridegroom's procession arrived, the bridegroom himself arrayed in the customary gorgeous robes, and bearing on his head the gilt and jewelled crown appropriate to his position. He was an intellectual-looking, spectacled young man of pleasing countenance, an Assistant

workers—including stonecutters and masons from Agra. Robert Grant Irving, *Indian Summer: Lutyens, Baker and Imperial Delhi* (Yale University Press, 1981), pp. 135–6.

Civil Surgeon of Delhi, who had brought with him forty or
fifty men friends. This was a wedding of a Kayasth family,
and the Kayasths have made for themselves a reforming reg-
ulation limiting the number of guests introduced by the
bridegroom at their weddings. We understood that there
were three classes, limited to 75, 50 and 40 guests respectively (or something like that); and this particular family had
elected for the second class. The Bridegroom had so far never
seen the Bride, who had of course been selected for him by
the negotiations of the two families. The Bridegroom was
seated on the seat of ceremony, and half a dozen Brahmins
performed the "Darwaza" ceremony, which consisted in the
presentation to him of various things, including some family
presents, and much recitation of Sanskrit formulae. The odd
thing was that this was not made in any way a central feature.
It was done in a corner of the covered courtyard, whilst the
guests sat at the long tables and ate and talked, paying no
attention to the ceremony—even a gramophone was playing
hideous Hindoo tunes part of the time. After this was over,
we went upstairs and had refreshments apart from the crowd;
and B.W. was taken inside to see the women, including the
bride, most of them never having seen at close quarters any
European woman. The actual marriage ceremony at which
the bride would be presented to the bridegroom was not to
take place until 2 a.m., that being the hour pronounced by
the Brahmins to be auspicious according to the horoscopes of
the parties. These people were all of the Kayasth caste, mostly in the Government service, or pleaders. They struck us as
extremely intellectual, refined and courteous—in their own
way highly civilised—but both unwilling and unable to free
themselves from superstitious uses and the conventions
which in India are both social and religious. Some, however,
had joined the Arya Somaj.

The women of the family were introduced to B.W. in the
refreshment room (their quarters which I had peeped into
were merely dark bedrooms) by one of the English speaking
men of the family; he had, however, to retire when the youn-

ger women appeared and his place was taken by a relative of the second generation, but even he had to turn his back before I could speak to the wife of the third generation. The women were prettily dressed and looked happy and intelligent. The bride was an especially pleasant looking little girl of 13—she was not yet in bridal dress as that had to be put together at the last moment.

At the wedding, an Arya Somaj member had pressed us to attend a meeting or service of the Agra Branch of the organisation, which we agreed to do the day after tomorrow. They seem thereupon to have hastily summoned a special meeting and at 5 p.m. six members, including the Secretary, came to the hotel with carriages to fetch S.W. to the function. (Whether or not they expected B.W. also is not clear, but she was too tired to go). The meeting place was a small plain house, having a large paved courtyard, in which under a wide awning the meeting took place. Something like 150 men were squatting down under this awning, facing a table and three chairs. But first four of them went and sat apart, facing each other, and gradually made a fire in their midst, piling on stick after stick, and then pouring on salt and clarified butter, and incense, the whole being accompanied by Sanskrit recitations or incantations. This was "Havan", a ceremony prescribed for morning, and for the beginning of every service or meeting, according to the prescription of the Vedas. It was expressly explained to be no more than an act of purification of the atmosphere, the substances burnt having purifying qualities, with the purpose of remedying as far as practicable the involuntary fouling of the atmosphere which human life involves. Here, again, what was noticeable was that it was only a "sideshow". It was not made the central feature of the service, but went on in a corner of the compound, without the waiting crowd (squatted under the awning) even turning round to look at it. Presently one of the crowd arose, in obedience to a call from the Chairman, and recited a long Sanskrit prayer or invocation from the Vedas. Then another man read an essay entitled "Is God a Reality" in English, proving the existence, the omnipotence, the omnipresence and the permanence of God, a paper of no intellectual value or logical strength. Finally, after brief speeches of welcome for S.W. and a reply by him, the meeting terminated with another Sanskrit recitation. It was noticeable that every quotation from the Vedas was chanted or intoned, never spoken naturally.

The meeting consisted almost entirely of intellectual-looking, cultivated, *young* men under 30 or so, there being only half a dozen grey heads among the whole hundred and fifty. This was explained by the hour of meeting, arranged for S.W.'s convenience, being too early to allow of attendance by men in business or Government service, so that the bulk of those present were said to be student class, or else superannuated persons. It was remarkable that such a meeting should have been got together at such short notice. They were obviously devout and apparently full of sincerity and zeal. At one point a dozen little children were brought in, being some of the orphans that the society had rescued from death and undertaken to support and educate—each member pays 1 per cent of his income as subscription.

We saw, in Agra, at dinner or otherwise four civilians—Reynolds who was just handing over charge as Commissioner on final retirement owing to age limit; Mardon, Collector, who received temporary charge as Commissioner, F. C. Chamier, Joint Magistrate about to act as Collector; and Dacres (cousin to Sir Sydney Olivier) a youthful Assistant Magistrate. Reynolds was old and worn out by 34 years service, and seemed a routine person, "wooden" and uninteresting. Chamier was a young man of charm and refinement, somewhat silent and modest, but apparently able and sympathetic. Dacres, on the other hand, was a mere "Society" rattle, a handsome, well-dressed youth, interested in nothing but dancing and sport, snobbish in opinion, and anti-Indian in prejudice, who served to remind us that even among the youngest and newest civilians there are some who have all the class and racial prejudices of the worst of the old generation.

Hardwar, 24/26 February 1912

Our three days here, as the guest of R. C. Hobart[1] (a subdivisional officer, virtually acting as Collector of this sub-division of 350,000 inhabitants, under the nominal supervision of the Collector of Saharanpur), have been full of interest. We stay with him in the "Municipal Bungalow", a building erected for his accommodation when visiting Hardwar (from Rurki, his headquarters) as Chairman of the Municipality. Hardwar is an immense pilgrimage centre, though just now only a few are coming. We went first to see the Gurukula,[2] a college established by the Arya Somaj for education according to the prescriptions of the Vedas. The boys enter at 7 years old, and they must remain until 25, never once visiting their homes or families, or their native villages, and living day and night under the closest scrutiny of, and in company with, their teachers. The idea, as explained, is to protect them against the polluting influences of the

[1] R.C.A.S. Hobart belonged to the Indian Civil Service. On his arrival in India in 1905 he started his career as an assistant commissioner in the United Provinces. In 1914 he became joint magistrate, and retired in 1931 as officiating commissioner.

[2] The Gurukul Kangri, set up in Hardwar in 1902, was the principal and model institution established by that section of the Arya Samaj which advocated the revival of the ancient Hindu system of education. Today it enjoys the status of a Deemed University.

world, including the average Hindoo home! No woman is even allowed to see the boys; and B. W. had to stay outside until they had been carefully packed away. Their parents are allowed to visit them, not more than once a month, but such visits are not encouraged except at long intervals, or in emergencies. The institution has been started only some 15 years, so that the effect of this 18 years rigid monasticism cannot yet be seen. Two youths, however, are being this year "graduated as M.A." and finished, they having started 15 years ago at a somewhat higher age than 7. The greatest attention is paid to personal character; a teacher sleeps with the boys in each dormitory, eats with them at each meal, and plays games with them. (Nevertheless during the year, 23 are noted in the medical report which S. W. saw as suffering from "onanism and debility"). The curriculum is a carefully planned combination of Sanskrit language, the Vedas, Vedic logic and philosophy on the one hand, and English, Western philosophy and elementary science on the other. There was a really extensive library, including good collections of English philosophy (and English translations of German, Greek and French)—they had Bergson's *Creative Evolution* for inst-ance, though it was only just published, and it was actually being read by one of the teachers—and also of English and American Economics and History. There were chemical and physical laboratories, and a practical elementary knowledge of chemical, physical and mechanical processes seemed to be imparted. The lectures were given in Hindi, the English and Sanskrit books being used for reference and independent reading. The teachers, who all seem to give their services free (or for bare subsistence) appeared generally intelligent and zealous. Altogether we were much impressed by the place. It was stated that it was hoped that the students would become Arya Somaj missionaries and lecturers, or teachers in similar institutions. They were all nominally admitted gratuitously, and maintained out of the donations and subscriptions of the members; but money was taken from wealthy parents in the beginning actually as fees; and now in the guise of donations, this fact being bitterly complained of as inconsistent with the Vedas by their critics and rivals, as all learning ought to be imparted freely to anyone. This institution has been, in the past, an object of the most absurd Government suspicion and has been watched by police to see if it was not secretly drilling the boys, and training an army! The Government seems to have been unable to understand why so much devotion should be put into an educational institution; and it certainly presents a contrast with the Government colleges, or with Aligarh, with their exclusively English teaching, total absence of personal supervision of the boys at night, practical freedom to come and go at will, government by masters of an alien race and creed, and (except at Aligarh) complete secularity and absence of religion, and a curiously superstitious reliance on the games and prefectorial system copied from "the English Public School"! The boys looked exceptionally healthy and happy. During the whole 15 years, only 20 out of the 300 had been lost by expulsion or resignation. Over 200 applied for admission this year, though only 20 could be admitted. And, one, at any rate, of the two new "graduates" who was to become a professor in the college, seemed a very charming and promising youth (who proposed to spend a year in England). The other, less prepossessing, was already editing his father's vernacular newspaper with, it was said, remarkable success.

Another day we visited two rival institutions, set up in the same place in opposition to the Gurukula. One, the Mahavidyalaya at Jawalapur was also Arya Somaj, and we could discover no assignable ground for its establishment or its hostility. Its fifty or sixty boys were being taught nothing but Sanskrit language and philosophy (though other subjects were said to be going to be added); and it was being run by a dismissed Hindoo Sub-Inspector of Police, Sita Ram, a man of bad character and unpleasing servility of manner. Its domestic arrangements were as good as those of the Gurukula, but the teaching seemed very poor, there was no library or laboratory; and the note of personal devotion seemed lacking. The other was an imitation started by the orthodox Hindoos in opposition to the Arya Somaj, with exclusively Sanskrit and Vedantic teaching without English or Science. It was only a few years old, and perhaps other subjects will be added later as the boys grow up. It was important only as showing how the Arya Somaj is stimulating Hindooism to rivalry.

We had a long day on the Upper Ganges going by train and carriage ten or fifteen miles up stream, and then walking three miles along its banks, amid the huts of the Saddhus and the "dharmsalas" or pious lodging houses erected for their accommodation. These Saddhus come and live here in the cold weather, and migrate to Hardwar in the rains, and travel further down to Muttra, etc. in the autumn. They seemed to us, in their simple reed huts, to be enjoying a pleasant holiday camp, and not in the least to be meditating! Some were nearly naked and smeared with ashes, generally half stupefied with hemp: others were clothed in yellow robes, and seemed fat and jovial. At Lakshman Jhula Bridge we embarked on Saknais, to float down stream for five hours, shooting innumerable rapids. These are simply the hides of Nilgais, a horse-like cow, inflated with air and the holes tightly fastened up. An Indian "charpoy" or bedstead is laid across two of them, and thus a safe raft is made, so buoyant that it rises on every wave. Two men, each astride his own Nilgai, floated on either side; and holding on to the raft by their hands, moved their legs in the water like paddle-wheels. Thus mounted, we floated down the stream, only a few inches above the water, from 1.30 to 6.30 p.m. going through gorges, past wide shallows, and down the most alarming rapids; disturbing flights of hundreds of small black herons, wild duck, beautiful swifts, and other river fowl—finally getting into an iron rowing boat with a picturesquely attired crew of five men, to be rowed swiftly in the gloaming past the lengthy esplanade of Hardwar itself, with its lofty lodging houses for pilgrims, its lighted temples and its long bathing ghats, just in time for S.W. to dress and go to dinner with no fewer than eight officers of the Irrigation Service, most of whom had met here to consult as to how to make a great dam across the Ganges in order to impound more water for their canals.

We omitted to give any account of our brief visit to Aligarh College. This college was started by a great Mahomedan leader, Sir Sayed Ahmed,[3] as the first English educational institution for Mahomedan wealthy men's sons. One of the first Principals was our friend Theodore Morison. Now it has 1000 pupils, and will be the centre round which the New Mahomedan University will grow. We had heard that there had been trouble between the English Principal and the Mahomedan teachers owing to "strikes" among the boys and the complaints of parents leading to the resignation of the late Principal, Mr. Archibald, and we understood that the college was no longer what it used to be. We saw very little of the boys as we came on a Friday, the Mahomedan Sabbath. But the Principal, with whom we stayed, drove us round the buildings and talked extensively to us. The buildings are scattered over a large site and make any kind of discipline with regard to coming and going of boys wholly impracticable. Mr. Towle did not seem to us the right sort of man to be Head of a big institution. In appearance and in manner and still more in conversation he was a colourless and evasive person. One could quite believe, what we afterwards heard on good authority, that he had lacked loyalty to his Chief and had, in fact, been chosen to succeed Archibald just because he had offered to do anything that the

[3] Sir Syed Ahmed Khan (1817–98) was the founder of the Muhammedan Anglo-Oriental College at Aligarh (now the Aligarh Muslim University) which produced many distinguished Muslim political and intellectual leaders. Sir Syed's own policy of loyalism towards the British government in India was based upon his conviction that it was futile to challenge the might of the Empire. He made a determined effort to introduce English as the medium of instruction, and to introduce Western scientific and liberal ideas into Islam through translations of scientific works into Urdu. The beginnings of Muslim political separatism are frequently attributed to him.

Trustees decided on. He was full of discreet but bitter criticism of the Trustees, of the boys, of their parents, of
Mahomedans and indeed of India and its inhabitants. He was
in fact a hireling—perhaps a conscientious hireling—and no
doubt fairly capable of the job of getting boys through examinations—but lacking any kind of personal influence over
his staff or his scholars. So when we saw at Lahore a leading
Mahomedan who was a Trustee of the College and would be
largely concerned in appointing the Principal of the new University we begged him to select a man of personality as Principal and we suggested Hope Simpson. Towle was only
another instance of the poor kind of personality that is in the
Indian educational administration.

At Hardwar we saw a great deal of two Indian officials;
one the secretary of the Municipality and the other the
M.O.H.[4] Both these men were Brahmins and belonged to
the orthodox school though approving much of the Arya
Somaj, and both were particularly upright and intelligent—
zealous—wholly devoid of servility or even of "plausibility".
The secretary of the Municipality told me that he could not
join the Arya Somaj because they neglected the worship of
ancestors and advocated inter-caste marriage; but that he was
wholly with them in their objection to Sadhus and in their
strenuous puritanism. He thought Hindu Society was, on the
whole, improving though he feared that *family obligation* was
disappearing, even before the larger public spirit, which
should take its place, had developed. He did not believe that
at present there was sufficient public spirit to run local government satisfactorily, leave alone provincial or national government. "At present every Indian is for himself and his
family—he cares little for the Public Good; he does not even
understand what you mean by it. He understands family
obligation, and religious obligation. But the idea that he has
any duty towards persons because they inhabit the same
town or country is strange to him. Indians who have had an

[4] Medical Officer of Health.

English education or who have mixed with Englishmen are getting this idea; but it is only limited to a few."

The Hobart brothers (one a civilian acting as subdivisional officer, i.e., virtually as Collector for the Rurki Sub-division under the nominal supervision of the Collector of the whole Saharanpur District), the other an R.E. officer (acting with a Native Sapper regiment) with whom we stayed for three nights, were exceptionally sympathetic to Indians and men of great personal charm. The civilian brother (Charterhouse and Oxford) was able and energetic though somewhat hasty— even slightly scatterbrained. They had been born and bred in Indian Public Service, either military or civilian, and though conservative in Home politics were extraordinarily appreciative and evidently much beloved by their respective Indian subordinates. After Hope Simpson, Hobart the sub-divisional officer for Hardwar and Rurki district, is the best civilian we have met for the executive work of a district.

At Amritsar we stayed only for the middle of a day, primarily to see the extraordinarily picturesque Sikh Golden Temple. We were taken over it by a Hindoo Fabian (Maheshwarry), a Rajputana "Bunya" by caste, who was a barrister, and an orthodox Hindoo. He (who had been in England and had joined the Fabian Society through the South London Ethical Society—he had lodged with Gunning, then Assistant Secretary to the A.S.E.)[5] and his cousin, the leader of the local bar, were the first of the "Bunya" or trader class whom we had consciously met to talk to. These two, at any rate, were quite distinguishable from the Brahmins and Kayasths: keen and alert intelligence, without aristocratic distinction, as if sharpened by generations of money-lending and trading. He was the first of the Maheshwarry clan or section of the caste to go to England, and he had not yet quite overcome that venture, several of his caste fellows still refusing to meet him, though most had done so. He thought it important to walk warily, and to be very conciliatory to them; or else no other

[5] Amalgamated Society of Engineers.

member of the clan would practically be able to enjoy the advantages of English education. He had therefore remained strictly orthodox, and did not favour the Arya Somaj. He was interested to point out the multitude of orthodox Hindoo shrines and images all around the Sikh temple, as demonstrating that the Sikhs were really only a section of the Hindoos. After visiting his law office and his cousins, he took us, at our request, to a wholesale dealer in Cashmere shawls, up a narrow stair to an upper storey of a house in the crowded "bazaar" street, the establishment of a family of Bikaner Jains, who had many tens of thousands of pounds worth of stock in that flimsy building, unprotected (as we learnt) by fire insurance. Here we turned over beautiful things, and bought a shawl and a tablecloth for under £ 10, on his assurance that these were lowest net wholesale prices. The headquarters of the firm is at Bikaner, in the Rajputana desert; they have hundreds of Cashmere families virtually in their employment, making them advances and collecting from them periodically their handwoven products.

We then went to tea with a Mussulman member of the Punjab Legislative Council (whom Maheshwarry declared to be an almost penniless person who supported himself in all probability by the gifts made him in the belief that he had influence with the Government—but this was, we imagine, merely the *nouveau riche* Bunya's way of suspecting everyone of destitution who is not plainly wealthy). This dignified and courteous old gentleman sent a good carriage for us, and lived in a spacious flat above a narrow street in the native city. He had the good common sense shrewdness of the educated Muhammedans, but did not show any particular ability or distinction. We learnt from Maheshwarry what no one, English or Indian, had so far told us, that there exists throughout India a network of local associations or Sabhas of orthodox Hindooism, each place having its own independent society, and the whole being in some way affiliated to a society at Benares, of which the wealthy Maharaja of Darbhanga is President. This organisation has for its object the protection of the interests of Hindoos and Hindooism; it evidently was in antagonism with the Brahmo Somaj, and the Arya Somaj and it has incidentally maintained asylums for decrepit old cows which are thus saved from death!

Lahore, 29 February to 3 March 1912

Arriving at Lahore at 6 p.m., we were met, to our surprise, by Rambaj Dutt Chowdhri,[1] the Arya Somaj pleader whom we had met at Calcutta, and whose wife we had so much admired. It is all part of the extraordinary politeness and courtesy of these educated Indians of all sections. As we preferred to stay at an hotel, rather than with him or with English officials, so as to be free to see all sides, and as his wife was temporarily absent, we have spent hours with him, driving to the sights. He has been President and is still Vice-President of the head or central branch of the Arya Somaj, and his clever wife, we believe, conducts some vernacular journal. But a certain simplicity of character, and plain honestness of purpose, even to naivety, has perhaps saved him from prosecution, though he went on a lecturing tour to England. He is quite convinced that the Arya Somaj is the true religion and

[1] Pandit Rambhaj Datta Chaudhuri (1866–1923) was one of the most prominent leaders of the Arya Samaj movement in Punjab. He was also an active Congressman and played a significant role in nationalist politics in the Punjab in 1919. After the Jallianwala Bagh massacre he was arrested and deported to Dera Ghazi Khan. Later he participated in the Khilafat and Non-Co-operation movements. With the assistance of his wife, Sarla Devi Chaudhrani, he edited two papers. Pandit Rambhaj Datta's name is particularly closely identified with the formation, all over the Punjab, of Hindu Sahayak sabhas to unify Hindu politicians on a common platform.

the only one, and that, without limitation of race or colour or creed, all the world will one day come over to it. To him it is not specially a Hindoo or an Indian religion, though incidentally he is a strong Nationalist. He has thrown himself with energy into its philanthropic side, busying himself in forming many local branches or societies having for their object the raising up of the "untouched" Castes, the maintenance of orphans and the management of elementary and other schools. All this perplexes the English official who cannot believe that it has not some underlying political motive. Without being personally bitter, he is estranged from the Government of India and regards the Punjabi officials as hostile to the race in education and self-reliance. He mentioned that the words underneath the statue of Lord Lawrence "Will you be governed by the sword or the pen"[2] had given dire

[2] The statue of Lord John Lawrence (1811–79), Chief Commissioner and then Lieutenant-Governor of the Punjab, and Viceroy and Governor-General of India (1864–9), presented by Sir Edgar Boehm to the Lahore Municipality, and unveiled by Sir Charles Aitchison in 1887, was actually erected on the Mall. The statue represented Lord Lawrence as offering to the people a choice 'By which will ye be governed—the pen or the sword?' The theme of the statue was inspired by an incident of 1848 when Lawrence was Commissioner in the Punjab and found himself confronted with rebellion by the discontented Rajas of Kangra, Jaswan, Datarpur and others, who had been dispossessed by the British annexation of the Punjab. Lawrence ordered his subordinates to issue a proclamation to the major landowners in the district saying, among other things: 'I have ruled this district three years by the sole agency of the pen, and if necessary, I will rule it by the sword. God forbid that matters should come to that.' Lawrence sent out forces to quell the rebellion, and at every halt these forces met the headmen of the surrounding villages. A pen and a sword were placed before the assembled headmen, who were asked to choose the instrument by which they would rather be ruled. It is recorded that the pen was enthusiastically grasped, and the rebellion aborted. This episode was considered by Lawrence's contemporaries as an example of his masterly skills of governance. In the 1930s, in response to a nationalist agitation in Lahore, the word 'governed' in the inscription was substituted by the word 'served'.

offence to Indians—the students of the University refusing to walk in that part of the gardens. We tried to explain that here they had taken offence without reason, the saying exemplifying the preference of the Englishman for civil over military government. But he clearly believed that the emphasis was entirely on the word "governed" and that it was meant to signify that Indians had to submit to one or other form of the British Raj.

We have had two long talks with Lajpat Rai,[3] a member of the Arya Somaj who was actually "deported" without trial on suspicion of "tampering with the native troops". He is a short thick-set man with a bullet shaped head, bright intelligent expression and somewhat thick lips and dark colour. A Bunya by caste (Trading Caste), and pleader by profession, he is quite clearly an agitator by preference. He has not an attractive personality—though he is pleasant tempered and open minded—but he has, at times, an unpleasant expression of successful intrigue. He looks *a Bunya*! With us he was apparently quite frank in his denunciations of the Government—especially the Punjab Government for its arbitrary proceedings and persistent desire to suppress the development of the race. He instances their suppression in the schools, of the teaching of English history on the one hand, and their steady prohibition of any heroic history of early In-

[3] Lala Lajpat Rai (1856–1928) was among the most influential and distinguished leaders of India's national movement. He was an Arya Samajist and founded the DAV College, Lahore, where he also worked for some time as a teacher. In 1888 he joined the Indian National Congress and was a part of its extremist faction. His leadership of the agitation against land legislation in the Punjab was punished by his deportation to Mandalay. In 1920 he presided over the special session of the Congress at Calcutta, but was again imprisoned during the Non-Co-operation Movement in 1921–2. In 1923, as a Swarajist, he entered the Central Legislative Assembly and then founded the Nationalist Party, which successfully contested the elections three years later. In 1928, while leading a demonstration against the Simon Commission, he was assaulted by the police and succumbed to his injuries.

dian civilisation. "They want to withdraw any subject that might stimulate the courage and patriotism of the Hindu— whether it is the love for his own race and religion or his growing desire for Western political freedom".

In their colonisation policy of the lands rendered fertile by irrigation, in all their land legislation Lajpat Rai contended that the British Government had legislated with the express object of excluding the Hindu as compared with the Mahomedan from the ownership and occupation of land. They suppressed free speech and free press—tried in every way to emasculate Indian life. They threatened officials who belonged to the Arya Somaj and persecuted private persons who preached the doctrine, the police always telling the people that the Government would be angry if they attended the meetings and sent the children to the schools. About the religious side of the Arya Somaj, Lajpat Rai seemed more or less indifferent, except that it freed the people from superstitions and fanaticism. The second morning he brought another Arya Somaj Bunya—a more spiritual minded man—and with him we discussed the prospects of Arya Somaj as a proselytising religion. I suggested that nowadays, it was difficult to maintain the Infallibility of the Book, and the fact that it had originated in the dim and distant past did not increase its authority, and that the absolute reliance of the Arya Somaj on the Inspiration of the Vedas—above and beyond that of all other scriptures—would eventually alienate the most intellectual Hindu from the Arya creed. The reply was that every Hindu was born and bred to Faith in the Vedas, and that the Infallibility and comprehensiveness of the Vedic teaching, was always assumed. We also suggested that in Hinduism and even in the writings of the Arya Somaj, there was little or no direct teaching of *Conduct*, nothing comparable to the Ten Commandments or to the Sermon on the Mount. "We assume that a man who has reached a certain stage of spiritual development will necessarily be moral—all our effort is to get to this stage by spiritual exercise. If the modern Hindu lacks conduct—and we admit that he does—it is because he has departed from the Truth of the Vedas and has become an idol-worshipper". There was, in their conversation, the usual reference to "Spiritual Science" and "Knowledge"—by which they always mean a sort of mystical metaphysics or metaphysical mysticism. And they were quite assured that the ancient Hindus had a sort of monopoly of spiritual development and that all other races and creeds were what they called "Primitive"—a stage in which "Ethics frequently submerged true Religion". We are struggling with books and pamphlets—mostly highly controversial—explanatory of the doctrine of the Arya Somaj, but to us they are very unreadable as they are elaborate explanations of every apparent inconsistency or blemish in the Vedas, and long arguments as to the Truth of all the dogmas very much in the style of the Commentary on the Bible by the old-fashioned evangelists, who believed in the literal Inspiration of the Christian scriptures. The only difference is that these Vedic "Protestants" have read the theology and the criticisms of the Christians, and use quotations with considerable skill and plausibility— they are in fact far more cosmopolitan in their culture than the analogous people among the Christian races. I doubt whether this side of the Arya Somaj will survive—visitors half suggested that the time had not arrived when patriotic Hindus could afford to indulge in the "Higher Criticism"! To fight orthodox Hinduism they must offer something that was equally dogmatic and exclusive—faith in the absolute inspiration of the Vedas.

On our way to Peshawar we stopped off at Gujranwala in order to attend the conference of the Arya Somaj at this Guru Kula. We arrived in time for the ceremony of Initiation of some 30 or 40 little boys who had recently joined the Guru Kula. The ceremony had that strangely informal even disorderly picturesqueness characteristic of Hinduism. Round the purifying fire squatted the little boys, clothed in yellow, with shaved heads, who were being "instructed"! An outer circle of older students (with hair intact and more ordinary costumes) were acting as a sort of chorus in the responses. A

Brahmin instructor was reading passages out of the Vedas and he and some of the boys were pouring "Ghee" or throwing sweet smelling wood and herbs into the fire. Meanwhile some twenty mothers clad in white, seated on a raised platform, were talking with each other, some 100 male parents, visitors and governors of the Guru Kula, seated European fashion on chairs, were on the other side—the space between the men and the women being filled by Arya Somaj converts from the "Untouchables" who were thus listening to the Vedas and taking part in the ceremonies from which they would be rigidly excluded by orthodox Hindus. The ceremony consisted in the vows of chastity, obedience, and "self-study" during the eight years' residence at the Guru Kula—the boys being given a symbolic cord wherewith to gird up their loins (signifying activity), and a staff to protect men from wild animals when they went out into the jungle "to relieve nature" instead of making use of fellow human beings as "sweepers" to remove nightsoil! The boys then went round the company "begging their bread"—a very perfunctory ceremony performed in memory of the old Vedic doctrine of the vow of poverty of the learned ones. This Guru Kula only takes boys up to the age of 16 and though it separates them from their parents for eight years, it does not prevent the parents from visiting them. The boys are supervised closely by a tutor (for every 25) day and night—the instruction seems inferior to that of the Hardwar Guru Kula, less money being forthcoming. The Headmaster, with whom we had a long talk, was a young spiritual minded intellectual (favourite philosopher William James)—a charming personality, disinterested and refined. The Principal was an elderly man who had retired from the Government Service in order to devote the whole of his energies (unpaid) to the establishment and working up of this Guru Kula—a strong man of sturdy independence—rather the type of the 18th century Quaker.

After the ceremony of initiation there was a religious address by a young "Guru"—of the simple spiritual type, and a fervent address by an able young official of the Baroda Government, an inspector of schools who had sent two of his boys to the Guru Kula. We could not understand either the one or the other, but it was clear from the rapt attention of some 200 persons including the 50 Untouchables, that the address was eloquent and persuasive. A collection was afterwards taken and a list of contributors of larger sums given, making some 2000 rupees (much of it, by the way, in sovereigns showing how these are getting into circulation). We talked with some other of the Professors and Governors and were shown round the buildings, and given tea and fruit in a tent set apart for us. Like the Hardwar Guru Kula there was the same note of disinterested devotion and patriotism— but as an educational institution it hardly looked efficient.

At Peshawar and again at Lyallpur we heard a good deal about the Arya Somaj. Every British administrator fears it as a political force. The Chief Engineer at Lyallpur told us that practically all his Indian officials and contractors were Arya Somaj and had managed to raise rates—wages and tenders— by at least 30% owing to their solidarity. He told us, too, something about the "Hindu Sabha"[4]—a purely political organisation started by the Arya Somaj to unite all Hindus in one body. A very intelligent Mussulman, a Government Pleader, who came to see us at Lyallpur, also complained that the Arya Somaj was now trying to *consolidate* Hinduism. This he said was illegitimate, since their original aims had been to *reform* Hinduism, i.e., to make another sect in antagonism to the orthodox Hinduism.

We have been studying the "Light of Truth", a weighty volume, dated 1882, of doctrine by the founder of the Arya Somaj—the famous "Guru" or "Ascetic"—Dayananda,[5]

[4] An offshoot of the Arya Samaj in Punjab. In addition to their religious and social functions, these Sabhas were designed to become tools of political action of the Hindus.

[5] Swami Dayanand Saraswati (1824–83), Hindu reformer and the founder of the Arya Samaj in 1875. He was the author of *Satyarth Prakash* (The Light of Truth), in which he attacked

who died shortly after its publication. This book is the most extraordinary jumble of Vedic lore, modern culture and acute and sometime subtle original philosophy and reflection. Certainly there is no lack of dogmatic teaching about *conduct*—since this work lays down not merely general moral maxims, but also detailed instructions on sexual acts, the duty of parents, the religious life, and also on the "Arts of War and Government". Incidentally it reveals the evils of the lascivious and idolatrous practices of Modern Hinduism. In this work you find the dogmatic insistence on the infallibility of the Vedas, the insistence on extreme austerity in restraint of animal passions, the inculcation of public spirit, and patriotism, and the proselytising fervour of the Arya Somaj—in their most authoritative forms. Idealisation of the religious and social organisation of Ancient Hinduism is combined with a measured and incidental denunciation of an Alien Government. It is, however, difficult to convict the author of "sedition" since the whole argument of the book is against political agitation *until the Hindus have made themselves fit for it by a purification of their religion and an advance in personal character—in truthfulness, in public spirit, in energetic industry*. In this work you find the same combination of intellectual subtlety, wide culture, with an almost childish lack of sense of perspective or of scientific critical faculty, that is so common among the Hindu gentlemen whom we have met. Some parts of the work—notably the chapter on the practice of "Yoga" are not to be understood by the ordinary Western mind and may be treasures of spiritual development which are fast locked to us. The curious rules laid down for holding the breath, and concentrating the attention, seem to the philistine mind of the Westerns, instructions in the art of self-hypnotism—a pathological process rather than a spiritual

---

polytheism, idol worship, superstition and the excessive ritualism of Hinduism as it was practised in northern India. He advocated a return to the original religion of the Vedas, rejecting all later religious thinking if it contradicted Vedic teaching.

exercise. But that is only another way of saying that one does not understand it.

The account of our Peshawar and Lyallpur visit will be found in another volume[6]—we use these last pages to continue our account of the Lahore Arya Somaj.

On our return to Lahore we went to dine with Rambaj Dutt Chanduri, whose clever, energetic wife had meanwhile returned. Their house is a somewhat strange mixture of European and Indian furniture, and the dinner, tho' vegetarian and including Indian dishes, was served in strict accordance with European fashion, from the hour, 8.30, to the disposition of the fruit and flowers on the table. The company consisted of ourselves and Alfred Ollivant,[7] whom we had introduced, and some dozen men and two Indian ladies— mostly but not exclusively Arya Somaj. It was not a social success—the two ladies and most of the men talking English with difficulty, and Ollivant being shy and reserved. Lajpat Rai and the Chaudhuris and I kept up some discussion but we were none of us at our ease. Far more interesting was a garden party at the house of Harkishen Lal,[8] a big Hindu capitalist, who had begun as a Pleader, a friend of both the Arya and Brahmo Somaj though not actually a member of either. He was an able man of the world with strong but moderate

[6] A reference to the completion of a volume (Volume 30) in the manuscript diary.

[7] Alfred Ollivant (1874–1927) held a Commission in the Royal Artillery, which he resigned in 1895. He was, however, much better known to his contemporaries as the author of popular novels such as *Owd Bob* (1898); *Danny* (1903); *The Gentleman* (1908); *The Royal Road* (1912); and others.

[8] Harkishen Lal (1864–1937) started practice as a barrister but eventually, inspired by the nationalist ideal of indigenous economic development, became a pioneer in the field of commerce, floating the Bharat Insurance Company, the Punjab National Bank of Lahore, some other banks, flour mills and ice and soap factories. In the Punjab he was widely known as a financial wizard. In 1920 he became a minister in the provincial government formed under the Montagu–Chelmsford reforms.

Nationalist views, believing that the British occupation had had its uses but that it ought to be superseded by a purely Indian administration. Indeed one of the remarkable facts about India is that *all Hindus are Nationalists*—and except for their jealousy of the Hindus—nearly all Mahomedans believe in the government of India by the Indians as the ultimate ideal. Harkishen Lal differs from the Arya Somaj in thinking that Indians have to adopt European education and in attaching really very little importance to Indian thought and Indian religion—he has in fact the same outlook as the little group of Japanese statesmen who caused the Japanese Revolutions and have built up modern Japan.

We have seen a good deal more of Lajpat Rai, and the more we have seen of him the more we like him. He is certainly not "loyal" to the British connection—but why should he be! He is dead against bombs and assassination, but believes in converting all classes of Hindus to faith in their power of self-government. At present he is going slow—he feels that it is useless to fight the British Government—all that can be done is to keep within the law and go on as straight ahead as is possible with a black wall of suppression always appearing when the direction of the Movement becomes known. It is this suppleness of policy which makes the English official fear and dislike him and call him "not straightforward". But obviously given his purpose, and the hostile force of the British Rule, his course cannot be straightforward. Certainly with us, trusting to our goodwill, he has been absolutely frank both about his objects and his methods.

He took us to see the Dayananda Anglo Vedic College (D.A.V. College) affiliated to the Punjab University, but receiving no grant. It was the policy of affiliation which produced the split in the ranks of the Arya Somaj 14 years ago—its dissentients leaving the governing body and founding the Hardwar Guru Kula. This college with 700 undergraduates and a preparatory school of 1500 students is the most live educational institution in Lahore. Its Principal and founder has laboured eighteen years without pay or reward—being maintained, on a small subsistence allowance (50 rupees per month), by his brother. The professors were most of them men of attractive personality and wide culture and the science equipment was certainly superior to the Islamic or Christian college of the Punjab University (though probably not to the Government College which we did not see). This college contributed a quarter of its whole yearly crop of graduates, and in an apparently successful attempt combined an elaborate education in Hindu learning with the modern requirements of the Punjab University. The elementary school is divided into two departments—the first two classes being held in various branch schools throughout the city, and the remainder in a large central school with good classrooms. The per centage of attendance of the boys seems exceptionally good, but the Punjab rule is that failing to attend for six consecutive days results in being struck off the registers, and this improves the per centages. As to this college and school we were amused to hear little malicious stories from Sir Louis Dane,[9] Lt. Governor, with whom we lunched. He professed to admire the Arya Somaj and had reversed the policy of his predecessor (Sir Denzil Ibbetson)[10] of blind suspicion and suppression. But he could not resist telling me that the college had been proved to be a centre of lawless sedition—two boys belonging to it having been discovered with pistols and with a press for printing violent leaflets just before the Durbar. When I enquired, I found that seditious leaflets *were* discovered, but that the boys were not living in the college; and that only the younger brother (who was not proved to have

[9] Sir Louis Dane (1856–1946), of the Indian Civil Service, served as Chief Secretary to the Punjab Government (1896–1900) and as Lieutenant-Governor in the Punjab (1908–13).

[10] Sir Denzil Ibbetson (1847–1908), of the Indian Civil Service, was member of the Viceroy's Executive Council and Lieutenant-Governor of the Punjab (1907) during a particularly stormy period which saw the deportation of Lala Lajpat Rai and Ajit Singh in connection with the agitation against the Canal Colony and Land Alienation Acts.

any share in the printing) was even attending as a day scholar; and that the pistols were ancient weapons belonging to the boys' deceased father—a Government official with the right to have them; and that the police had eventually *withdrawn all charges* (this was in the newspaper of the day following). Also he told me that the college authorities were fighting among themselves and had kicked out the Principal and founder. As the Principal had shown us round himself and had told us that he was presently retiring, *to become President of the Governing Body*, I was a little surprised. It is curious how all the British officials talk loosely about Indians or Indian institutions on the supposition that, as a tourist, you will not have heard the other side. When you cite your information, they shelter themselves behind some equivocal re-statement of the case. Certainly we have found the British officials more inaccurate and more disingenuous than the Indians—the Indian Nationalists showing a most laudable desire not to mis-state facts. Of course this must be discounted by the fact that we appear important persons to the Indian, whereas the officials think that anything will do for two globe trotters who have no particular right to official information.

Interesting to note that Lajpat Rai and many other Nationalists object altogether to the present system of government of the Native States and would like to see them absorbed in British India. "Under Native state rule we have neither the reign of law of the British Government nor the sympathy of an Indian administration. Many of the Chiefs would like to administer their states on progressive Nationalist lines, but whenever they try to do so they are stopped by the British Resident. On the other hand, as their authority over their subjects is autocratic, they can be more capricious and arbitrary than is possible under the redtape administration of the British officials." He quoted the recent persecutions in Patiala—the Maharajah was really against them but he was in deadly fear of displeasing the British Government by whom he might be deposed. Once his ministers started on the path of suppression they were not restrained by the routine of British administration, and some 100 officials and others were arrested and kept in prison on mere suspicion of being seditious for about a year without any kind of trial or conviction—which could not have happened without public scandal in British India. The hope of the Nationalist lay in an appeal to the Liberal and Labour parties of the British Parliament—in so far as they had any hope from sources outside themselves. The native Chiefs were bound to be hangers-on of the British Government, and like all hangers-on would be more intolerant than their Chiefs.

I ask Lajpat Rai what Act of Parliament he would like best—if he were limited to one—and he answered after a moment's thought "Liberty to educate the people", by which, of course, he meant Liberty to Agitate among all sorts and conditions of men!

Our admiration of the Arya Somaj brought us into a heated controversy with a Christian missionary in Delhi in which I certainly lost my temper and became really abusive! Andrews,[11] an ardent member of the Cambridge Mission at Delhi, to whom we had an introduction from Bishop Talbot, had been cited to us as the most "nationalist" of Englishmen, in India, and that reputation threw us off our guard. He is a somewhat "saintly" and disingenuous missionary, bent on the redemption of Indians through Christianity. Like all the

[11] C. F. Andrews (1871–1940), a British missionary who came to India in 1904 to teach at St Stephen's College, Delhi. During his eight years at this institution his political outlook was revolutionized. He came into contact with many Indians in public life, and it was on Gokhale's suggestion that he visited South Africa in 1913. Here, working with Gandhi, he helped the Indian community in its fight against discriminatory legislation and took up the cause of indentured labour. After the War Andrews publicly proclaimed his support for complete independence. He was by Gandhi's side at the Second Round Table Conference, and subsequently acted as a mediator between Gandhi and the British government. His efforts to improve the lot of seamen, cotton workers, tea-estate workers, forced labour and, above all, of untouchables in many parts of India, won him the title 'Deenabandhu' or friend of the poor.

missionaries we have met, he is subconsciously bitter at the
ill-success of missionary effort in actual conversions. So
when we began to admire the Arya Somaj, expecting agree-
ment from him he started off by damning them—not with
faint praises—but with little malicious stories of their sedition
and association with political crime, and complained of their
underhand attitude towards Christianity— "they take all its
teaching and ascribe it to the Vedas". By this time we had
already become heated, and had asked him for chapter and
verse proving that Lajpat Rai and the Arya Somaj had "tam-
pered with the soldiers". He maintained that as all the Punjab
cultivators had relatives in the army, any conversion of these
to Nationalist sentiments must mean disaffection in the
army! "It is a crime to make a soldier disloyal to the *Colonel
whose salt he takes*." "What do you mean by that" we exclaimed hotly, "The salt of the soldier, like the salt of the
Colonel, is paid for by the natives of India. Not a penny that
is spent on the army of India is British money. How *dare* you
say that the soldier is unfaithful to the country that supports
him when he becomes an Indian Nationalist". Afterwards I
felt I had misbehaved myself and was sorry. But these missionaries with their perpetual assertion that "they love the Indians" and their equally perpetual malicious abuse of them to
English people as immoral and unworthy, are not attractive
controversialists. The Nationalists, on the other hand, are
curiously indifferent and even kindly disposed towards the
Christian missionaries, as providing a great deal of education—especially as pioneers—which would have otherwise
been absent. Perhaps it is easy to be generous when you are
getting the best of the bargain! The Christian missionaries,
hoping to get converts, have offered free education—the Indians like the Japanese have taken the education but have
ignored the Christianity. Hence the bitterness. Now the
Arya Somaj are threatening the only preserve of the Christian
missionaries—the depressed classes—and therefore in spite of
the obvious self-devotion and piety of the Arya Somaj they
are in real disfavour with earnest Christians. The Brahmo

Somaj, on the other hand, with its idealisation of Christ and the Christian scriptures, its detachment from Hinduism in all its forms, and, be it added, its incapacity to proselytise, is in high favour as the only "pure movement" in India. (One of the leaders of the Brahmo Somaj, by the way, when he heard that I came from a Unitarian family, introduced me to a group of Brahmos as belonging to the European branch of their Church!)

Peshawar, 4 to 6 March 1912

We begin this book on the North Western edge of the Indian Empire, to which we are paying a flying visit. Arriving at 6 a.m. we sallied out after tea and a hot bath to call on the Director of Public Instruction, the only person to whom we have an introduction (the Deputy Commissioner to whom we sent on a letter, has just left on promotion to the Secretariat at Calcutta—this constant shifting being typical). The Director (Richey), an energetic man of about 35, has only been here a year, having come from an educational post in Eastern Bengal. And the matter is made worse by the absence of anything in the nature of specialist journals which should make known to all India what is being done in each part. Thus, we have been inspecting the Muktabs[1] or Common Mosque Schools, where Mussulman boys learn the Koran by heart, in various places in the United Provinces. There (and as we learn also in the North West Frontier Province) they are quite outside Government aid. As there are throughout India thousands of these schools, attended by, perhaps, hundreds of thousands of boys; and as they cannot be abolished

[1] Islamic primary education was designed to teach the pupils the alphabet and religious observances and prayers. This was done in the *maktabs*, or schools attached to mosques. The word *maktab* is derived from the Arabic word *kutub* which means a place where writing is taught.

(seeing that the religion of Islam makes them obligatory); we have been exercised in our minds as to what could be done. It is impossible to force them into a Government system, and it does not seem either creditable or administratively expedient to leave hundreds of thousands of Indian boys without any real education, even elementary. We have therefore been asking what could be done, and suggesting the possibility of the Government leaving the schools under the Mulvis, but offering (1) to supply them with books, maps, etc., and (2) to provide peripatetic visiting teachers, being Mussulmans, who should teach secular subjects, if invited by the Mosques. None of the officials in the United Provinces and none of the prominent Mussulmans whom we consulted, were aware that in the Province of Sind, in the Bombay presidency, this very problem was tackled in 1873, thirty-nine years ago, and after various experiments and checks (due very largely to the constant shifting of officials) a system of very loose Government recognition and inspection, with liberal Grants-in-Aid for instruction in secular subjects, over and above the teaching of the Koran, has resulted in some 12,000 boys in such schools, in this one Province, being brought under instruction in reading and writing their mother tongue, in arithmetic and in geography, under a very simple Code. We have learnt this today only from a confidential memorandum by the Sind Director of Public Instruction, of which the Director here happened accidentally to have got a copy. This Sind plan, though after 39 years of effort, so far successful, leaves unsolved the problem of what to do for the boys in the Mosque schools which will not adopt even this simple Code, and are thus in the position of all the Mosque schools in the U.P. and N.W.F. Province, and probably elsewhere in India, for all of which our own suggestion stands. What these (and other) facts suggested to us is the desirability of there being a weekly or monthly journal, devoted to popular description of new administrative experiments in the different provinces of India, for the information of all the other provinces. In this country it is not possible for such a journal to be run by pri-

vate enterprise, and it is clearly a case for a Government publication, to be run perhaps semi-officially, without Government responsibility (like the Colonial Office List), or actually
by a Government Department (like the Board of Trade
Labour Gazette). The editorship might very well be held by
an Indian official of education and discretion.

We went to see the Church Missionary Society (Edwardes)
College, here, an excellently built structure, elaborately furnished up to English standards, with living rooms for the
students in quadrangular form. The three or four English
clergy are engaged in teaching about 24 Muhammedan youths
up to the "First Arts" examination of Lahore University
(now being extended to the B.A.), without any science
laboratory or science teaching, and with only the nucleus of a
library. There are simple Christian services each morning,
but otherwise no proselytism; and the youths, in fact, do not
become Christians. It is difficult not to feel that this work,
which seems typical of Christian work in Northern India, is
not what the British public subscribes for. Useful as it may
be in supplementing the educational work of the Government and the independent efforts now being made by the
Hindoo and Mussulman communities, it is a dead failure
from the standpoint of the Christian missionary. This fact
may account for a certain lack of straightforwardness, and a
disagreeable attitude of dislike for the Indians, and of contempt for their views and aspirations, that we find characteristic of such missionaries as we have met (who happen all to
have been Anglican or Congregationalist). These missionaries are in a false position with regard to the mission-
subsidizing folks at home. They seem to be secretly irritated
with India, and really annoyed at any attempts at Indian
progress such as the Arya Somaj, outside their own panacea,
and none of those we have seen manifests any admiration or
love for the people whom they are professedly trying to influence. We feel that the first and fundamental requisite for
successful missionary work must be a genuine admiration of
the people among whom it is to be carried on, a real apprecia-

tion of the good qualities of their race, and a generous recognition of those special excellencies which make possible a sincere attitude of "reciprocal superiority". If a man cannot feel towards the Indians that "best form of equality", as John Stuart Mill termed it, he is not fit to come out here as a missionary. We have not found among such missionaries as we have seen, any glimmering of appreciation that the Indians may be, in certain race qualities, actually equal to the English, let alone their superiors—in spirituality, in subtlety of thought and in intellectual humility or national modesty, for instance. The theological representatives of England in India seem to be as cocksure as our military or civilian or commercial representatives, that we are in all respects the superior people, kindly vouchsafing to stoop to administer at liberal salaries the affairs of an inferior "subject race". (We have not seen any Roman Catholic missionaries in India; and things may be different, even as regards Protestants, in the Madras Presidency, where most of the Christian converts are to be found.)

We have met here Alfred Ollivant, the author of "Owd Bob" (who has been a couple of months in India, chiefly with soldier and civilian cousins and other relations), and have spent a pleasant day with him at the Khyber Pass: meeting and passing the caravans escorted by armed soldiers which traverse the pass in each direction on the Tuesdays and Fridays when the "truce of the road" prevails and (what is perhaps of greater security) when it is picketed at intervals by the Khyber Rifles, who at other times merely occupy the dozen small forts and blockhouses that we garrison between Jamrud (at this end) and Lundi Kotal (near the true Afghan border). The wild and desolate hills between the two frontiers are sparsely inhabited by Afridis, who live in fortified mud castles, each sheltering a family group, with walls and towers, and who intersperse the cultivation of their little patches of arable land and the herding of their goats, with promiscuous plundering of passersby and almost continuous blood feuds between families—the Corsican vendetta—when they lie in wait for each other and shoot at sight. It is a lawless land, where every man goes armed, and over which there is no magisterial jurisdiction. This belt of mountains, a sort of "No man's land" seems here to exist all along the border. The N. W. Frontier Province Government has now settled down to a policy of mingled bribery and reprisals, so as to secure (1) that there shall be no raids on British territory or attacks on the British officials and soldiers who garrison isolated forts or traverse the passes; and (2) that no person shall actually be attacked on the road itself, though he may be followed and attacked on the road if he merely takes refuge on it. Otherwise the Afridis are left severely alone to murder and plunder each other as they will. Their adhesion to these conditions is secured by (1) the enlisting of several thousands of them in the Indian army, especially the Khyber Rifles; (2) the regular payment to them of subventions, in compensation, so to speak, for their loss by abstaining to plunder the caravans on the road; (3) occasional employment at wages in roadmaking, etc. and (4) stern reprisals on any tribes which make raids or infringe these conditions. Reprisals seem to take the form of secretly and simultaneously arresting and detaining all persons of a particular tribe, together with whatever camels, oxen or other property they have about them, who are found in British territory or within grasp of British forces on a given day; and then informing the tribe that unless they pay a fine there and then imposed on them, the property detained will be sold. In graver cases, the tribal villages will be invaded and captured by a punitive expedition.

The British forces claim to do as they like, whether in keeping the peace, erecting forts, maintaining garrisons or road-making, along the Khyber road itself and for fifty yards right and left of it; but whether or not even this much is technically British territory is not clear. Visitors are allowed up the Pass, even on Tuesdays and Fridays, only by special permit, and are now stopped at Ali Masjid, half way up—chiefly so as to shorten the day for the pickets who are withdrawn practically as soon as the two caravans have got through. Apparently, no European is allowed to go through to Afghanistan, unless he has a special permit from the Amir. He would be turned back at the Afghan frontier; and therefore the Indian Government's prohibition is not questioned. We were told by the officer or Commissioner of the Khyber Rifles (Bickford) that when, some years ago, Pierre Loti[2] was in India, the Government of India believed he would try to pass through the Khyber in the caravans, disguised as a woman; and severe orders were given that every person was to be closely scrutinised so as to detect and arrest him. But they never found anyone like him; and presently he was authentically known to have returned quite unromantically by steamer to Europe.

The "caravans" consisted of four men of the Khyber Rifles marching in front; then a straggling crowd of one or two hundred men, with a few women, walking; then several dozen pack donkeys; several score of laden camels, some shaggy creatures from the Bactrian desert, others lean and bare, and finally four more men of the Khyber Rifles, the whole dragging out to something like a mile. The outward camels were laden with sheet and rod iron, petroleum, and packing cases and bales presumably containing cotton goods and miscellaneous European products. The inward camels were less heavily laden, but they were bringing skins, bales of wool, and nondescript bundles which may have contained carpets. It looked as if we were witnessing, in tangible form, part of the "drain" of excess of exports over imports, which the Indian patriots complain of! The outward caravan was swollen by Afghans returning from service or peddling in India during the cold weather, and some of them were driving

[2] Pierre Loti (1850–1923), French novelist, noted for his picturesque romances, located in the places he visited during his extensive travels in Salonika, Constantinople, Tahiti, Senegal and Japan. His travelogue, *Vers Ispahan*, published in 1904, presented an unusual picture of an Islamic country before its commercial exploitation by the West, a development that Loti condemned.

young oxen and cows which they had apparently bought out of their earnings. It was noticeable that hardly anyone rode, except a few young children. The animals were used almost exclusively for the transport of goods; and the wild, unkempt, curiously garbed figures of all ages strode along, gossiping or silent, sometimes quarrelling and wrangling, often looking like our idea of Abraham, Isaac and Jacob.

Opposite Jamrud Fort is a well-built four-square caravan-serai, where the caravans halt for the night, and pay a fee or toll for each animal, which is taken by the Government as part of its revenue. We went to tea with the Officer Com-manding at the Fort (Bickford), a healthy and clean but unin-tellectual soldier, who had (we were told) been somewhat unduly advanced by the favour of the present Chief Com-missioner of the N.W.F. Province (Sir George Roos Keppel), under whom he had served.

In the evening we dined with Maffey, the "Political Agent" for the Khyber, an I.C.S. of charm and ability. (From him we learnt that J. A. Spender, the Editor of the "Westminster Gazette" who was out here for the Durbar, had just written privately to say that the Liberal Government would be "out" within six months, wrecked by the unpopu-larity of the Insurance Act and the difficulties of the Home Rule Bill!). On the following day we lunched with two other Civil Servants (Richey, Director of Public Instruction of an Educational service, and Howell, I.C.S., temporarily acting in revenue administration).

We are amused at the universal praise of the wild Pathans (Afridis and Afghans) of these parts. Everyone says they are fine fellows, far superior to the Hindoos! We learn on cross-examination that they are cruel and treacherous, shockingly addicted to unnatural vice and habitually given to stealing each other's wives; that murder and robbery are so common as not to be deemed crimes; that the men do little work, leav-ing their agriculture and the care of their goats mostly to the women and boys; and that the only occupation considered worthy of manhood is the promiscuous shooting at each other, taken unawares, which they call war. When we ask why a people is admired which breaks nearly every Commandment, and is apparently of no earthly use in the universe, we are told that they are fine manly fellows, "good sportsmen", with a sense of humour! Verily, our English standards are peculiar. The fact is that the British officer likes them because (1) they admire and respect him and his special qualities; (2) they make good soldiers under him; and (3) they in no way compete with him or "claim equality", or excel in directions in which he feels himself deficient. When we ask a thoughtful Civilian whether he sees any reason to believe that, even in a couple of centuries, the Pathans will have developed into anything like a civilised people, or into anything else of use in the world, he is bound to admit that there is no sign of any such possibility.

Peshawar itself is a picturesque and crowded walled city, full of little square shops opening on the streets, nearly all exactly alike, each with its occupier, his son or his apprentice squatting on the floor plying their handicrafts—here the coppersmiths in a group, there the primitive shoemakers, or the tailors working Singer's sewing machines; with innumerable sellers of coffee, sweetstuffs and fruit interspersed among them, and a whole narrow lane of butcher's shops, the first we have noticed in India. The first day we traversed its crowded streets they were thickly picketed by armed police, though there was no sign of disturbance; but we learn that two years ago at this season, when a solemn Mussulman commemoration of the death of Ali coincides with the Hindoo saturnalia called "Holi", there was a serious riot and fight between the two religions with loss of life. So this year special precautions were taken. Only a few years ago the wild Afridis made a successful raid on the richest bazaar in Peshawar itself, and got clear away with much loot. This carefully planned exploit, done by a few dozen men, was organised by a youthful recruit of our own army, who induced "Rahab the harlot", who, as in the Old Testament story, dwelt "on the wall", to let the men be drawn up into her dwelling. They then erected barricades at each end of the bazaar they had chosen for plunder, and set them on fire! These fires kept out the stray police who appeared, long enough to permit the band to secure their plunder and escape by the way they came!

With Richey, the Director of Public Instruction, we have inspected (1) the Government Normal School, temporarily housed in a modern palace, built to accommodate the Amir of Afghanistan and other distinguished Oriental visitors; (2) the Municipal High School, with some 450 boys, under an Anglicised German Headmaster, housed in quite insufficient buildings; and (3) a Hindoo High School of 600 boys, in still worse accommodation. These were all, in their several ways, surprisingly good; the Normal School small but having its own practising school, and turning out astonishingly well drilled teachers; the Municipal High School admirably organised and administered, and doing real educational work; and the Hindoo High School, up to now despising any Grant from Government and maintained by private subscriptions by local men of means, being under an eager, zealous and pushing young headmaster, a member of the Arya Somaj, and achieving good examination results, with very poor school appliances.

Altogether we get a vision that the N.W.F. Province, hitherto much neglected, is seemingly making more actual progress in education than any other province of North India. The Chief Commissioner (Sir G. Roos Keppel) is very keen on making up leeway; Richey, the Director, is an able, energetic, zealous and resourceful man; both Hindoos and Muhammedans are now eager for schooling; and, alone in India, the Provincial Government has abolished school fees. Richey, by the way, from Rugby and Balliol, was one of "Milner's young men" in South Africa;[3] and married there a rather pretty and charming girl who was apparently teaching

___

[3] Viscount Alfred Milner, who had served as British High Commissioner in South Africa during the Boer War, has been described

in a Normal School, her people being English and Scotch at Johannesburg. On retrenchment he was found a post as Assistant Director in Eastern Bengal, whence he has a year ago been promoted higher.

It may be worth noting that the formation of a separate N.W.F. Province, so keenly pursued by Lord Curzon, has by no means universally commended itself. In the desire to get a Government specializing on frontier problems, which involve so largely political and military considerations, the revenue and general administration of the by no means trivial strip of territory taken out of the Punjab is said to have suffered. Moreover what was created is not an independent Province, as autonomous as that of the Punjab or the U.P., but an administrative district very directly subordinate to the Government of India. We learn that the officials of the N.W.F. Province do not constitute a service by themselves, but are reckoned as part of the Political Department of the Government of India; and they are interchangeable with the Political Agents etc., in and for the Native States. A considerable proportion of them seem to be military officers, who are now engaged in the work elsewhere done by the Civilians.

---

as 'a well-nigh perfect expression of social-imperialism' (Bernard Semmel, *Imperialism and Social Reform*, 1960, p. 81). He gathered around himself, in South Africa, a group of young men from Oxford who came to be known as 'Milner's Kindergarten'. They included Leopold S. Amery, Lionel Curtis, Lord Lothian and other notable representatives of British Liberal-Imperialism.

Lyallpur, 6 to 8 March 1912

A flying visit to this centre of the great Chenab Canal colony has given us a vision of the most extensive and reputedly most successful of the Indian irrigation schemes. A tract of some 5,000 square miles, a quarter of a century ago almost barren desert, inhabited by under 100,000 wild nomads, has been turned into a highly productive wheatfield (with cotton, sugar-cane, oil-seeds and vegetables as subsidiary crops), having something like two million inhabitants who are extremely prosperous, and quite free from danger of famine. This has been done by a great scheme of bringing water from the Chenab, and distributing it all over the area by ramifying distributory canals. Owing to the Deputy Commissioner being down with enteric, and other officers' bungalows being full up, we were sent to the Dak Bungalow where we found the rooms far more commodious and comfortable than that we occupied at the hotel at Peshawar or at the hotel at Allahabad; though the food and cooking were more primitive. We spent the morning going over a fragment of the Colony, tramping from canal to canal, under the guidance of one of the Canal engineers (Yeoman) and one of the Indian Canal officials. The Indian spoke no English, and the English engineer, who may have been good at his technical job, neither knew nor cared anything about the people, or their social and economic arrangements; and was, indeed, after more than twenty years in India, as ignorant of and as uninterested in the country that he was serving, as the ordinary sailor is about the ports at which he touches. All he had picked up were the common prejudices and dislikes of the English community. Certainly, from the three "Coopers Hill men"[1] whom we have met (Yeoman, Clutterbuck, Tullock) and the half-a-dozen others with whom S.W. dined at Hardwar, we can only derive the impression that "Coopers Hill" failed to produce any cultivation of mind, or to turn out men of real education or breadth of view. They have for the most part proved far inferior to the members of the I.C.S., prejudiced and snobbish and unenlightened as some few of these are.

The Chenab Colony is clearly a success in the main essentials, and thus reflects credit on the engineers, though it seems that at the start the levels were very roughly taken, so that some of the first settlers found that they could get no water and threw up their allotments; and some of the allotting was badly done. But we were not so much impressed with the Colony, as a social and economic experiment, as its repute had led us to expect. We have enlarged and corrected our impression from the official reports (Gazetteer of the Colony and "Punjab Colony Manual"). We were taken first to an inconceivably squalid mud compound, housing half-a-dozen families, with their buffaloes, in one hideous confusion. These turned out to be tenants—apparently rackrented tenants paying half of all their gross produce in kind, as well as bearing all the Government demands for land tax, canal charges and local cess—of a small landlord owing six "squares", or 160 acres. The Government whilst wishing to have a majority of peasant owners, had given some land to capitalist owners, thinking it desirable to have "leaders of society". By common consent, they had been a failure. Yet we were told that Sir Louis Dane, the present Lt. Governor of the Punjab, was in favour of having them in the new Colonies.

---

[1] The Royal Indian Engineering College, Coopers Hill.

We went next to a regular Canal village, laid out officially at the outset, and inhabited by sixty families cultivating thirty squares, so that each family had about 13 acres, for which it was said to pay to the Government altogether, about 75 rupees (£5). This was more prosperous in appearance than the tenants' mud huts. The mud dwellings had extensive compounds; they were equipped with elaborate wooden doors; and the house of the headman into which we were allowed to peer had a good deal of household possessions. They had built themselves a small mosque, and they supported a Mulvi whom we saw, and who taught the boys the Koran. But the people looked very wild and barbarous; the cattle and children were very promiscuously mixed up in the dirty compounds; and there was, after some twenty years of colonisation, no sign of education, sanitation or medical aid—scarcely even decent roads or any really effective police (as regards protection of village property) being provided by the Government which attracted all these people to this spot. We learn that, at the start, there was no thought of doing anything at all but allot the land. No provision whatever was made—hardly any is yet made—for the conditions of civilised life. It was regarded exclusively as a question of water engineering and land allotment—neither the Educational nor the Medical Officers were asked to report what such a Colony required, and no one seems to have planned out anything like a model settlement.

Truly Indian Government is a thing of contrasts. In the afternoon we visited the Lyallpur Agricultural College, some four years old. Here we found a very extensive, handsome, really well-built, of quite good "oriental" design, splendidly equipped with science laboratories, apparatus and library; with its own oil-gas plant making electric light; having excellent lodging accommodation for over 100 youths; under an able English chemist of expert skill, with two other English professors and several Indian assistants; working its own extensive farm and experimental grounds of hundreds of acres—the whole done apparently regardless of cost, and containing only some 45 youths, half of whom were bribed to come by scholarships covering their whole maintenance. On this College the Government had spent between fifty and a hundred thousand pounds, and was incurring a heavy annual charge; whilst ninety per cent of the boys, even on its own Colony, could not be provided with elementary schooling, on the plea that there was no money available!

Barnes, the Principal, struck us as an able scientist and ambitious for discoveries—not really interested in teaching, and least of all in teaching Indians. It appears that the small demand for agricultural instruction is rendered even smaller by the refusal of the Government to admit any Hindoo students not belonging to an agricultural caste, professedly part of a policy to prevent the alienation of the land to Bunnyas and money-lenders, but (the Hindoos said), really part of the policy of retaining the land for the Muhammedans.

In the evening we dined with Gwythyr, the principal local engineer, a quiet able man, who had been born in India and trained at Rurki. There we met Gibb, a Coopers Hill man superior in distinction to any yet seen, inventor of "Gibb's Module" (a water measuring device), and ridiculously like Sir William Ramsay. We had seen in the afternoon Abdul Kadir, a Mussulman pleader (getting the Government briefs) who was like other educated Mussulmans in quiet charm, but like them also servile in dependence on the British Government, and horribly conscious (in spite of claiming to be a ruling race) of inability to organise or initiate or maintain anything without Government aid.

Lahore, 9 to 12 March 1912

Our second brief stay in Lahore was, besides visits to the Fort, and the Shahdara tombs,[1] marked by (1) a Hindoo dinner party; (2) an interesting meeting with a score of leading Muhammedans at a Judge's house; (3) a garden party at a Hindoo capitalist's, to meet the leading Hindoos; (4) lunch at the Lt. Governor's; (5) a visit to the Islamia College; (6) a long visit with Lajpat Rai to the Arya Somaj school and college; (7) a visit to the Aitchison Chiefs College; (8) a dinner party of officials at the house of the Director of Public Instruction; and (9) tea with the Agnews (District Judge)—no bad record for three days! We failed to find time to utilise our introductions to the Anglican Bishop and the leading Anglican Deaconess.

The dinner party at Rambaj Dutt Chowdhri's has been already described. These dozen Hindoo gentlemen and ladies (one "enlightened orthodox", two Brahmo Samaj and the rest Arya Samaj), together with the garden party of similarly mixed Hindooism, left on our minds the impression that the Hindoos of Lahore, as compared with those of Calcutta, were a little "provincial" in manners and ideas, much as Manchester or Newcastle would compare with London—

[1] The tombs of Emperor Jahangir, his wife Nur Jehan, and her brother Asaf Khan.

perhaps a little sturdier but with that somewhat "rougher". They were at least equally "Nationalist".

There seems to be a vigorous branch of the Brahmo Samaj at Lahore, quite independent of Calcutta and Bombay, small in membership, but having substantial endowments which support a local newspaper (Tribune)[2] and a local College. From the Editor of the one and the Principal of the other, and from the Cambridge Wrangler who was Professor of Mathematics at the Government College (Chowla, with a refined and educated wife from Cashmere, as white as any Englishwoman), we gathered that the Brahmo Samaj here, though thus relatively wealthy (again like English Unitarianism) was not really more "alive" or popularly influential than those at Calcutta and Bombay. The individual members were people of grace and charm and refinement, who found in their abstract religion a resting place and freedom to contract legal marriages, but hardly desired propaganda or proselytism.

The Islamia College, housed in a new brick building without amenity provided a hundred or more Moslem youths with the means of getting a Punjab University degree without resorting to Christian or Arya Samaj Colleges on the one hand, or the completely secular Government College on the other. It had had a succession of Moslem Principals, who had more or less failed, partly because of the inveterate habit of the Moslem Governing Body of interfering with internal discipline; and it was now under a somewhat second-rate English Oxford man (Martin) who had been promoted from being an Assistant Master at Aligarh. It struck us as a place poor in spirit, with inferior Moslem professors, concerned only to get its youths through the B.A. examination. But it aspired to become a constituent College of the new Islamic Univers-

[2] *The Tribune*, founded in 1881, was already by this time more than a local newspaper. It was certainly the most influential nationalist paper in the Punjab, with a reputation for fearlessness and independence.

ity. It had, however, a department in which the "Yunani" or
Mussulman medicine was taught by Hakims, which might
usefully be developed into a practical teaching of hygiene and
physiology alongside of the weird "materia medica" and traditional therapeutics of the Muhammedan doctors. We have,
however, found no one prepared to accept, or even to understand the idea of such a development.

The Aitchison Chiefs College, a Government foundation
of a generation ago, lived in the most magnificent College
buildings that we have yet seen, built in charming
"Saracenic" style, with gorgeous amplitude of space, amid
groves and gardens and playing fields, of opulent magnitude.
Here about a hundred sons of Native Chiefs, either ruling or
practically noble, were educated from 7 to 17 or 20, up to
Matriculation standard. Each had his own servants (from 3 to
25!) and horses, and provided his own food. (A common
dining room had lately been started, as an innovation to increase corporate feeling.) It was the young Raja of Faridkot, a
tiny independent state, who had 25 servants for himself and a
brother. The family had asked that he should have sixty! The
College Authorities compromised on 25, including a domestic tutor, a Maulvi to attend to devotions, cooks and coachmen, etc. and a special "Chowkidar" or Watchman.

The boys were reading, and playing games as they chose,
it being Sunday. Our host (Cornah) an energetic and viva-
cious young Englishman, was Assistant Principal, whose
vocation was school-mastering, which he probably did well.
(Practically no supervision over the boys at night, though
they slept in two's and three's in adjoining small rooms).

The Director of Public Instruction (Godley) was a
"stick"—a dull, wooden, though doubtless honest and conscientious cousin of the late Under Secretary of State at the
Indian Office—probably "jobbed" into his present billet, after coming out as professor in the Government College. He
seemed to have no particular knowledge of educational administration, and was certainly unaware of the expedients being
tried in other parts of India—indeed, he appeared uncon-

scious that there *were* any problems to be solved. To him, it was merely a question of getting enough trained teachers, and of securing from the Lieutenant Governor sufficient money to pay them. The brightest of the company at his house was G. R. Wathen, a professor at the Government College (married to a connection of the Buxtons), who deplored the obstruction which the Deputy Commissioners usually offered to educational progress (thinking roads much more necessary and much more certainly useful than schools), and the fact that the Government always consulted these Deputy Commissioners on educational problems, yet never the Principals and Professors of Colleges, nor the heads of schools. For instance, Gokhale's Bill was sent out broadcast for opinions (which, as expected, were usually hostile) to the civilian officers, but not to anyone concerned in educational work. He strongly advocated making the educational service an integral part of the I.C.S.

The Mussulman party at the house of Mr. Justice Shah Din[3] was distinctly interesting. B.W. went an hour earlier to meet the "Purdah" ladies, several dozen of them, in gorgeous raiment, one a Begum of high rank in magnificent jewels, several speaking English having been (or actually being) pupils of the English Anglican Girls School, which gains their presence by having a Maulvi to teach the Koran.

The score of men whom we both talked with later included the leading Islamic Pleaders and Barristers, an Editor or two, professors and Government officials. They all wished British rule to continue, for fear of succumbing be-

---

[3] Justice Shah Din (1868–1918), an important judicial administrator of the Punjab, Judge of the Chief Court (1908–18) and also, for a time, its acting Chief Judge. A conservative by temperament, Shah Din, like Sir Syed Ahmed Khan, was a believer in liberal education through a synthesis of Eastern and Western values, and an advocate of female education. In 1893 he became a Fellow of Punjab University and in 1895 a Trustee of the MAO College, Aligarh. He was actively involved in Muslim politics, being the organizer of the Muslim League in the Punjab, and its first President.

fore the Hindoos; they would be glad if Government would aid the Muktabs by peripatetic teachers; they nearly all desired a prompt modification and gradual cessation of the Purdah system, though none of them would begin; they despaired of getting their girls educated (only a tiny few being rich enough to go in carriages to a school, even if their families would allow this). Here, again, the Mussulmans were despairing of achieving anything without Government aid. They said that, until quite lately, no Muhammedan above the labouring class would take to any occupation other than War and Government; even now there were far fewer Muhammedan lawyers than Hindoo lawyers; and there were hardly any in business. Nor will the landowners take up agriculture as a profession, and devote themselves to developing their estates—they like to be mere rent receivers.

We are struck by the enormous value to the Muhammedan community in India of the work done by Sir Syed Ahmed in founding and building up Aligarh College. It looks as if, but for Aligarh, there would today be scarcely any Mussulman in India able to rise above the rank of an artisan or a subordinate of police. The Hindoos would perforce have held, not only the whole legal profession, but also the whole Government service. We meet practically no Mussulman judge, barrister or Civil Servant of standing who is not an ex-student of Aligarh. It is instructive to remember that Sir Syed Ahmed was almost to the end, opposed by the bulk of the Mulvis and by a very large proportion of the wealthy Muhammedans. And to this day they don't like "Western learning", or anything else not emanating from Islam itself. Their present thirst for education is avowedly only in order that they may not be ousted by the Hindoos.

A garden party of Hindoos was given for us by Harkishen Lal, at the instance of Lajpat Rai (who has already been described). Harkishen Lal is a Hindoo barrister who has gone into business on a large scale—government contracting, banking, flour-mill owning and what not. He seems to be in all the big business undertakings of the Punjab, where English capitalism does not seem to prevail to any great extent; and he may be anything between a millionaire or (as Agnew somewhat maliciously suggested) a manipulator of balances among his manifold undertakings. He seemed to us a shrewd and able business man; free from prejudices or enthusiasms, cool and a little cynical; good friends with both the Brahmo Samaj and the Arya Samaj, but not actually a member of either body. His wife, a pleasant looking silent Hindoo, was not "purdah", and appeared to welcome us when we called; and was present also at the garden party to meet some fifty Hindoo men and half-a-dozen Brahmo Samaj ladies. The men were Pleaders, Editors, Professors and Government Officials; exclusively Hindoos, and mostly Arya Somaj or Brahmo Samaj. The conversation turned on the same points as with other educated Hindoos: they were all "Nationalist" in sympathy; and they had the usual grievances. Among the ladies was the Maharaja Dulip Singh's daughter, who had married a local Hindoo "bourgeois", and was supposed to hold distinctly "seditious" opinions!

We were distinctly glad that we had not accepted the Agnew's proffered hospitality, though Mrs. Agnew seemed a nice woman, with intelligence and open-mindedness. He turned out to be the officer who, as Magistrate, had begun the proceedings against Lajpat Rai which led to the latter's arbitrary deportation without trial. It would have been awkward for us, if we had stayed at Agnew's house, to have had our four separate meetings with Lajpat Rai! He told us that Penton, the Financial Commissioner of the Punjab, had suggested the expedient of deportation and had drawn attention to the long-forgotten power to deport. The Government, as Agnew admitted to us, never formulated any charge against Lajpat Rai, or revealed the cause of his deportation or made any excuse or apology or explanation of their high-handed proceedings. Agnew, who talked loosely and carelessly (relying on our ignorance), made out that Lajpat Rai had suffered nothing! "He had the time of his life: he was taken to the station in a motor car, and given a pleasant holiday in Burma". "Treated like a King", said Bosworth Smith, a Deputy Commissioner of the Punjab, to us on board the boat. As if it was nothing to carry off a lawyer for six months away from his practice; to exile him from his wife and family; to make no allowance for their maintenance; and to keep him a prisoner under close custody (never allowed out without a warder) during the hot weather in Mandalay! What happened was that Sir D. Ibbetson the Lt. Governor asked half-a-dozen people who were the people most influential in fomenting discontent, and they all gave Lajpat Rai as a leader. When we innocently enquired what was alleged against Lajpat Rai, Agnew mysteriously said that this was strictly confidential and had never been published—he seemed to think it of no consequence that Lajpat Rai accordingly had no chance of denying, disproving or explaining— but Agnew accidentally let out that the Government thought that Lajpat Rai was tampering with the troops. Of this, we can discover no sort of evidence. But as we have had it put to us by naive Englishmen, it comes only to this, that the Punjab furnishes the mainstay of the Indian Army (apart from the Gurkhas); and these Punjabee soldiers are nearly all themselves cultivators or of cultivators families; so that any stirring up of discontent among the Punjabee cultivators excites discontent among those Punjabees who are serving in the army—hence any agitation in the Punjab is in effect, to excite disaffection among the soldiers! This has been quite seriously urged upon us, more than once as a reason why all agitation in the Punjab must be stopped at once however peaceful and constitutional, and whatever the grievance. In confirmation of this, we may record the gossip that, when the new Canal Act was arousing great discontent in 1907–8, as an infringement of the promises made to the Colonists (it was on this that a foul-mouthed agitator Ajit Singh[4] was operating,

[4] Ajit Singh came into political prominence when he joined Lala Lajpat Rai to protest against the government's agrarian policy which sought to raise revenue assessments and the rates for irrigation facilities. In 1907 an excited mob set fire to government build-

when he was summarily deported at the same time as Lajpat Rai), Lord Kitchener is said to have insisted on the Government of India vetoing the Act (which it did), saying that otherwise he would not answer for the loyalty of the Sikhs in the army—Agnew, of course, did not explain this to us; but we believe it to be the view on which the Punjab Government acted. We learn that Lord Morley telegraphed out that there were to be no prosecutions for the vague crime of "sedition"; if the Government prosecuted it was to be for some definite offence.

Ajit Singh, by the way, appears to have been a person of no importance, who railed at everybody in turn; a mob orator and journalist, quite unconnected with Lajpat Rai. The English officials were ignorant of what had happened to him and told us all sorts of stories. The truth is that, when brought back from deportation, he discreetly went away to avoid police persecution—first to Persia where he embraced Muhammedanism, and then to Constantinople, where he is now editing a local newspaper.

Agnew was curiously like Sydney Buxton[5] in physical appearance, manners and speech; and had even the same kind of narrow precision of intellect, but he lacked Sydney Buxton's fundamental Liberalism and fair-mindedness. We

---

ings on hearing a speech he made. As a consequence he was deported, with Lala Lajpat Rai, to Mandalay for six months. He returned to become the editor of *Peshwa*, a revolutionary paper, but eventually, out of sympathy with the strategies of the Congress, he fled to Persia and thence to Italy and South America. By an odd coincidence he died on 15 August 1947, the very day of India's independence.

[5] Sydney Charles, first Earl Buxton (1853–1934) was a Radical politician and a member of the London School Board (1876–82). He was the author of the Fair Wages Resolution and was also partly responsible for the first National Insurance Act. In *My Apprenticeship* Beatrice Webb refers to the Buxtons as one of the families which 'represented money power in the London Society of the seventies and eighties. *My Apprenticeship* (Penguin edition, 1971), p. 73.

talked to him about the tremendous powers of imprisonment without conviction given to all Magistrates in India by their power of requiring anyone to find sureties, or in default to go to prison ("rigorous imprisonment") for as much as two or three years. This is habitually used with regard to people whom the police report as "of bad life", and it is not infrequently employed for "political" agitators or lecturers. The magistrate may even stipulate that the two or three sureties to be found, for some quite large sum, shall be residents in the locality, of known loyalty and good character, and payers of so much in direct taxation. He can thus make it quite impracticable for the prisoner to find the sureties, *and he habitually does this*, intending and wishing to send him to prison for a year or so in default—without conviction of any offence! This procedure appears to be regularly used throughout India with regard to reputed "bad characters", who are, of course, usually humble folk; when crime is rife and evidence cannot be obtained. Agnew said it was a very "successful device". Dacoity or cattle stealing would be prevalent; no evidence could be obtained; the police ran in a dozen men; the magistrate committed them to prison in default of finding sureties; and the crimes ceased! He admitted that it was theoretically indefensible, and said, of course, that the magistrate ought not to impose plainly impossible conditions; but he asserted that the Indian Government must have some such power of summary imprisonment owing to the difficulty of getting evidence. When we pointed out that it was used in cases where full evidence was available (as in the case of the Arya Samaj lecturer at Jhansi) he evaded the issue. Someone ought to ask for a return of men imprisoned without conviction, merely in default of finding sureties. It is a case of oppressing the poor and weak, when rich men do not suffer; and it lends a very potent handle to police persecution of unpopular persons.

Our lunch at Government House was the usual formality. Sir Louis Dane seemed a kindly, genial administrator, of commonsense and practical judgment in avoiding trouble.

He had retired from the I.C.S. ten or twelve years ago, and become a Resident Magistrate in Ireland; but his wife found this intolerable after India, and he asked and was given the post of Resident at Kashmir, whence on Sir Denzil Ibbetson's death, he was made Lieutenant Governor of the Punjab—apparently as a man capable of smoothing down things after Ibbetson had stirred them up. But though out of practical English commonsense he smoothed things down, he had all the usual Anglo-Indian prejudices, and he had even more than the common Anglo-Indian disingenuousness in talking to inquisitive tourists whom he thought ignorant (vide the story of the two Arya Samaj students, and the pistols already given). Lady Dane thought that no friendly intercourse with Indians was possible because they had nothing to talk about! We have never quite understood this complaint, seeing how much we found to talk about with both Hindoos and Muhammedans. The conversation at the luncheon table between the two A.D.C.'s and the daughters made us realise what was meant. It turned exclusively on lawn tennis, polo and the various race meetings and tournaments. Now, it may be that races are separated from each other more by their amusements (and, as regards the English, by their incessant talking about their peculiar amusements) than by their differences of religion, of language, of dress, or even of cookery. Because the educated Indians don't talk tennis or polo, the average Englishman thinks they can have nothing to talk about! Whereas it is he who is conversationally destitute. The educated Indians seem to us as ready as we are to talk about public affairs, about social and economic problems, about music and art, about philosophy, and even about religion. But then, all these topics are banished from a large section of English society.

Delhi, 12 to 16 March 1912

We were disappointed in Delhi, which, fine as some of its things are, does not show well after Agra. But we were whirled to the Kutab Minar in the Commissioner's motor car, and spent an hour wandering about these wonderful ruins, with great satisfaction. It is perhaps the best column of victory in the world; and the neighbouring village had various interesting sights. On our way back, among other sights we were interested in Humayun's Mausoleum as the forerunner of the Taj, of which it exhibits nearly all the features, missing only the perfection of the whole. This disposes of the characteristic story repeated by Anglo Indian after Anglo Indian that the Taj was built by Italians! There is not a fragment of evidence that any "Italian" of artistic competence was ever at the Mogul Court; and the Italians at the time the Taj was building were putting up the terrible Renaissance churches denounced by Ruskin. The idle story is only an instance of the English lack of generosity to the Indians, and of inability to recognise any point in which Indians could conceivably excel Europeans.

We saw at Delhi, as usual, some leading Muhammedans, who were as elsewhere. Out of a local bar of fifty or sixty, only six or eight were Muhammedans; though Delhi has nearly as many Muhammedans as Hindoos. The bank where we got money had only Hindoo clerks. The majority of the

Government officials were Hindoos. The business is nearly all in the hands of Hindoos. The Muhammedans are mostly artisans, labourers and cultivators. There is no Muhammedan College, only one (inferior) Muhammedan High School for all Delhi, and apparently very few primary schools (apart from the dwindling Muktabs at the Mosques). Our Muhammedan friends deplored all this, but seemed to despair of altering it. The most attractive of them in many ways was Latifi, an Anglicised Indian (St. John's Oxford) in the I.C.S., married to an educated Indian wife, out of purdah. He was officiating as District Judge, but had lately spent a year in describing all the industries of the Punjab, published as a book—quite ably done, with many minor suggestions for Government aid in their improvement. He attributed the Muhammedan backwardness in business to their inability to accept interest. When pressed as to how that interfered with the ordinary commercial enterprise, which needed to borrow, but never had occasion to lend money, he said that the Muhammedan in business was at a disadvantage in borrowing, because he could not usually find any willing lender who knew him intimately, or as a friend—such being usually his co-religionists, and therefore unable to lend at interest. He thus always had to pay high interest to a stranger, instead of the lower rate that an intimate knowing his character would be willing to lend at. (He said they were unwilling to lend without interest, and hence did not lend at all, but always invested in land, to get the rents). This disadvantage seems to us unsubstantial. The explanation may be psychological.

We were interested to find that both the Commissioner (Dallas) and the Deputy Commissioner (Beadon) of Delhi were ex-officers: the Punjab service seems to be full of these army officers, and this goes far to explain to us the ill-success of its administration compared with that of the U.P. Certainly those we have met or heard of, at Lahore, Amritsar, and Delhi, appeared most unsympathetic administrators, neither understanding nor caring about the feelings of the educated Indian; and blandly unconscious of there being anything to study in the art of administration, of which they were entirely ignorant. They were doubtless upright magistrates and honest officials, incapable of being bribed, though not at all incapable of being prejudiced.

The Deputy Commissioner of Delhi was giving a garden party to "Natives", to which we were invited, as it was understood that we "wished to meet natives". It appeared that there were two garden parties on successive days, one to the English and their wives, and one for the "natives". Latifi (being of the I.C.S.) and his wife were the only "natives" present at the former. At the latter the only English present were the Deputy Commissioner (Beadon) and his wife as hostess, the Commissioner (Dallas) and his wife; the Editor of the local newspaper, and the Chairman of the local (English) Chamber of Commerce, both rather ineligible, lower-middle class men; a missionary (Andrews) and a couple of clergy, who had been specially told to come; and ourselves. Among the Indians were the descendant of the Mogul Emperor, and one or two other "princes", various great Muhammedan "nobles", all the Indian officials of a certain status; and pleaders, lecturers, etc. For their amusement, an Indian conjuring performance was provided, which no one attended to. The whole arrangement seemed a monument of invidious race distinction and snobbishness, which does the English administration no credit.

We dined and also went to tea at the Cambridge Mission which carried on practically the only University College at Delhi[1] (there is one other, a feeble Hindoo College,[2] of in-

---

[1] An obvious reference to St Stephen's College, founded in 1882 and maintained and staffed by the Cambridge Mission to Delhi. Before the establishment of the University of Delhi in 1922 it was affiliated to the Punjab University.

[2] Hindu College, founded in 1899 (incorporated in the University of Delhi, 1922). A traditional rival of St Stephen's, Hindu College was established to provide an alternative for those Delhi Hindus who did not wish to send their sons to a Christian College. Over time the college came to acquire a distinctly nationalist profile.

ferior grade, only recognised up to the Intermediate Arts examination and always on the point of being closed) besides schools, dispensaries and zenana work. The Principal (Allnutt), who had been 32 years at his post, was pathetically like a tired millhorse, wearied and worn out by his perpetual grind; but genial, kindly and broadminded to the last. His 200 college students were more than half Hindoo, less than a third Muhammedan, and about an eighth Christians. No attempt at proselytism was made, though simple Christian services were held; and only an infinitesimal fraction had ever been converted in all that time. He had thus brought up innumerable masters for Hindoo and Muhammedan schools all over the Punjab. They had had some successful girls' schools for Muhammedans, conducted by lady teachers, *with a Mulvi to teach the Koran*; but it was decided (by whom?) that this latter piece of toleration was going too far for a Christian mission; and when the teaching of the Koran was dropped, the attendance at once fell to nothing. Now they were trying to re-open one school, and with great difficulty they were getting three girls to promise to attend.

The other man in whom we were interested was the person in command, Andrews, who had been greatly commended to us by various people as the only enthusiastic 'pro-native" among the missionaries. He proved to be a somewhat "smooth" and seemingly disingenuous "ecclesiastic"; clean-shaven and celibate, of the "priestly" type. We unfortunately fell out with him straightaway, as he proved to be full of rather malicious slanders against the Arya Samaj, Lajpat Rai, and others whom we knew and respected—the statements being, plainly, to our own knowledge, loose and even disingenuous aspersions which it was, to say the least of it, uncharitable to pass on to presumably ignorant enquirers. At our subsequent meeting, we avoided this dangerous topic; but Andrews manifested the same "mauvaise langue" about the Indians, and their character and characteristics—making us feel that he had the same jealous annoyance that we have noticed in other missionaries in North India.

Jaipur, 17/19 March 1912

A night journey brought us at five in the morning to the British Residency here, to which we had been spontaneously invited by Col. Showers, to whom the Impeys had written from Chhatarpur. The Residency is a two-centuries old marble palace, in wide and pleasant grounds, with large and lofty rooms, somewhat splendidly furnished in quite good taste, apparently at the expense of the Jaipur State, to which it belongs. Col. Showers turned out to be a kindly, genial and simple minded soldier; so deaf that he could hear only when he put up his ear-trumpet to one's mouth, an excellent host so far as letting us do what we like is concerned; but not able to be very communicative. As usual, the wife is in England.

We gather from him that Political Agents at the Native States tend to interfere less rather than more as time goes on; and to interfere very little indeed with the larger States, unless invited to give advice, which is not often the case. He sees the Maharaja regularly once a week, on Thursday afternoon. He tells us that only Hyderabad, Mysore, Kashmir, Nepaul and Baroda have Residents all to themselves: all the others, even Gwalior, Jaipur, Bhopal and Patiala, are grouped with other and smaller States—perhaps to diminish the invidiousness of there being a "Resident" in a State. The principal business is now the conduct of correspondence between the States and the Government of India. But the

"Resident" has summary magisterial powers over all British subjects in the State: he was not sure whether he had over European foreigners.

We did not see the Maharajah[1]—an old gentleman of bad reputation—selfish, sensual and intensely superstitious—like so many chiefs, childless, and refusing to nominate his heir. Colonel Showers suggested that the childlessness of so many of these ruling chiefs is deliberate because they are so intensely jealous and fearful of an "heir apparent"—and he pointed to the fact that this man has numerous illegitimate children and three legitimate wives but no heir. The Prime Minister was a Mahomedan—an Aligarh boy to whom Morison introduced us—a great landed proprietor in the U.P.—a dignified and sensible elderly man but not interesting. Sidney saw also the private secretary to the Maharajah, a cultivated and plausible Bengalee Brahmin. Perhaps we learnt most from the refined and intelligent young Brahmin student who was deputed to attend us. From what he said and implied we gathered that the Maharajah's government was priest-ridden, narrow-minded and despotic—no new movements being tolerated—enormous sums being spent on priests, Saddhus, and religious mendicants, and such education as is given being entirely in the hands of men brought up in Jaipur. The Arya Somaj had some dozen members among officials and professors but they had to keep very quiet as the Maharajah objected to them on religious and political grounds. To Mahomedans and Christians he was cordially tolerant. No beef was allowed in the State; to kill a cow meant imprisonment for life—exactly the same punishment as for the murder of a man. We visited two Rajput noblemen's houses—one a comfortable European bungalow, the other a more resplen-

[1] H.H. Sir Sawai Madho Singh Bahadur (1861–1922), a generous contributor to famine relief, the First World War and the All-India Victoria Memorial. He attended the coronation of King Edward VII in 1902, travelling to England with 125 officers and attendants, on a chartered ship, carrying not only food but also drinking water from India.

dent and distinctively Indian residence with fine formal gardens, tanks, and running water channels with innumerable flower pots alongside them. In both cases our hosts were tall, handsome, accomplished men, speaking English fluently, devotees of sport, and polo, with a large family of boys surrounding them—handsome, smartly dressed little urchins with pretty manners. But these Rajput grandees seemed to be leading somewhat aimless lives—they ought all to have been in the army but this the British Government denies them except in subordinate positions which their rank and wealth makes impossible to accept; and all part in the government of the country is denied them by the constitution of the native state.

We learnt that it was felt as a drawback by the young student, and by his class, that they were excluded, as being not British subjects, from eligibility for the I.C.S., and indeed also the Provincial Service. He said that only two Jaypore men had ever got into the Indian Medical Service, and that only by making out that they were British subjects—perhaps as the sons of British subjects. He admitted that, as regards subordinate posts in the Provincial Service, no great strictness was observed, and a very short term of residence in the Province might suffice to qualify. We learnt afterwards that the technical disqualification was often ignored, or got over, in cases where, through influence, it was really desired to appoint—though this does not make the matter any better! The result is to make it rather hopeless for clever and ambitious young men in backward Native States. At the Jaypore College (which is a full B.A. and B.Sc. College affiliated to Allahabad University), the hundred and odd students nearly all hoped for Jaypore Government employment, which most of them would fail to get. Our informant himself thought of going to the Rurki Engineering College, in order to get an engineering post. He had thought of medicine, but had been unlucky: he was simultaneously a candidate for admission to Lahore and Lucknow Medical Colleges, and failed to pass at the former. For the latter he did pass, but was rejected on the

ground that he had sat also at Lahore. We thought that, probably (as his father was a retired Superintendent of Jaypore
Customs and his relations were in Jaypore Government
employ) he would also get a small appointment.

It is part of the State feeling that all the nine Professors at
the Maharaja's College (except the Principal whom we saw
who had gone to Muir College to get his M.S.) were of that
College only. Two of them taught between them all Natural
Science, and others Mathematics and the Arts subjects. We
took the opportunity of suggesting the establishment of post-
graduate scholarships tenable elsewhere; and in particular of
sending new Professors to see the other colleges of India at
least. There was also a Sanskrit College with a hundred students, a High School of several hundreds, and lower
schools—all for boys together with a small Nobles School (of
15) for the sons of great folk. We heard also of Jain Schools
and Muhammedan Schools, so that Jaypore City seems
rather well-provided educationally.

Udaipur, 23 to 25 March 1912[1]

We came here via Chitorgarh which we stopped to see, involving a night in a quite comfortable Dak Bungalow. We found the State Elephant, which came to meet us at the station, altogether too slow a method of progression—the poor beast had an open sore on the leg which made it whimper when it knelt down—so we hired a tonga to go up the fort, which is a great hill like that of Gwalior. The two towers, one Jain and one Hindoo, were well worth seeing, as was also the confused mass of ruins of palaces, temples, tanks, etc.

At Udaipur we had the State Guest House to ourselves, and enjoyed two restful days driving out morning and evening, and browsing over an armful of books borrowed from the youthful Scottish missionary in the heat of the day. Of this State (Mewar) we saw only a youthful Private Secretary, a Bengalee Brahmin whose father was a judicial officer in the service. The Maharana,[2] as the ruler is styled, was away ti-

[1] In the manuscript diary, this entry appears before that for 19–21 March (Ajmer). The following entry explains the apparent discrepancy.

[2] H.H. Maharana Sir Fateh Singh Bahadur of Udaipur (1849–1930), was a Grand Commander of the Order of the Star of India, but refused to wear the sash and badge because he said it made him look like a messenger in a government office. Fateh Singh belonged to the tradition of the proud Rajput, kept his distance from the British government, generally contriving to fall ill when called upon to meet its representatives. It is said that if perchance he could

ger-shooting to which he devotes every possible moment.
He is a man of 65, intensely Conservative and priest-ridden,
opposed to all innovations, scoffing at those Hindoos he calls
"knife and fork wallahs", spending the revenue on his
amusements and doing nothing for progress, though his
State seems to be getting more and more barren, and a great
scheme of irrigation is (we were told) well within his power.
Here there is no College, and no educational or other opportunity for the young men—the place seemed to us dead, partly because the population was diminished by flight from the
plague, which was mildly raging. The Scottish Presbyterians
have had a mission here for thirty-five years and have gradually won their way into the Maharana's favour by the
medical skill and tact of Dr. Shepherd, who is an M.D. and
runs a free hospital. He told us he had, in the whole state, 140
Indian Christians. A nice young Aberdeenian (A.C. Grant)
had just come out as his assistant, and it was from him that
we borrowed books.

The British Resident (Col. Kaye) was away "in camp"
visiting his other States. His wife entertained us and nearly all
the other English residents to dinner—the Agency Surgeon,
the Railway Engineer, the Adjutant to the Imperial Service
Force here, and their wives—a rather "terrible" party, the
hostess and her lady friends in extremely decollete and ultra-
smart gowns, the conversation more than usually "Anglo-
Indian" in its contempt for the "natives", its concentration
on petty grievances, and its snobbishness. But these English
in such Native States as this have nothing to do, and it is just
as well that those who are fit for nothing better should be
sent there.

---

not avoid such an encounter, he would bathe immediately afterwards, in ritual cleansing. As a ruler he preferred to centralize all
administrative powers in his own hands, refusing to co-operate
with the British government which wanted him to suppress
peasant agitations in his state. Eventually, the animosity between
him and the British resulted in his being forced to abdicate in 1921,
in favour of the more loyal Maharaj Kumar.

Ajmere, 19–21 March 1912

We omitted to describe our two nights stay at Ajmere, where we slept at the Railway Station Refreshment Rooms, as the British Resident was away and the Waddingtons'[1] house was full. When the train arrived at 10.15 p.m., an hour late, we tumbled out into a crowd of a dozen Hindoo gentlemen, bowing and salaaming; these turned out to be the leading members of the Arya Samaj, who had come to welcome us, and (as we rather feared) for a talk! We were dead tired, and could only dismiss them abruptly, and sit down to our belated dinner. Next morning, one of the principal among them (Ram Bilas Sarda),[2] a man having four shops selling piece goods and a Municipal Commissioner, drove round with us for two hours to the sights. We spent two hours more inspecting the Arya Samaj institutions. And in the evening half-a-dozen of the deputation of the night before

[1] Charles Willoughby Waddington of the Indian Educational Service was Principal of Mayo College, Ajmer, from 1903 to 1916, and later guardian successively to the Maharaja and Maharaj Kumar of Jodhpur.

[2] Probably *Har* Bilas Sarda (1867–1955), scholar, social reformer and legislator from Ajmer. Sarda was an Arya Samajist, Municipal Commissioner for many years, and a member of the Central Legislative Assembly, best known for his successful introduction of the Child Marriage Restraint Act (1930).

came and talked with us for a couple of hours. These educated and progressive Arya Samajists are certainly remarkable men (pleaders, officials and business men), who in
Ajmere have shown great organising and managing ability.
They have a successful, printing and publishing establishment, where they were producing cheap editions of the Vedas
and of Dayanand's writings, as well as school books and
pamphlets. The compositors worked only 45 hours per
week. The adjacent orphanage provided for some two hundred and more boys and girls, who were being brought up
and educated. This was rather a crude sort of "institution",
the girls especially looking depressed and unduly docile. But
the upbringing of girls is a difficult problem in India. These
girls were apparently "married by advertisement" so to
speak, the bridegroom being required to deposit some 2000
rupees as security that the bride would not have to be provided for again by the Orphanage. Some of the boys, the
mentally dull ones, were being taught carpentering. Otherwise the education seemed commonplace. It was rather an
"amateur" orphange, dealing with the most hopeless class of
waifs and strays, foundlings abandoned by their parents, and
so on. But its officers seemed devoted, the management eco-
nomical, and the intention excellent. The Arya Samaj day
school had grown into a large affair, including altogether
some six or seven hundred boys, and reaching up to the entrance examination of Allahabad University. It was attended
by boys of all creeds and classes, three fourths of them not
being children of Arya Samajists. Here, too, the school
seemed to have a good spirit, though it did not strike us as
particularly advanced educationally. There was only a tiny
nucleus of a library. We gathered that the actual membership
of the Arya Samaj in Ajmere was small—a couple of hundred
or so—and that it was not increasing; though the Society
counted a large number of sympathisers who preferred to not
actually join as members. A voluble pleader (author of "Hindoo Superiority", a somewhat worthless because indiscri-
minate and uncritical compilation of extracts proving the

greatness of Hindoo civilization in the past), who was among our evening party, said that the first apostolic fervour had passed away, and that the society now suffered from dissensions and splits, between those who wanted to observe, verbally and precisely, the letter of Dayanand's writings, and those who claimed freedom to progress in their spirit—the latter being termed the "flesheaters", because one of their innovations was to eat meat if they chose.

We lunched and spent the afternoon at the Mayo College, the best of the four "Chiefs Colleges" of North India, now under a man of mark, the first educational personality we have met in India (Waddington). The really beautiful buildings for which Sir Swinton Jacob is responsible, were built partly by the Government of India, partly by the ruling Chiefs themselves, each State having its own house (Jaypore, Udaipur, Jodhpore, Kashmir, etc.)—some nine or ten in all—and sending free of charge as many pupils as it chooses, in return for an original donation. The boys from 7 to 25 in age, have their own horses and servants, and eat each by himself (even those in each State House not messing together). A few have English guardians who are in charge of them, living in houses of their own (including a son of the Gaikwar of Baroda, after being successively in half-a-dozen schools in England). Waddington himself had the young Rajah of Idar (grandson of Sir Pertab Singh now Regent of Jodhpore)[3] living in his house. The hundred or more boys were playing cricket and tennis in the beautiful and extensive grounds. No "chapel" was visible, but we were pointed a Hindoo Temple right away in an obscure corner, to which all the Hindoo boys were compulsorily taken every afternoon to enable them to "do Pujah" for a few minutes. There was a Brahman whose duty it was to instruct them, but we gathered from Waddington that the whole thing was perfunctory, and that

[3] H.H. Maharajadhiraj Lieutenant-General Sır Pratap Singhji Bahadur succeeded to the *gaddi* of Idar in 1902, but abdicated in 1911 to assume charge as Maharaja Regent at Jodhpur, consequent on the death of his nephew Maharaja Sardarsinghji of Jodhpur.

although the Chiefs insisted on the performance of the necessary rites, they were not keen on anything more. There was
one Muhammedan House (that of the State of Tonk) which
had its own Mulvi and Mosque. The schooling is not very
thorough or advanced, the boys finding some difficulty in intellectual work, and are not spurred onward by parental
pressure. The Assistant Masters seemed undistinguished
young men interested in cricket and sport.

But Waddington is fully conscious that it is not enough
and he has gradually, after 37 years' existence of the College,
managed to develop a "post diploma course", for boys who
have already passed the entrance examination. This he now
hopes to see split off into a separate "Chiefs University",
which some of the Chiefs wish to establish at Delhi, the new
capital!

He was pessimistic as to the education of the Chiefs—
could not say what was the best course to pursue—was definitely against English schools for them—thought, on the
whole, that Mayo College with the proposed new Chiefs
University was the best that could be done for them—with
perhaps a year's post-graduate study in England at an advanced age, or better still, a year's leisurely travel with a wise
"bearleader".

It is noteworthy that Waddington, though a man of exceptional force and personality, was not really interested in India
or Indian problems; and applied himself solely to his job of
directing a school for the sons of these proud Chiefs, without
apparently any ulterior thoughts. We did not gather that he
had a high opinion of the Chiefs, either for capacity, conduct
or ability to do business.

Ahmedabad 28 March to 1 April 1912

We had a delightful two days at Mount Abu seeing its fantastically beautiful Dilwara Temples, and journeying in two Indian Rickshaws (far inferior in comfort and commonsense to the Japanese) right into the mountains, with wonderful views of the great desert plain to the ruined Temples of Achalgarh. We were staying with an attractive, refined and sensible Political officer—Sir Elliot Colvin—the Agent of the Governor General for Rajputana, and controlling about thirty states. He confirmed our other information that the British Government was interfering less and less with the government of these States. He also thought that all natives of India, even those in Native States, should be eligible for appointments. He was a somewhat stiff conservative in general opinions, with the usual nervous dread of criticism of the British Government as a kind of sedition which must not be played with. Like Colonel Impey he was not much interested in the problem of British India apart from the Native States, and wholly unsympathetic to nationalist aspirations. All the same, his modesty and general good sense and personal charm made the atmosphere of his home quite sympathetic, even to two such obstreperous reformers as ourselves!

Here in Ahmedabad we are living in quite a different atmosphere. The Commissioner of the place (Barrow—a grand-nephew of Charles Dickens) telegraphed to Mount

Abu to ask us to stay with him and we drove out some three miles from the station and found ourselves in a roomy old Mohammedan Palace or Garden House, with a broad terrace on to the river, now meandering within its broad, dried up basin. The situation is picturesque, and the establishment most comfortable. But our host is a problem. He is a tall, thick boned, somewhat coarsely featured man—the remnants of a fine countenance which has quite obviously grown coarse with the experience of life. His wife is a confirmed invalid and lives in England with their three daughters. Our host seems to live a life of isolation—both from the "Natives" whom he despises, and from the few English people with whom he seems on very distant terms. We rather suspect some "skeleton" stored away in the roomy old palace or in a humble establishment near by. He is most hospitable and quite anxious to tell us everything, and refreshingly frank. For instance he implied, and even expressly admitted, that "Commissioners" were no longer wanted. He showed us all the papers with which he had to deal—all cases which did not seem to us, or even to him, to require his intervention between the Collector and the Government of Bombay. There are only three Commissioners for all Bombay Presidency, and he has himself six Collectors and two Political Agents more or less under his direction—the three Commissioners meet regularly during the year to discuss questions which arise in the Presidency and to send reports to Bombay. Our impression is that Commissioner Barrow is biding out his extreme limit of time, with the minimum of exertion rather than take his pension to live in retirement with his wife and daughters. He is hopelessly out of sympathy with anything Indian—looks on all natives, except a few British educated aristocrats as "niggers" who have to be kept in their proper place. He violently resented the suggestion that the day might come when an exceptionally accomplished Indian might be appointed as Lieutenant Governor, or even as Governor of one of the Presidencies and he thought it had been a mistake to let Indians rise to the rank of Commissioner or even Collector. In fact, Barrow, in his general attitude on Indian affairs, and, I suspect, in private life, represents the old Anglo-Indian officer of fifty years ago. As might be expected, he complained that the young men who are now coming out are of a lower social status and "no good" as a governing race.

We have mostly spent our mornings and evenings in driving about, seeing the very large number of beautiful mosques and tombs and Jain temples. But one afternoon was devoted to an "At Home" given by the Gujerat Branch of the National Indian Association[1] to meet us. Here we shook hands and said a few words with one or two hundred Indian men and women—mostly Hindoos, Jains and Parsees—the men being pleaders, professors, officials, millowners and retired pensioners; and the women mostly Parsees, or enlightened Hindoos who have no purdah (common in Bombay Presidency) or members of the Bombay analogue of the Brahmo Samaj.[2] All spoke English more or less and the party was just what it would have been in an English provincial town, except for more graceful manners, somewhat greater intellectuality, and more idealism; and on the other hand, somewhat greater shyness and diffidence among the women and somewhat less of "forcefulness" among the men.

One morning we spent in going over the great cotton mills of Sir Chinubhai Madholal,[3] established some sixty years

[1] This could be a reference to the Indian Association founded in 1876 with the object of organizing public opinion all over India, unifying the Indian people on the basis of common political aspirations, and promoting Hindu-Muslim friendship.

[2] The Prarthana Samaj, founded in 1867, inspired by a visit to Bombay of Keshub Chandra Sen. Like the Brahmo Samaj, it rejected idolatry and adopted the ideals of congregational worship and social reform.

[3] Sir Chinubhai Madhavlal was the grandson of Ranchhodlal Chhotalal, the pioneer of the cotton textile mill industry in Ahmedabad. The industries founded by Ranchhodlal (the Ahmedabad Spinning and Weaving Company, 1858) and his son (the Ahmedabad Ginning and Manufacturing Company, 1876) were

ago, and now employing 4000 hands, mostly men and boys. The owner is a Brahmin, a millionaire, very benevolent with his wealth, and he seemed to us a man of quiet power, calm wisdom and wise moderation of opinions. The machinery and organisation seemed excellent: there was one Lancashire "mill-manager" and two other English employed in some other capacities, the rest of the 4000 being Hindoo or Mohammedan. These operatives were working well and regularly, in marked contrast with those in John's mills at Agra. But they were largely the descendants of past operatives, and not newly gathered together as in John's mills. They seemed also much more self-respectful and independent. They worked 12 hours a day in summer (13–1) and 11 in winter (12–1), but the new Factory Act would prevent women working for more than 11. Boys began "when they passed the Doctor", said the Lancashire manager; or from 9 years old, said Sir Chinubhai. The latter agreed that the hours were too long, and suggested that they were too early in beginning, especially in the summer, as it was difficult to get any sleep before midnight, and the men came to the mill only half awake. Sir Chinubhai wanted a tariff against foreign imports, with Free Trade within the Empire. He was beginning to feel the competition of Japanese imports. There were 40 mills in Ahmedabad, all in Indian hands; none of them boarded or lodged their hands.

Another morning we spent with the Collector [Painter, a man of 40, strong, energetic and practically commonplace, without idealism, imagination or (as it seemed to us) much knowledge of India outside his daily work], visiting his "Cattle-Kitchens". The famine here is mainly a "fodder famine", and the cattle, the renowned Gujerat breed, would

---

later managed by Chinubhai Madhavlal. By the 1930s, however, this family was virtually wiped off the industrial map of the city. Sir Chinubhai, significantly, was Chairman of a Committee of Management appointed in 1910 by the Government to supersede, on grounds of incompetence, the elected Ahmedabad Municipality, restored only in 1915.

die by thousands but for help. The Government is distributing fodder, subsidizing the railway to bring it in at a quarter freight, and making cash advances. In addition this Collector has got up a charitable fund and a voluntary committee, which is feeding over 3000 cattle in five or six camps; the cattle being brought in and attended to by their owners but remaining with these permanently in the camp, which supplies only the site, organisation and food. It has proved very successful in calling out the people's own energies, and saving the cattle without involving the Government in the purchase and care of thousands of animals.

Ahmedabad, with a population of 185,000, with great wealth, and many rich people, is strangely free from English residents or English business. There seem to be only two or three Civil servants, two or three railway officials, two or three soldiers, and two or three banking people—not a dozen in all—together with half-a-dozen clergy or missionaries and not a single business man. There is only one "English" bank, and apparently no "English" shop whatever. It is a new experience to us in India to see all these wealthy villas and carriages and mills, entirely in Indian hands. It seems equally free from all "movements" for the redemption of India— both the Commissioner and the Collector explaining this absence of sedition to the fact that the people were too busy and successfully busy in getting rich. The Arya Somaj hardly exists, the Nationalist organisation is very weak and sends no delegate to the National Congress: the Brahmo Somaj alone has one or two small philanthropic institutions. There is no bad feeling between the Hindus and Mahomedans—in fact very little movement whatsoever. The municipality had to be squashed and a nominated body put in its stead—the Collector would have preferred one man—an official—and evidently thought any attempt on the part of the Ahmedabad people to interfere by act or thought with the work of a Government was a dire mistake.

Godhra, 1 to 3 April 1912

"Ghosal is not Indian[1]—he is British—in education and in manners—we should not regard him as a native" had said Commissioner Barrow of his Collector. That surprised us, as we knew he was the brother of the ultra-Indian-Nationalist—Mrs. Rambaj Dutt Chowdhri, nephew of the Indian poet Tagore, and belonged to an old Brahmin family distinguished for its learning and its patriotism. Moreover he had married the daughter of a Ruling Chief—the Maharajah of Cooch-Behar. However when we came here we realised the truth of the Commissioner's commendation. Ghosal has modelled himself exactly on what he *believes an English official ought to be.* He is silent and reserved, ultra-conservative in opinion, zealous and industrious in the executive business of his district, devoid of intellectual curiosity and sumptuously clothed according to fashionable English standards for each part of the day's work—indeed he overdoes the part in this respect—his dress is too immaculately correct and his manners too perfect—a reproduction of the most conventional

[1] Jyotsnanath Ghosal, the son of Rabindranath Tagore's sister Swarna Kumari joined the Indian Civil Service in 1895 as assistant collector in Bombay. In 1912, he was joint collector and Political Agent, and in 1913, was awarded the Kaiser-i-Hind medal. Later in his career, he became a member of the Legislative Council, and temporary member of the Governor's Council at Bombay.

Public School and University man. When one remembers the fervent and inconsequential talk and the slumacking[2] and dirty garments of our friend, the good-hearted Hindu Pleader—his brother-in-law—one realises why his sister never mentioned her connection to the Admirable Crichton. The Arya Somaj and all its works he evidently holds in detestation—though he is far too discreet to express his feeling in so many words: "India is going too fast" is the only remark he has let fall of a general nature. He expresses no general views and vouchsafes no general information. But he has done his best, in a well-bred, taciturn way to give all the information we have had the energy to ask for—and I should imagine that his facts were generally correct, though his judgment is devoid of any illuminating insight.

His wife is a pretty little lady, who appears as a picturesque Hindu girl in the early morning, as a beautifully attired Hindu Princess for dejeuner, and as a neatly garbed English tennis player in the late afternoon and a fashionable lady at dinner. There are no books in the house beyond third class novels—Marie Corelli figures largely—no newspapers beyond the *Times of India*, "The Pink-un" and a few illustrated London Prints; the furniture is ultra-European and the walls are covered with portraits of English officers, society ladies, Maharajahs, inscribed to "Darling Babs" or "from loving . . .". Curiously enough the husband talks English with a strong foreign accent and with difficulty, though he was seven years in England—the wife talks it as an Englishwoman. There is a French governess for the two children—boy and girl—and the boy goes this autumn to a preparatory school for Eton. As our Commissioner said, the Ghosals mean to be more British than the British. What his real feelings are it is impossible to say. But it is dull work talking to him, as one dare not assume that he is an Indian, and one knows he is not an Englishman—the result being that we

---

[2] Probably slummocking, a colloquialism, meaning to move or speak in an awkward and disorderly way; slovenly, untidy.

have felt less free to discuss Indian problems with him than with anyone else except perhaps the effete colonels and mayors who act as civil administrators in the Punjab. All this is ungrateful as the house is extraordinarily comfortable, and the Ghosals leave one alone, in the hot hours, and have the great advantage of two good motors. He has two English assistants—the one I talked to was rigidly Anglo-Indian. Altogether this glimpse of Bombay administration—of a Commissioner, three Collectors (two Indian) and two Assistant Collectors, does not reveal the sympathetic side of the British Raj.

The famine relief works that we had come to Godhra to inspect were both minor operations—one the making of a road on which some 1100 persons had been employed, and the other the deepening of a dried up tank, which was occupying between 400 and 500. But the "famine" was itself a minor affair, existing as regards human distress, only in this one district of the Panch Mahals (and in some parts of the State of Baroda). It is a local scarcity, due to an almost complete absence of rain in the last rainy season. The lack of fodder for cattle is a little more widely spread, as we saw at Ahmedabad; but the rest of India has had a good year. The relief works had the usual features of crowds of men and women engaged in the simplest manual labour, the men digging soft earth and the women carrying it in small baskets to where it had to be dumped. The operations had been planned in advance as relief work to be resorted to when necessary. The work was set out by the Public Works Department and supervised by (Indian) subordinate officials temporarily borrowed from different departments. There were hospital tents, casks of water under reed roofs, shelters for nursing mothers and their infants, latrines—all of the simplest and flimsiest kind. The Assistant Surgeon (a Goanese, who had studied at Dublin and Edinburgh) visited all the works frequently, on the watch for cholera. The special feature of these works was the absence of any arrangement for lodging the workers. These primitive tribes flatly refused to sleep away from their huts, and preferred to starve rather than do so—partly from blind conservatism, partly because they feared to lose their little possessions whilst absent, and partly, we were told, from the not unjustifiable fear of disease and death if they herded together in a famine relief camp. (It appears that, in the great Gujerat famine of ten years before, cholera played havoc in the camps). So the Government had had to start numerous small works, to and from which the starving men and women walked night and morning, four miles, six miles, and in some cases even ten miles each way. Those too old or too weak to work, or prevented by purdah were relieved by doles of food distributed in the villages themselves. But none who were adult and ablebodied were given such doles: these had to come and work at piece work rates for wages calculated so as to be just sufficient for bare subsistence at current prices—the men getting 1¾ annas per day and the women 1½ annas per day. Or, rather a whole gang of about 50 being given a task to do, which was calculated to yield such a wage if the task was completed, and the sum payable being reduced in proportion to every part of the task left undone at the end of the day. The grouping of the men and women in gangs was largely left to themselves, each village keeping to itself; and it was left to the gang to appoint its own ganger, a man of influence among them who got a fractionally larger share and directed instead of digging. But the Government object not being economy but relief, the regulations were evidently not very precisely adhered to; and the gang was paid each night enough for its members to live on for twenty-four hours, the elaborate calculations of task and rates being used as a means of getting the work done and of affording some check on the total expenditure. Indeed, the whole "Famine Code" that we studied, an elaborate printed volume the outcome of a whole generation of experiment, reads much more like a guide to relief, so that no one should be permitted to die of starvation, than like any precise checking of the "labour cost" of each work. We did not see in it anything applicable to English conditions; nor did we pick up from it any hint or suggestion for dealing with our own "unemployed". The Indian administrator has to deal with (1) workers homogeneous as to occupation, all cultivators of the soil; (2) under purely temporary stress, from which it is certain that they will presently regain their normal occupations; (3) without fear of the works being swamped by numbers of "underemployed" or loafers, attracted by the Government wage; and (4) without being subject to pressure to raise that bare subsistence wage to the "Trade Union rate". We learnt that the weaver or other artisan was not expected to come to these relief works; and that wherever necessary other relief was afforded to him—sometimes the Government bought his unsaleable product or ordered more, using it to clothe the naked; sometimes as with the bangle makers the Government advanced him subsistence whilst he went on working for stock. The part of the problem which most nearly resembles that of England was therefore outside the Famine Code! It is interesting here to remember that we were told that the Ahmedabad cotton mills had never, in all their half century of existence, had to go on "short time" or shut down altogether.

The men and women on these relief works looked well nourished. We saw no signs of semi-starvation and no dreadful living skeletons. Hardly any boys under 14 were at work, though they might have got their penny a day; and we were told that the families preferred to leave them at home to look after the cattle etc. This was a matter of policy—the Collector, with Government approval as he explained, thinking it better to relieve *before* the people had been brought low in health, in order that they might not succumb to disease. This policy had so far been justified by the death rate of the district being actually lower than usual, so the doctor told us, though he lived in dread of cholera. Those whose clothes had worn to rags had only to ask, when they were given new ones out of charitable funds at the Collector's disposal. We heard several complaints, all to the effect that the pay was not enough, because it left nothing over for the little luxuries to which they were accustomed.

Baroda, 3 to 5 April 1912

A few hours railway journey brought us to this capital of a Native State—to be met at the station by our Arya Samaj friend the School Inspector (Atma Ram) and by minor officials, on behalf of the Gaikwar and his ministers. After dinner S.W. saw the Dewan (G. L. Gupta) the lifelong friend and son-in-law, and the biographer of R. C. Dutt[1] whom (after retiring from the I.C.S. as High Court Judge) he accompanied into Baroda service. He proved to be an able, genial, hospitable but uncommunicative man of about 62. [His daughter and another young Indian girl, with her husband, a young Indian man (Mukerji, who had been an Oxford Fabian) and another (an Indian officer in the Gaikwar's army) were just then, at 9.30 p.m., starting out on a magnificent elephant on some pleasure jaunt—which showed how little "purdah" there is here!] Gupta said that the condition of the Indian cultivator had undoubtedly improved within his recollection; his standard of living had gone up considerably,

[1] Romesh Chunder Dutt (1848–1909), of the Indian Civil Service, who retired in 1897 and presided over the Indian National Congress two years later. He became Prime Minister of Baroda in 1909. Dutt is best-known for his *Economic History of India*, and his translations, in English verse, of the Ramayana and the Mahabharata. He was a member of the Royal Asiatic Society and a Fellow of the Royal Society of Literature.

wages had risen more than prices, and various social advantages had been added, in the way of hospitals, schools, etc.
He was quite clear that India would always wish to remain
part of the British Empire, for obvious self-interest, however
much self-government it obtained.

Masani, the Minister for Education, who had introduced
compulsion, took us the next morning to see the boys and
girls high school, the technical institute, and elementary
school for girls, the training college for women, the State
Free Library and two palaces.

The palaces were both furnished entirely in European
style. In the one now in use, we were shown into every
room, including the bedrooms of the Gaikwar, his Rani, the
young Princes, the young Princess, etc., even to the dressing
rooms in which their clothes were laid out, and their baths
were being prepared, for their momentarily expected arrival.
There were practically no books in the so-called "library",
and very few in the intimate living rooms; but it is noteworthy that we saw in the Princess's room a copy of Pierre Loti's
"L'Inde, sans les Anglais", of which the very title strikes the
Anglo-Indian as seditious, and which we have accordingly
found to be quite unknown to the officials and their wives.

The various educational institutions that we saw were
somewhat primitive—the principals were mostly absent for
one reason or another, the classes were thin, the apparatus
was poor; and it seems as if the schemes were ahead of the
capacity or integrity of the subordinate officials available.
But the elementary school for girls was a reality. These hundreds of girls from 6 or 7 up to 12, and a few older, had been
gathered in by the compulsory law alone. They were under
the direction of a competent woman, knowing no English,
who had been "trained" five and twenty years before, and
now had several women and several men teachers under her.
She was drawing 60 rupees per month (£48 a year), a good
salary as Indian teachers' salaries go. Baroda now has 94.3 per
cent of its boys at school between 7 and 12; and 66.3 per cent
of its girls between 7 and 11—comparing the actual number

of pupils with the children of school age revealed by the Census of 1911. Out of 3095 villages, more than 2138 have got schools, most of the others having fewer than 15 children of school age. About 94 per cent of the whole population have schools accessible to their children. All this is enormously ahead of the rest of India, and reflects great credit on the State, even if the average attendance is only something like 60 per cent of the school roll, and even if many of the schools and teachers leave much to be desired. The total gross expenditure (1911–2) for education is 16 lakhs of rupees or £107,000 a year, for a population of two millions; which would be equal to £13,000,000 a year for all British India; or about three times as much as the Government does spend. The Education Minister hopes to get his budget up to 20 lakhs, or £133,000 a year, which would be equivalent to 15 or 16 millions sterling for British India.

The following morning we journeyed out to the Summer Palace and to a neighbouring village to see the schools. Here we found the school divided into three buildings—the Headmaster, an intelligent and trained Hindoo, who was also the Postmaster, holding the higher classes in the Post Office; an assistant master taking the lower classes in an adjoining building; and a separate school for the "Untouchables" in the isolated group of cottages belonging to these outcasts, in the house of one of them, and taught by a member of this strange community (he has passed the Seventh Standard and gets 7 rupees a month). A very small proportion of the students were attending in the two first classes we came to, but by the time we got to the third a good attendance had been evidently whipped up. There were a good many children of school age in the streets and quite clearly Baroda is only at the beginning of the task of getting the children actually to attend school, even if it gets them on the school roll. The Minister explained the low attendance by the lowness of the castes (not a single Brahmin among the children)—they did not care for education and it was not wise to push compulsion too far. He told us that he had started medical inspection, but as the parents were too poor to make up deficiencies—(glasses for defective eyesight and extra food for anaemic children)—it was useless to go on with it. For the same reason he had stopped physical exercises, as the children were not strong enough to do them after their mental work. Altogether he was quite aware that primary education in Baroda had only just begun, and that universal education was still only on paper. Masani, who had begun service in Baroda as Professor of Biology at the College and then became Secretary to the Gaikwar, was a Parsee from Bombay—a strong, able, good-looking man—with what seems to be the typical Parsee attitude—detached but benevolent, feeling that Parsees are not *of India*, but are *in India* for their own advantage, and have therefore an obligation towards India—not in the least nervous or touchy about getting their rightful share of influence—assured that their superior enlightenment and education will give them as much influence as they deserve. His son is Science Professor at the College—an attractive and alert young man who is coming to England to get his D.Sc. and hopes to find superior employment in British India.

We went over the College and High School—housed in fine buildings. The High School had a Parsee as Headmaster—a man of the same strong virile type as the Parsee Minister of Education. The classes were full (over 700 boys present, and two or three Parsee girls) and the boys looked very intelligent, and the masters competent. The College has as Principal—Clark—an Englishman (Cambridge) who has been twelve years in the Baroda service. He was a strong, rather handsome man, with a hard, conceited and unpleasant expression and he excited our antipathy. He was clearly not on very cordial terms with the Minister of Education. We were left with no particular impression about the College (300–400 students mostly in arts) as Clark was uncommunicative in the presence of the Minister; and though polite to us, was not in the least anxious to see us again. We heard afterwards from the Headmistress of the Girls' School and also from Mr. Gokhale and other official sources that Clark was a notorious slacker and that he was merely hanging on for his pension, and that the Gaikwar had been "taken in" in his appointment for twenty years.

On our return to the Guest House we found a letter from the Maharajah asking us to breakfast at 11 a.m. The Gaikwar[2] impressed us very favourably and the Rani was extraordinarily attractive and charmingly clothed. The family is now under a cloud owing to the "Gaikwar incident" at the Delhi Durbar,[3] the assumed disloyalty of the Rani, and the scandalous rumours about the daughter. We should gather, from what we have heard from the different Indian officials of Baroda, that the Gaikwar had been fretting for some time under what he considers the unjustifiable interference of the British Resident with regard to the internal administration of his Dominion; the Rani is said to be bitter about the probable inheritance to the throne of the little grandson of the late Rani, which she believes will be insisted on by the British

[2] H.H. Maharaja Gaekwar Sir Sayaji Rao III (1863–1939), Indian representative at the Imperial Conference, 1937, and author of *From Caesar to Sultan* and *Famine Notes*. The Gaekwar was a man of literary tastes who read Plato (in Greek), Spencer and Bentham; and was so moved by *Alice in Wonderland* that he had the book translated into Marathi.

[3] A reference to an incident which assumed a curious importance at the time. It pertained to the appearance at the Delhi Durbar of the Gaekwar, who—unable to attend the rehearsal and unobservant of the deportment of his immediate predecessor, the Nizam of Hyderabad—omitted to wear the sash of the Star of India and made only one bow when presented to the king and queen. In an attempt to find the exit he then wheeled around, thereby presenting his back to monarch and consort. The following day Gokhale called on him to say that his behaviour had caused a sensation and that an apology was expected from him. The apology was duly tendered to the Viceroy and made public through the columns of *The Times*, which nevertheless used this opportunity to make severe comments on the conduct of the Gaekwar since 1905, alleging that Baroda harboured and sheltered many extremists. Matters were not helped by Keir Hardie's praise of the Gaekwar and press criticism continued for the next two years.

Government; whilst the whole family is sympathetic to the Nationalists' aspirations, and feel themselves born to be leaders of the Indian people. However that may be, the Gaikwar and his Consort struck us as real enthusiasts for social reform. The Gaikwar is not what one would call a gentleman—he is a clever and ambitious man—sympathetic, emotional and appreciative—liable to be led away by a stronger personality. He is said to suffer from chronic indecision. He talked quite frankly and was delighted that we admired the Arya Somaj, and asked Sidney whether he would be right to employ them as educationalists, and whether he should ask the Government of India's permission. "Employ them without asking" was Sidney's reply. The Rani is charming to look at, and very intelligent. But though she was also frank, her frankness was tinged with bitterness. I can quite believe that "India without the English" is her ideal. But at present the Gaikwar is on his good behaviour. He has made a mistake—a bad mistake. If he had paid elaborate respect to the British Raj, whilst trying, in his own kingdom to build up a self-governing race, the British Government could not have seriously interfered with him, or diminished his prestige in India. By bad manners he has risked the substance as well as damaged the form of his sovereignty. And the whole family seem to have suffered from an absence of self-restraint and domestic respectability (their personal conduct is in a state of unstable equilibrium, the clash of two hostile codes of manners). All the same, we like both the Gaikwar and the Rani—both seem to us genuine in their devotion to India, and he at least, was taking his disgrace in good part, and not relaxing the vigour of his efforts to raise the standards of his people. The sons of his present Rani, like her daughter, seem to be somewhat addicted to "irregular conduct". One just returned from Harvard, looked rather stupid and dissipated. We had seen a younger boy at Mayo College, who had been in succession at several English schools. The son of the first wife died at 24, it is said from dissipation—the little grandson is being watched over by the widow and a devoted nurse, and rumour is busy as to the precautions that have to be taken to safeguard him from the ill will of the charming lady. But these rumours would be rife in the Court of an Indian Ruler whether or not there was any reason for them. The Princess Indra about whom were the negotiations for marriage to the Maharaja of Gwalior, did not appear at breakfast.

The city of Baroda, though possessing no old buildings, has the charm and good order of the capital of a native state, as distinguished from the squalor and disorder of the native cities in British India. Ghosal, the Collector of Godhra, told us that even the villages in the Baroda State were distinguished by amenity, and that the police were superior—life and property being more secure. He attributed the latter generally to the better administration of Justice—all sorts of technicalities preventing the discovery and punishment of crime in British India. That is of course only the other side of the greater respect for personal liberty under the British Raj, and the greater difficulty of good government by alien Rulers.

Among the other institutions that we visited was a boarding school for the most promising students of the Antaryas (Untouchables), in order to train them as teachers for their own community, or as leaders to raise their fellows. The boarding school though a government institution was under the charge of our friend, the Arya Somaj inspector of schools (Atma Ram) whose salary is 110 rupees per month—£87 per annum). He and his wife and six children with a young Brahmin teacher (also Arya Somaj) were living with these 30 boys, and 12 girls. They were being brought up in the rites of the Arya Somaj cult, and looked models of attention and careful physical and mental training. This little group of enthusiasts were evidently inspired by deep religious humanitarian feeling and the experiment looked more promising than similar work by the Salvation Army, as the religion the children were being taught and the customs and habits they were learning were in no way a breach of their own race feeling and were in fact an intensification of it on the highest lines. If the Gaikwar, instead of being rude to the Viceroy and the King Emperor in order to assert his own sovereignty, had introduced Arya Somaj teachers in all his schools, and established Boy Scouts, he would have done a good deal more towards making possible the ideal of "India without the English", and yet not given the British Government the chance of administering a big snub to the most progresssive ruler in India.

With regard to the compulsory education experiment, it appears that there is as yet practically no attempt to secure *regularity* of attendance as distinguished from occasional attendance. Until a child has failed to put in an appearance for six consecutive days (at first it was ten), nothing is done. Consequently the "regular irregulars" are suffered to pull down the average attendance without check. (We suggested notice from the teacher after two absences, and a personal visit after four). After six consecutive days' absences, notice is sent by the teacher to the village Headman, and the machinery of prosecution and fine is set going (Usual fine 2d or 4d). There are no School Attendance Officers, but the Headman is supposed to make out annually a list of children liable to attend school. The occurrence of the Census was naturally used by the Minister to check these lists, with the result that many girls were found omitted. The Minister did not think there was much bribery or oppression, but he had summarily dismissed two or three minor officials, and could only hope that his Assistant Inspectors would keep things straight. The Gaikwar offered a 50 per cent increase in salary to Hindoo teachers who would go to "Untouchable" schools, but practically none accepted, so strong is the prejudice. They had to rely for such schools on a few Mohammedan teachers and on teachers sprung from the "Untouchables" themselves. It is certainly a wonderful achievement to have got going no fewer than 300 schools for these "Untouchables" and to have brought thousands of them on the school roll.

We learnt that since Lord Curzon's time there had been

much less interference by the British Government. But the Resident toured through the State, and therefore inevitably had complaints poured out to him, besides derogating, by his very presence, from the Gaikwar's position. Every detail about railway, telegraph, telephone and postal business had to be specially submitted to him. The British Government insists on the excise duty being levied on the mills in Baroda State; and prevents the export of salt from the Baroda ports. It appears that the Baroda born are precluded (as not being British subjects) from English Government employment: books published in Baroda do not thereby gain copyright in British India. Hence Baroda authors, whom the Gaikwar tries to encourage, have to get their books published in Bombay or Ahmedabad. This exclusion of the Native States from copyright seems wanton rudeness.

Before leaving our description of Baroda, we may add what we heard about the Gaikwar at Bombay Government House and from Mr. Gokhale whilst staying with him at Poona. Sir G. and Lady Clarke[4] were both of them contemptuously bitter and suspicious about the Gaikwar and the Rani. It appears that Sir George and his former wife, and his daughter (who died lately), were on intimate terms with the Baroda family and that Miss Clarke had stayed for a fortnight at a time actually with the Rani. Now nothing is too bad to be said about the Gaikwar and the Rani and the children. Lady Clarke told me the long tale as to the discovery of a centre of active and violent sedition (bombs etc.) in Baroda, which she asserted must have been known about by the Gaikwar (this was never alleged to be more than a printing press), and she represented the Gaikwar as being quite ready to take arms against the British, and the incident at Delhi being his way of testing the feeling of the other native rulers.

[4] George Sydenham Clarke (1848–1933), in 1913 created Sydenham of Combe, 1st Baron. Secretary to the Committee of Imperial Defence (1904–7) and Governor of Bombay (1907–13). Author of *Studies of an Imperialist* (1928) and *My Working Life* (1927).

Mr. Gokhale who is friendly to the Gaikwar attributed the incident to a combination of causes—a certain amount of ill-will, brought about by the vexatious interference of successive British Residents, to the unduly great consideration that the Barodas had received from foreign Courts which made them resent their treatment as subordinates by Viceroys and British officials, and lastly by genuine absentmindedness or nervousness on the morning of the Delhi function, due to the fact that the Gaikwar had *that morning* received notice of the pending divorce proceedings brought against him by an English solicitor (Statham) with whose wife he had been on too friendly terms. (This case was dismissed the Gaikwar's plea of being a sovereign ruler and therefore exempt from the jurisdiction of Courts of Law being upheld). Gokhale gave us a dramatic account of the episode which he had seen. The "disloyal" rudeness to the King Emperor had been complicated by the Gaikwar's refusal to stand up at the entry of the Viceroy, on a previous occasion—the British Resident, Cobb, having practically forced him to rise for a moment, and having reported his behaviour to the Viceroy. It appears that the day after the Durbar, Gokhale, who was in the Viceroy's camp, heard that the Government of India was actually considering his deposition. Anxious to save the Gaikwar, Gokhale hurried to his camp early the next morning and had him roused from his slumbers. Seddon, his Prime Minister (an I.C.S. who was immediately afterwards withdrawn by the Government of India), had also hurried to the Gaikwar Camp, and Gokhale, he and the Gaikwar had a consultation as to what should be done. The Gaikwar was wholly unaware of the gravity of his offence, but he was induced to sign the letter of apology which Gokhale and Seddon drafted there and then. The Viceroy sent a stiff answer refusing to accept the apology, as a sufficient explanation of the two incidents, and asking whether he could publish the Gaikwar's letter. The Gaikwar answered, with equal stiffness, that he could do as he pleased, and the letter was published. Since then the relations have been very strained, and the Gaikwar has been forced by Cobb to dismiss two officials, who had connections with extreme Nationalists, and to issue a proclamation against sedition. He is, in fact, still in a precarious position. I doubt whether the Government of India would be so foolish as to make a martyr of him but one can understand his state of nervousness and the Rani's state of anger.

Arriving at Bombay in the early morning of the 8th we were met by one of the A.D.C.s and escorted in a motor to Government House. It is a most attractive residence, consisting of various bungalows in beautiful wooded grounds, overhanging the sea, with one central suite of reception rooms. Our bungalow (No. 1 India) was actually perched on the rocks, and from our verandah we could watch the waves of the Indian Ocean dashing against the very wall of our abode. Very delightful were the moonlight nights—I sleeping on a sofa on the verandah, and alternating the hours of sound sleep, with intervals of watching the fishing smacks, sailing close under me—so close that I could distinguish the voices of the fishermen—perhaps discussing the white ghost appearing just above them! The charm and luxurious quiet of this official sanctuary was enhanced by the cool breeze of the Homeward Sea—refreshing after the parched heat of Baroda and Ahmedabad, and reminding us that we should soon be sailing away to our home and our work. But the etiquette at Government House was stiff and the company not congenial—less so than we expected. Sir G. Clarke, whom Sidney knew twenty years ago, and who had the reputation of a liberal minded and progressive administrator, has grown old and bitterly reactionary, both as regards Home politics and, what is more important, as regards Indian affairs. Poor man, he looked unhappy; his eyes had that lifeless, sullen, and suspicious expression which betokens disillusionment. Since he came to India, as Governor of Bombay, he has lost his wife and only child, and though he has married another lady, to whom he seems very much attached, she has not evidently filled up the blank. The former Lady Clarke and the daughter had been both enthusiastic devotees of the task of "bridging the gulf", and were much beloved by the Indians. The present lady is of the worldly-widow-mould, no doubt sensible and devoted to her present lord, but stupid and snobbish (more than once she talked of *birth* as a requisite for the art of government) and disliking "lower races" and "lower classes", and resenting their desire for self-government. She complained with asperity of a Governor being "shackled" by Legislative Councils and talked of India as a veritable volcano of sedition. As for Clarke himself, he was somewhat taciturn; when he did talk he uttered the usual commonplaces. "Hindus were mere talkers"; and when I referred to the capacity for organisation and self-devotion shown by the Arya Somaj he dismissed this activity as "political" as if that necessarily damned it morally. There were one or two stupid but harmless A.D.C.s and one or two able and alert secretaries and politicals—one Enthoven (formerly Secretary to the Government of Bombay, now Secretary to the Commercial Department of the Government of India under W. H. Clark), of whom Clarke spoke highly, but who was a bad type of pedant and bureaucrat—and showed a good deal of nasty temper about Gokhale, or any other Indian who claimed a share in the Government. He denied that the Indians of the present day had any capacity whatsoever—except the capacity of making themselves troublesome to the British Raj. When I suggested that whatever were the rights of the case, there would be, in fifty years time, more Indians in the Government of India, he flatly denied it. They had reached "saturation point" and any further admission of Indians would be inconsistent with British Rule and would be reversed even if it were introduced. He even resented my using the word "Indians" instead of "Natives"—there was no *race* of Indians! Claud Hill, now member of Executive Council, Bombay, was equally reactionary but more discreet and outwardly sympathetic to, and respectful of, Indians. Altogether we came away, grateful for the hospitable kindness of the Clarkes—all the more so because they could not have liked either our reputation or ourselves—but not impressed with the prospects of a Rule represented by Clarke and his entourage.

Staying at Government House was a very Anglicised native Ruler, the Jam of Nawanagar, formerly the noted British cricketer "Ranjit Singhji";[5] and as the Governor told me much bored by his relegation to the Rule of an Indian State, after victories on an English cricket field. He is now somewhat in disgrace, having overspent himself scandalously. He has now been cut down to an allowance of £10,000 a year and told to live in Europe whilst the British Government administers his State. It was interesting to note that *both evenings* he sat on the left of His Excellency—Claud Hill taking precedence of him, apparently as a member of the Executive Council of Bombay. Indeed this well-bred, quiet but uninteresting Indian gentleman, in spite of his position as a ruling sovereign and his title of His Highness, was decidedly kept "in his place" and made to feel his unimportance, the Governor barely speaking to him.

Our impression of the Clarkes was confirmed by the wife of the Editor of the *Times of India* (Stanley Reed). She said that they were even more unpopular with the Europeans than with the "Natives", and that their staff was equally so. It appears that the stiffness of the etiquette at Government House and Lady Clarke's assumption of regal airs is ridiculed—specially as the lady is known to have "lived in a cottage" prior to her third marriage—and that Clarke, whatever may be his abilities, does not belong to the aristocracy. So says the tittle tattle of British society! Moreover Clarke has "stood up" to the Europeans both as regards the granting of fresh sites for their sports, and in his Bill for the suppression of bookmakers on the race course.

Sir G. Clarke agreed that the Government of India was

[5] H.H. Maharaja Kumar Singh Ranjitsinghji, Jam Saheb of Nawanagar (1872–1933), a well-known cricketer and an especially talented batsman. He represented India twice in the League of Nations and in 1932–3 was Chancellor of the Chamber of Princes.

faint-hearted, especially about borrowing capital, dreading the incubus of heavy fixed interest charges in lean years. This greatly retarded desirable Government enterprise, even if estimated to be productive. He agreed that the forests could be further developed, as well as irrigation and railways. He had himself recommended that the companies and shareholders should be got rid of, and especially the obstructive and costly board of directors in London. But on the whole he said very little, always diverging off into irrelevancies, which frequently included depreciations and aspersions of the Nationalists.

We may put here what we learnt at Government House and elsewhere as to the King's visit. No one will ever realise the nervousness of the Government about his safety, or the extent of the precautions taken. Sir Edward Henry, late of the Indian Service, and now Commander of the Metropolitan Police, came and took special charge. The precautions began months before. For instance, special reports were laid before him relating to all the various organisations in India including the Arya Somaj and Mr. Gokhale's "Servants of India",[6] so that he might decide what steps should be taken with regard to each of them when the King arrived; many hundreds of people were quietly arrested and kept in custody until he had gone—not that they were accused, or even suspected of any designs, but merely as being people who might make a disturbance. Lady Clarke said that 400 were thus arrested in Bombay alone. Every "native" house on the line

---

[6] The Servants of India Society, founded in 1905 by Gopal Krishna Gokhale, aimed at training 'national missionaries' to work for the unification and self-government of India. Recruits to the Society were chosen for their intellectual qualities and their capacity for devotion to duty. They were required to live on a modest allowance for a five-year probationary period, while working for the social uplift and education of women and backward classes; the organization of political education and agitation; the promotion of good will among communities; and the scientific, technological and industrial progress of India.

of route had a policeman posted inside it (this was probably none the less annoying because these men were English clerks sworn in as special constables, who thus got a good view for nothing—so one of the English told us); and the householder was informed that he would be "held responsible" for the good behaviour of all its inmates. At Delhi, in the big procession on the first day the Queen had all the usual insignia of royalty, but the King rode in the midst of a group of officers so that no one should be able to pick him out. Something similar was done at Delhi (as at Bombay) with regard to policemen being stationed in every "native" house. We were told in the U.P. that the Government telegraphed that A. and B., well-known Nationalists, had left Calcutta for Delhi. The officer in charge telegraphed back asking what was meant, should he arrest them? In reply he was told that this was for him to decide, and he thereupon arrested them and detained them in custody, remarking to us that "he was not taking any risks". After the first few days, when the immense popular approval was perceived, the precautions were relaxed, until, at Calcutta, the King drove freely among the crowds. What had been feared was not so much an attack on the life of the King, which it was believed that Indian superstitious reverence for a King would prevent; but some attack on an officer in the king's presence, as a protest and a demonstration unwarranted, and it merely serves to prove how little the officials know of the Indian mind.

Poona, 8/10 April 1912

We went straight from the luxurious and materialistic and intensely "official" atmosphere of Government House, with its ungenerous belittling of the whole Indian people, mingled with innuendoes and aspersions even of the most distinguished of them, for a brief visit to Mr. Gokhale, at the home of the "Servants of India". We, of course, make no concealment of our destination; but "Government House" is far too self-satisfied and is also far too obtuse, to have any sense of the extent to which the contrast jarred upon us, and how it made us ashamed of our official representatives in India. For Poona is not only remarkable as an educational and intellectual centre, having evidently far above the average of Hindoo intellectualism: largely under the influence of Gokhale it has become the centre of two remarkable Hindoo organisations, both of them extraordinary in their spirit of devotion, and in their practical achievements.

The first of these is the Fergusson College (named after Sir J. Fergusson, who was Governor). This, in spite of its misleading name, is not a Government institution. It was started some thirty years ago by a little band of highly educated Hindoos, high caste Brahmins, who felt that what was specially needed was Higher Education, under Hindoo control. They had no money and no position, but they set to work, themselves becoming the teachers, and living from hand to mouth on such fees and subscriptions as they could get. They formed themselves into a sort of brotherhood (having twenty members), which took vows to serve the College for twenty years, without remuneration beyond the subsistence allowance that they permitted themselves to draw from the funds—at first 30 rupees a month, then raised to 50, and now to 75 (£5), as funds came in. This is not to be increased. For this £60 a year each, these twenty Professors who are all married, their families living in modest little huts close to the College, run what is now one of the greatest Colleges in India, having over 700 undergraduate students, besides still more extensive school departments. They form a republic of equals, their weekly meeting assigning work to each of its members, and practically governing the College. For official purposes one of them is styled Principal; there is a Board of Management consisting of twenty of the subscribers and the twenty Professors; and there is even an Executive Committee of three subscribers and three Professors. But the whole thing is in the hands of the Brotherhood, for without their virtually gratuitous service it would come to an end. They recruit their number by admitting a promising graduate of distinction on probation. Apparently there is no difficulty in attracting clever young men, whose devotion makes them willing to bind themselves for twenty years. The vow, we are told, is never broken. But the Brotherhood itself has released a few, and has offered to release others (who declined to be released). Thus, the present Principal is an attractive young man of thirty or so, who went to Cambridge with a Government scholarship and became Senior Wrangler. He could have had very high official appointments, and the Brotherhood spontaneously offered to release him. But he elected to remain with them at £60 a year. Gokhale was among the founders, and was one of the leaders. As great public opportunities opened out to him, the Brotherhood offered to release him. But he resolutely served out his twenty years like the rest, and only on its expiration did he give himself to his own political career and his own great project. And he does this on the modest superannuation allowance of

30 rupees a month (£24 a year), which the Brotherhood accords to those who complete their term of service. We met the Principal and all the other members of the Brotherhood, and were much impressed with their personalities, their great culture, their gentle and attractive natures, their obvious intellectual ability. So much disinterested zeal, and such a life of combined devotion and practical work reminds us, of course of the best of the Catholic Orders. Yet these men have done it for thirty years under the inspiration only of "Nationalism". They are, of course, Hindoos by religion, and we should infer, not particularly pious or orthodox Hindoos. They have found a religion in their cause. The curious thing is that no official, no Englishman, ever tells you of this organisation, which is perhaps unique in the world. Sir George Clarke told us to see a Government Normal School at Poona, and to call on the Commissioner and the Collector. But he did not mention Fergusson College, and did not seem to be aware of its remarkable and peculiar organisation. The Anglo-Indian apparently cannot take in the self-sacrifice and devotion of these people, even when it assumes so practical a form as a great and flourshing University College. Accordingly, as a part of parsimony and "Early Victorian" Administrative Nihilism, the Government policy has been to do directly as little for Secondary and University education as it could, but to encourage private enterprise. This has led, on the one hand, to the Missionary Schools and Colleges that we have repeatedly described, which seem to us to be, to the great bulk of Indian students, virtually secular institutions, and, on the other hand, to the upgrowth of great and influential colleges (like Mr. Surendra Nath Banerjee's at Calcutta, the D.A.V. College at Lahore, and the Fergusson College at Poona), *in the hands of the Indian Nationalists*. Thus, by the very policy of Government itself, a large proportion of the educated men are, year after year, actually moulded by the Nationalist party. This is going on all over India. This is what Lord Curzon really wished to curb and prevent, by some of his educational reforms. But, after thirty years, these

colleges are in too strong a position to be uprooted, especially as the Government can't afford to run many colleges of its own, and often runs these very badly, with merely hireling second-rate Englishmen as teachers. And hence the futility of the feeble little attempts to check the constant spread of the desire for self-government that we see in the substitution of "Cowper's Letters" for Burke's political essays (Calcutta); in the attempted suppression of English history from the B.A. curriculum (Bombay) in the prescription of nambypamby books of pure literature in the English course (Punjab) instead of anything intellectually stimulating, and in the refusal to develop a school of investigation and research in economics which Mr. Ratan Tata[1] actually offered to endow at Bangalore. The Government having first wished the Indians to get educated (Macaulay); then refused to do the work itself as being beyond the duties of Government (Administrative Nihilism); is now afraid of any intellectual development among the Indians, because it finds that intellectual development always leads to a desire for self-government!

To come back to Fergusson College. Their only serious trouble was over Tilak.[2] He was one of them and gradually developed what may be called "extremist" insurgent views.

[1] Ratan Tata (1871–1918) was the younger son of Jamshedji M. Tata and a partner in Tata Sons and Co. Ltd, Bombay. He was also Chairman of the Indian Hotels Company Ltd; the Tata Iron and Steel Works; and the Tata Hydro-Electric Power Supply Company.

[2] Bal Gangadhar Tilak (1856–1920), a prominent nationalist leader of the extremist school, helped to found the Fergusson College at Poona and the newspapers *Mahratta* and *Kesari*. Through the columns of the latter he spread the message of *swadeshi* and *swarajya* throughout the country, voicing the demand—unusual for his time—of self-government. In 1916 he founded the Home Rule League. In view of the fact that he was friendly with George Lansbury, J. Ramsay MacDonald and other representatives of the British Labour movement, it seems reasonable to suppose that he would have met the Webbs had he not, at the time of their visit, been serving a six-year sentence at Mandalay jail in Burma.

He, not content with the silent influence of an institution under such a Brotherhood, wanted to make the College a centre of revolutionary propaganda. Gokhale fought this, in the interests of the College itself, on the "larger expediency" line; and after some years of struggle Tilak and a few followers seceded.

Naturally such a college, after such an episode, has been under Government suspicion, but apparently Government can find nothing to take hold of; and the educational work is so patently good, and the results are so marked, that the Government makes a considerable grant.

The other organisation centred at Poona is that of the Servants of India. This was founded by Gokhale when he left Fergusson College on completion of service; and is an attempt deliberately to train men for "public service", either as teachers, as writers, as members of public bodies, as philanthropists, etc. These men are very carefully selected by Gokhale himself; they come on long probation; they are put through prolonged training under Gokhale; they are sent about India to see other parts; and the intention is gradually to form a body of trained and devoted men for any kind of public work. They get only a bare subsistence; and they vow to serve as required for a long term (20 years). The organisation has been going now for some seven years, and the membership, of one grade or another, has reached nearly 50. It is a proof of Gokhale's great wisdom and practical skill that he had managed to steer this body through the troublous years that have lately passed (1907–10) without giving the Government or the police the slightest excuse for a prosecution. There is a branch at Madras, and others are in course of formation. But all the recruits must come to Poona for their first three years, 24 months of which they spend under the direct personal tuition and influence of Gokhale himself.

We naturally saw a great deal of Gokhale himself, both at Poona, and afterwards at Bombay, where he took no end of trouble to enable us to see people. The more we know about him and his work, the more highly we appreciate him. About fifty years of age, a Chitpavan Brahmin, apparently vaguely mystical in religion, he is a man of singular sweetness of disposition, full of charm. He is remarkably well-read in English history, economics and philosophy, and even to some extent keeps up with English novels. But what strikes us most is his political sagacity and calm statesmanship. He is by repute an impressive speaker, persuasive and convincing; and he seems to have a great deal of political skill. He is evidently making a party of great and growing influence in the Imperial Council; and though he is always outvoted by the official members, he is apparently building up a force of public opinion outside, amongst all sections of educated Indians (Mussulmans and Parsees as well as Hindoos) which the Government has to defer to. He demurs to our suggestions for developing the forests, railways, canals and Government workshops, on the ground that without extensive further popular control, any such increase in Government action would only be used against the Hindoos. He is not even very keen on getting more of the higher posts filled by Indians because he says that, without increased popular control and a change of spirit, such Indian officials are (1) never put in positions of real power or authority; (2) apt themselves to become Anglicised, or at any rate so timid as to be even less favourable to Indian aspirations than the English; and (3) almost bound, by the nature of the case, to be more rigorous in dealing with Indians accused of disaffection than the English. Moreover, even if all the officials were Indians, the present system, without popular control, would still be evil. Hence, whilst not opposing Simultaneous Examinations, etc., Gokhale aims persistently at popular control. He puts his trust in popular education, steady pressure to increase the power of the Legislative Councils, creation of local bodies, etc. But he feels that a great deal must come from England. The Government of India won't move unless forced by England, or by a Governor General fresh from England.

In the course of conversation he gave us an interesting account of the different schools of extremists. Tilak, of whom Gokhale spoke with much admiration, in spite of his bitter fights with him, desired to make English rule so disagreeable to the Rulers as to force them to make concessions, and even perhaps to quit the country. Like the South Wales Syndicalists he proposed to pursue the "irritating strike"[3]— never to take part in anything that the British desired should be done, and always to do what they disliked. From Gokhale's account, Tilak was a shrewd politician in choosing his devices of irritation—he was, in fact, a sort of Parnell of Indian Nationalism. Then there was the Punjab school of extreme politicians—centring round Lajpat Rai. Lajpat Rai wanted eventually to drive the British out of India. But he recognised that this was wholly impracticable whilst the Hindus remained undisciplined, under-educated and divided. Hence he advised his followers to throw themselves into social and educational work for the present, always keeping before their eyes the ideal of an independent India. In ultimate purpose he was perhaps more extreme than Tilak, but in methods he was more moral and practical—he would have denounced illegality until war could be openly declared, and the Indians could fight to the finish. He did not believe in wringing reforms out of the British Government. Finally there were the Bengalee extremists. These men were religious mystics—political assassination was a righteous revenge on behalf of an outraged religion—the British were mere marauders whom the Hindoo had to resist to the death—and this immediately. These were, in fact, a distant echo of the worship of Kali, and the sacrifice of the "White

[3] It was in South Wales that syndicalism was particularly powerful in its appeal to British workers—a fact that was amply demonstrated in the miners' strike of 1912 when the militancy of the workers in this region became especially widely known. The Webbs saw in syndicalism a revival of the Marxist and Anarchist ideas most repugnant to them—namely the theory of the class-war and a preference for strikes and sabotage over reformist and collectivist methods.

Goat" to the great goddess angered by the desecration of her country by impious foreigners.

Gokhale himself believed in the self-education and self-discipline of the Indian people; and in persistent pressure on English public opinion to grant self-government by instalments. He realises that these two complementary tasks are tasks of supreme difficulty, which can only be accomplished by lifelong devotion on the part of large numbers of Indian patriots. He looks to English public opinion as the ultimate arbiter of the fate of India, and he is perpetually revolving in his mind [the problem of] how to awaken the conscience of England, and how to bring it to bear on Anglo-Indian officialdom. Perhaps he is more optimistic about English opinion, and more pessimistic about Anglo-Indian opinion, than is quite justified. I asked him why cultivated Indians see so little of intellectual Anglo-Indian Society, and he answered somewhat dryly—where is it? And certainly we have found far more capacity for sympathetic intellectual intercourse with cultivated Indians than with any of the English in India whom we have met; even the best of them, like Hope Simpson and Hobart, sympathetic and sensible men, are hardly the intellectual equals of Gokhale and the Fergusson College Professors, or of the staff of the Gurukula. As for the ruck of the British Civil Service—leave alone the ordinary army officers and the inferior administrative servants and the "commercials"—they are too far below the highly educated Hindu, to find anything in common with him. That is one of the great difficulties in our Government of India—a stupid people find themselves governing an intellectual aristocracy—the explanation being, as Gokhale more than once remarked, that the *Average man of the British race*, is far superior to the *Average man* of the Indian peoples. Until the average has been raised the aristocracy of India will be subject to the mediocrity of Great Britain—with the melancholy result of aloofness and disaffection on the part of the honourable Indians, and clever servile duplicity on the part of the dishonourable Indians. Hence the mutual misunderstanding of Government House and the "Servants of India".

Whilst at Poona we met one breezy and sympathetic Englishman—Dr. Mann, Principal of the Government Agricultural College. Mann is a Yorkshire radical and non-conformist—with a strong Yorkshire accent—a refined optimist, whose pleasant manner and obvious ability and enthusiasm for his work, has enabled him to become almost one of the Poona Nationalists, whilst keeping on the right side of the Government of India. He had been eight years in India and confirmed substantially all our views of the relations between the English and the cultivated Indians. Quite clearly, he preferred the society of the "Servants of India" to that of the Poona Cantonment; and as he is not what the Poona Cantonment would call "a gentleman" he found no difficulty in avoiding the English. His flourishing agricultural college was a remarkable contrast to the more pretentious establishment at Lyallpur—there were many students and little plant, instead of much plant and few students. After Waddington, he was the most inspiring personality in the Anglo-Indian educational service; and the contrast between the wellbred Waddington with his distinguished manners, public school and university training and sportsman's tastes, and the small and dowdy Mann with his warm feeling and quick intellect, was coincident with the contrast between their respective tasks—the training of the Chief's sons—destined to a life of leisure—and the education of the expert and the working landholder, who will succeed in life according to his industry and his brains. Mann had introduced the experiment of a Vernacular class, where cultivators' sons knowing no English, could be taught how to be good agriculturalists. The boys we saw (aged 12–16) were sons of considerable landholders, owning several hundred acres, but cultivating it themselves, with some hired labour. He had, by the way, incurred Government censure for too prominently taking part in an aggressive temperance movement, which tried to "picket" liquor shops. We are inclined to suggest that the

Government of India should bring out first-rate middle class men—the best type of elementary or science teachers—rather than the leavings of the university world—unless they can afford to pay the salaries which would attract men of Waddington's standards. The hireling upper-middle class person who accepts a position in India, because he can't get one in England—and who is a hanger-on of the English club—is a rotten element in Indian education. It seems that the very best policy would be to train clever well-bred Indians for the educational service; but that the Government will not do for fear of sedition.

There was staying with Gokhale an Indian I.C.S. (Bilgrani?) who was a District Judge in Bombay Presidency. He had been a Wrangler at Cambridge (St. John's College). He was a determined Nationalist, more bitter in his complaints of the Government than any we have met. He described to us case after case of unfair treatment of the Indian members of the I.C.S., how they were always presumed to be inefficient (unless they actually forced their capacity to notice) and how accordingly any little mistake or fault was taken as proving it—how they were always sent to the most unhealthy districts, irrespective of the fact that men from other parts of India suffered as much from the Bombay climate as the English: he himself was from the Punjab, and he suffered acutely from the low-lying coastal districts, in which he nevertheless was invariably stationed, whilst the English had a monopoly of the healthier districts—how an Indian Collector was never trusted by the Government, was always specially supervised by the Commissioner, and always had an Englishman placed with him as Assistant Magistrate and as Assistant Superintendent of Police, who were relied on to keep him in order. As he said, such charges of partiality could not be proved; he could only assert that they were felt, and that there were far too many instances to permit of any other interpretation.

Without necessarily accepting as true all that he alleged, it is clear that there is much feeling that the Indian members of the I.C.S. are unfairly treated. Some have resigned (his own brother resigned from the post of Assistant Traffic Manager on the railways because he was given no responsible work, and was put under a Eurasian of inferior official status); others remain on in bitterness; and the total number does not increase. Add to this that some (like Ghosal) set themselves to become more English than the English, and one can understand Gokhale's disbelief in anything like Simultaneous Examinations as a cure.

Gokhale, by the way, in his solicitude for our comfort, had put it in the hands of Bilgrani, as knowing English ways, to see that we got food etc. in every detail up to the English standards of luxury.

We saw at Poona, two other institutions, one an immense and surprisingly good girls school, run by the Deccan Educational Society (a Hindoo Voluntary trust), and officered (with one exception) by Indian teachers, mostly women but some men. The headmistress was an Indian unmarried lady of great personality (aged 40?), highly cultivated, speaking English perfectly, a native Christian by the way, governing her huge school and extensive mixed staff with perfect success, and withal, very attractive and charming. This seems to be the best Hindoo girls' school in India; and here again these people, "who are all talk", have shown very great executive capacity. The institution comprised (a) a Training College, (b) a primary school for practising purposes, and (c) a High School—altogether I think some 800 pupils.

The other institution was a philanthropic working and training home for Indian widows, of sufficiently high caste to be forbidden to marry again. This was run by an ex-member of the Fergusson College Brotherhood, who was devoting the rest of his life to it. Here several scores of women of all ages were being taught to read and write, and also to some extent trained to become teachers (all by men teachers which seems wrong); and also taught to do weaving and various kinds of needlework. An extension was being built, designed to take in unmarried daughters, whose parents wished to keep them unmarried until maturity, but who found it difficult to withstand the pressure if the growing girls remained at home. It was said that they would trust them to the Widows Home in preference to the Girls High School, because the former had a greater reputation for conservative orthodoxy.

We also saw a great Oriental scholar (Indian) whom European universities had delighted to honour with degrees, but no English university. He was getting old, but was still active in his retirement, translating inscriptions, etc. He confirmed our impression that the Arya Samaj citations from the Vedas were not to be trusted. (He himself was Prarthana Samaj, the Bombay analogue of Brahmo Samaj).

Gokhale, the Fergusson College Professor and the Servants of India all took the modern historical criticism attitude towards the Vedas and doubted whether the Arya Somaj with the fanatical adhesion to the inspiration of the Vedas would spread among educated Indians outside the Punjab. But they were warmly admiring of the spirit and work of the organisation. In fact, there is none of the detraction of "other people's effort" among the Indian Reformers—which is unfortunately common in England. Even towards the English official they preserve a kindly attitude, and blame the inevitable tendency of alien rule, rather than the individual. Moreover, most of them recognise that a certain measure of alien rule is necessary at present.

Taj Hotel, Bombay, 10 to 15 April 1912

On the eve of our departure For the last five days we have been seeing the Indians to whom we have been introduced by Gokhale—chiefly the leading Parsees—Petits,[1] Tatas,[2] etc., with whom Gokhale seems on intimate terms. These millionaire financiers, merchants, and manufacturers, are attractive, cultivated persons—enlightened and discreetly patriotic—the women attractive, good-looking, charmingly dressed and highly educated, and the men able and refined. They live in sumptuous palaces and bungalows with a plenitude of motors, and make frequent journeys to Europe. The

[1] The Petits were an old Bombay family of merchants and mill-owners, with interests in cotton, coal and insurance. The pioneer was Sir Dinshaw Petit (1823–1901), also a well-known philanthropist. His descendants not merely contributed to the expansion of the business interests they inherited but were also active in public life.

[2] Pioneers of industrial development in India. The founder of the House of Tata, today one of the largest and most diversified industrial empires in the country, was Jamsetji Nusserwanji Tata (1839–1904), who started his career with the successful modernization of the cotton textile industry through his Empress Mills and Swadeshi Mills. In 1907 he established the Tata Iron and Steel Company, a pathbreaking effort that resulted in the first manufacture of iron and steel in 1911–12. Equally pioneering was the Tata Hydroelectric Power Supply Company (1910) which generated and sold energy to industries in Bombay.

Tatas have houses and flats in London and Paris and are completely cosmopolitan. At these houses we met one or two Europeans—the Editor of *The Times of India* (Stanley Reed) and his wife, and one or two of the leading European commercial magnates—but no officials or Government House young men—partly no doubt because Government House is moving to the Hills. A few wealthy and enlightened Mahommedans, with their women out of Purdah, and a few more millionaire Hindus—complete the circle. The atmosphere is distinctly Nationalist, though enthusiastically loyal to the King-Emperor, and the Imperial connection. There is a distinct resentment at the exclusiveness of the European society—the notorious exclusion of all Indians from the Yacht Club and the refusal of the Collector and other officials to return the calls of Indian magnates. Otherwise the relations seem far more friendly than in Calcutta and other great centres of population. Baronets abound, especially amongst the Parsees. Compared to other Plutocracies, these Indians are aristocratic, in appearance, manners and cultivation; and far superior in personal distinction, to Government House or the English Indian official world—not to mention the Anglo-Indian commercial man—who is a very distinct commoner in body and mind.

One or two of the Parsees engaged in shipping and foreign trade spoke enthusiastically of the uprightness and honourable dealing of the larger Japanese firms. Their explanation of the contrary representation was that the Japanese had been so cheated by the Europeans, that they retaliated in dealing with Europeans and practised a lower standard of honesty deliberately as they thought such was the European custom!

We attended a meeting of the Municipal Council—partly because it was expected that there would be a heated debate on the chairmanship for the ensuing year. J. Baptista[3] (a

---

[3] Joseph Baptista (1864–1930) worked for the formation of the Indian Home Rule League and was its first President. He was active in the Bombay Municipal Corporation and was Mayor of that city

member of the Fabian Society, an able and ultra progressive Indian Christian barrister who had defended Tilak) had been nominated and had been promised the support of a large majority of the Council—had even been seconded by a leading English official. But Government House intervened, Sir. G. Clark actually sending for various members of the Council to persuade them to withdraw their support, and having ordered the English official to nominate a nonentity against Baptista. Gradually, as Baptista told us, he found his friends melting away under Government pressure. At the last moment he retired and it was clear that he would be supported by a small minority only.

Another manifestation of what we should call improper Government interference was the drafting of rules and regulations by Sir G. Clarke for the discipline of all schools and colleges. These rules, which were printed in the Agenda, were arbitrary and somewhat childish. The parents were to hand over the *whole* control of their children in and *out* of school to the Headmaster of the school. No boy or youth was to attend *any* public meeting, to join any association, to subscribe to or collect any fund for any purpose whatsoever, without the express permission of the Headmaster—and so on. Here the Government got a distinct snub, the Council replying that the spirit of the rules had already been embodied as far as practicable and desirable in their own regulations. In the schools run by the District Boards (that is, the rural schools) the Government had simply insisted on these rules being adopted.

We had several talks with the great leader of the Municipality (he was just retiring from the Chairmanship) and of the Bombay University—Sir Pherozeshah Mehta.[4] A very suc-

---

in 1926. In the same year he was elected to the Central Legislative Assembly. He organized two textile strikes and one postal strike and represented India as a Labour Delegate at the International Labour Conference at Geneva in 1924.

[4] Sir Pherozeshah Merwanjee Mehta (1845–1915) was among the founders of the Indian National Congress and its President in 1890.

cessful barrister, long the leader of the Bombay Bar, he had made himself leader of the two independent organisations of Bombay by sheer ability, persistence and public spirit. A Parsee by race and religion, he was in sentiment entirely Nationalist but he took his own line, and preferred the organising of local centres of independent action to Gokhale's general political reforms. Perhaps he was too much concerned to have his own way, and to score his little triumphs over the Government in local matters to be able quite enthusiastically to work for India at large. Thus, he was not in sympathy with Gokhale's Education Bill, holding that it was better to multiply university education and let it "filter downwards". He had had a terrific fight with the Government of India and Sir George Clarke over their proposed reforms of Bombay University, apparently resisting both the good proposals and the bad, because these were one and all tainted with the evil that they tended to deprive the University of its independence, and make it really an organ of the local Government. In the fight to maintain an independent Senate he had failed, as the Government of India proceeded by statute, which swept away the old, swollen and much degenerated Senate, and replaced it by a smaller one (of 100) mainly nominated by Government. But Mehta threw himself energetically into the New Senate, and by sheer weight of argument, converted the Government nominees, who were mostly well-chosen unofficial people. The last fight had been over English History which used to be compulsory for B.A. The Governor, without actually avowing his reason that English History made for Nationalism, tried to get it excluded, except as a special study. Mehta failed to keep it compulsory, but succeeded in keeping it in as an optional subject

He was a stalwart of the moderate school of nationalist thinking and a distinguished member of the Bombay Legislative Council and the Imperial Council of India. His contributions in the sphere of local self-government are particularly notable: he was virtually the maker of the Bombay Corporation and its member for forty-six years.

which any student can take. He was more successful with regard to the Matriculation examination. This the Governor sought to make the University relinquish to the College, so that each college might make its own examination, fix its own subjects and set its own standard. So extraordinary a proposal required explanation, and the only one we could get on the Government side was that the existing University Matriculation examination was open to criticism and that the Oxford and Cambridge Colleges had their own entrance examinations—which, be it noted (though the Indians were not told this), are over and above what the Universities of Oxford and Cambridge require for their first examinations—not alternatives to these. The real reason, so the Indians thought, was to get the control out of the hands of the Senate which, in spite of its emasculation, was still (under Mehta) obstinate and pretty independent, into the hands of the Colleges which were mainly under Government control (wholly so as regards Medicine and Engineering, predominantly so as regards Science, and largely so as regards Arts). Once the Colleges could fix their own Matriculation Examinations, it was believed that the Government, in its new policy of restricting university education, would compel them to raise the standard of entrance, so as greatly to limit the numbers. Here Mehta beat the Government. By his passionate eloquence and tireless persuasion, he kept a majority even of the Government nominees; and Sir G. Clarke had just approved the new regulations which fell far short of what he had asked for; and (as he told Sir P. Mehta) had approved them with great reluctance.

In all this contest with Bombay University our impression is that Sir G. Clarke, and the Government generally, comes out very badly. It is not that the University did not need reform; but that in all the proposals for reform the Government took the opportunity of withdrawing such autonomy as the University had previously been granted. It is not that the Governor interfered in the University, for as Chancellor he had a right to intervene and make proposals; but that he intervened as Governor, and used all the influence of Government, legitimate and illegitimate, to carry his points, which he formulated without consultation with the University, and pressed with bitter personal obstinacy. We cannot help feeling that it is a bad case of reaction, of taking back from the Indians opportunities for self-government which had actually been accorded to them.

We visited two of the Bombay cotton mills, one under the guidance of the proprietor, the other under that of the Factory inspector whom the Government deputed to take us. They both had efficient English machinery, in crowded and insanitary premises (one much worse than the other). In both, it struck us that the shafting and moving parts were much less securely fenced than in Lancashire; and there is no Employers' Liability, and (we are told) naturally frequent accidents. Both were under Indian management almost exclusively, though each had one Lancashire man: in one case as foreman and in the other case as weaving master. In both, the working day was 13 hours, less one hour for meals, with Sunday a holiday unless some Hindu festival was substituted for it. Both told us that other mills did a lot of "cribbing time", and that the factory inspection was very inefficient. There are only four factory inspectors in all India: all men and Englishmen, apparently promoted from subordinate services (our man was from the Customs). There is no restriction on the hours of opening and closing—only on the hours worked by each operative—and as there is no requirement that half-timers should go to school, and no provision for checking evasions, our Factory Inspector declared that it was practically impossible to get evidence that half-time boys were not putting in their free half time there or elsewhere, and that women were not working illegal hours. The ventilation was extremely imperfect, and dust and dirt abounded. In case of fire, the mill would be a death trap. Both mills were making large profits, and had never worked short time except in the famine years. Altogether we felt that if the Indian mills had a grievance in being subjected to the Excise Duty, this ought

not to be given up except as part of a bargain with the mill-
owners to accept a Factory Act up to the latest Lancashire
standard; and our own Workmen's Compensation Act. The
operatives were mostly recruited from the coast districts
around Bombay, not from Bombay itself; and they are said
to insist on frequently going home for longer or shorter
periods on their private affairs. They came somewhat irregu-
larly to work; and there was a system of taking on temporary
substitutes, a crowd of whom attended daily at the factory
gates. There was said to be no scarcity of labour (though just
now some extensive engineering works were somewhat
competing for hands); and no organisation for recruiting in
the country. The operatives were said to be very independent, shifting from mill to mill for the very slightest reason.
They were paid only once a month. The methods of remuneration, terms and conditions were said to vary from mill to
mill, there being no uniform rate or common rules, though
naturally competition among the mills kept the terms fairly
equivalent to each other. There was said to be no Trade Union, though there were inchoate associations among the mill-
hands for special purposes. Caste restrictions were said to be
dying out and to be unimportant: the mills now contained
people of all castes high and low, and no objection was made.
Piecework was the rule, and usually individual contracts;
though in some cases a whole room would be on collective
piecework, the leading hands getting a (specified) larger rate
than the others. The doffing boys and the piecers on the (few)
mules were always paid by the firm direct. There were a few
mules, but mostly ringframes (all worked by men). The
women only did such work as winding. The looms were
worked by men, each minding two only.

One of the firms employed no half-timers, declaring that it
was impossible to prevent their tiring themselves out by
working the other half, *sometimes actually at another mill.*

Both these mills were owned by Hindoos. In one case, the
father had started the mill some forty years ago, and had been
uniformly successful. The 1000 rupee shares were worth

2700 rupees. The Company was virtually a family one, the family having three Directors out of five. The family claimed to be Kshatriyas or warriors by caste. The young proprietor who took us over was this year Sheriff of Bombay. He had not been to England, as his caste did not permit it, though they allowed voyages to Zanzibar, etc., and they would presently give way about England. The other mill belonged virtually to a Bunnia family. It was far inferior in amenity.

This latter mill had its own dyeing and bleaching department which we visited, and which only did work for other firms when it happened to have nothing to do. It had imported much German machinery for dyeing, which was said to be in advance of English: also the English machinery makers were too obstinate: they would not make what they were told to make, and thought they knew better! Thus, though a screw press was normally much superior to a lever press, the latter was better for India, as the former got out of order in Indian hands).

Neither mill seemed to compete directly with Lancashire or Japan, making somewhat different products. One sold most of its yarn to dealers who supplied the Indian hand-loom weavers. (one-third of the total Indian consumption of cotton cloth is still made on hand looms in the Indian factories; and less than half is imported). Its cotton cloth was sold mostly in India and Central Asia. The other mill sent its cotton cloth mostly to Zanzibar for East Africa.

The women at work were nearly all married, their husbands mostly also working in mills. A few were widows, but these mostly married again. No definite or reliable information as to morality.

Altogether the mills of Bombay are not a pleasing development. But they prove that the Indians, Hindus as well as Parsees, can successfully manage business enterprise on a large scale. We were told that nine-tenths of the business of Bombay was in Indian hands; in contrast with Calcutta where nine-tenths is in European hands.

We went to Elephanta in a Government electric launch,

which Sir G. Clarke very kindly lent us, and we took with us a gentle and attractive Hindu friend of Gokhale, the Hon. Lalubhai Samaldas, who had been very attentive in looking after us, as well as another Hindu, the youthful Chairman of the Standing Committee of the Municipality. The latter was not interesting but the former, apparently a well-to-do commercial person, had been nominated to the Bombay Legislative Council and the University, as a well-disposed, moderate person. This he was, but it is significant that his Government nominee was a fervent admirer of Gokhale, and essentially a Nationalist; and he had not hesitated to oppose Sir G. Clarke when he thought he was wrong. He asked about the Fabian Society and expressed a wish to join. At his request S.W. saw his son, an attractive boy of twenty who had just taken his B.A. with distinction, and was determined to join the Servants of India. The father did not altogether disapprove, but wished him to spend two years in his own business office, and then visit England and the London School of Economics before finally deciding. It is noteworthy that the boy of twenty had been married for two years, to a girl now seventeen, but they have not yet commenced co-habitation.

We pass over the rest of our doings at Bombay—the Towers of Silence; the drives along the seashore; the lunches and teas and receptions where we met the cultivated Parsee, Hindu and Mohammedan, but scarcely any English; the stray English we saw at the Hotel and elsewhere. We did not present various introductions to English people, as there was little time to spare and we were tired. There is, however, just one more item to record. Ratan Tata (the second son of the Tata who started the great steel works and hydraulic electric works and the great Technical Institute at Bangalore) had wished to found and endow a corresponding Institute for Economic Research. He had formulated this proposal and made a definite offer of a large sum to promote economic investigation and study in India. He wished to locate this at Bangalore, alongside his father's Institute for Technological Research. He laid this offer before the Principal and Council of the latter Institute, by whom the whole project was rejected, lock, stock and barrel; and the money refused! The ground of refusal was that any economic research was bound to be, or to seem, "political", and likely to bring down on the Technological Institute Government displeasure. The refusal seems to have been accompanied by contemptuous references by the science men at Bangalore to the futility of any investigation into economic matters. And the Government, far from encouraging Tata's desires, or helping to get economic investigation started, has also thrown cold water on it. Hence Tata has let the matter drop. Meanwhile he has made an offer to London University to endow an enquiry into the problem of destitution, on which Miers[5] seems to have consulted Leonard Hobhouse[6] and Urwick,[7] and a draft scheme has been submitted to Tata (which his Manager Padshah gave S.W. in confidence, and on which S.W. wrote a long memo.) which may lead to £1000 a year or so coming within the sphere of the London School of Economics.

Sir G. Clarke's own project of an Institute or School of Commerce as to which he got out Lees Smith[8] to lecture three years ago, seems to have made little progress. He has some promises of money, but he seems to be so pigheadedly obstinate on having his own way, so ungracious about other

[5] Sir Henry Alexander Miers (1858–1942), Principal of the University of London (1908–15) and Vice-Chancellor at Manchester (1915–26).

[6] Leonard Trelawny Hobhouse (1864–1929), Professor of Sociology. London University, author of *The Labour Movement* and *Morals in Evolution*.

[7] Edward John Urwick (1867–1945), Professor of Social Philosophy, University of London, and later Professor Emeritus of Political Economy, University of Toronto. Author of *A Philosophy of Social Progress* and *The Social Good*.

[8] Rt. Hon. Hastings Bertrand Lees-Smith (1878–1941), associated with Ruskin College from its foundation in 1899. Liberal MP (1910–18) and Acting Chairman of the Parliamentary Labour Party from 1940. Author of *Studies in Indian Economics* and *India and the Tariff Problem*.

people's help, and really so half-hearted about the project at all, that we doubt whether it will lead to anything. The fact is that he has become afraid of any kind of education! The sooner this worn-out, tired, saddened and embittered man goes home into retirement the better. It is said that Lord Chelmsford[9] is to succeed him, which would be excellent.

[9] Lord Chelmsford, Frederic John Napier Thesiger, Viceroy and Governor-General of India, 1916–21.

On the "Homeward" Sea, 16 to 25 April 1912

On a crowded ship, disturbed by three crying babies and two dogs, in unpleasant moist heat which only the cool draughts of the incessantly going fans make endurable, it is not easy to sum up India!

First may be noted the fact, whatever it may be worth, that the more we saw of India, the more we learned about the Government and the officials, and the longer we lived among the people *the graver became our tone*, and the more subdued our optimism. At first, after China, India seemed hopeful. Great as were the difficulties, they did not appear insurmountable. We could look with confidence on the future. I still think that the problems can be solved, and that the future may be made bright. But as our acquaintance with the Indian bureaucracy has increased, and as we have more and more appreciated its alliance in the main with reactionary Imperialism and commercial selfishness in England we are less confident. Three months' acquaintance has greatly increased our estimate of the Indians, and greatly lessened our admiration for, and our trust in, this Government of officials.

Does this bureaucracy succeed in supplying a good Government? Our impression is that the I.C.S. has succeeded fairly well in carrying out its ideals of government, but its ideals are still those of 1840! Its conception of government is to put down internal war, brigandage and violent crime; decide civil suits and maintain order, and for the rest to leave people alone. These things it has very fairly achieved, and it is no doubt a great achievement to have done this for so huge a territory, out of its own resources, with so limited a staff of English, and with so imperfect a subordinate staff of Indians. Hence its self-complacency and, indeed, conceit, which is a serious obstacle to its learning anything, or improving. There are shortcomings even in this limited realm. There is still a great deal of theft and extortion from poor folk; cattle stealing, petty thefts on the railway, and even burglaries (dacoities) seem such more common than in Europe. Our law courts are honest and unbribable, but they are by no means racially unprejudiced; the magistrates commit many oppressions on poor and humble folk, largely because they do not regard their liberty as anything like so sacred as that of a white man; our procedure has encouraged an enormous amount of litigation and chicanery; its very excellence and rigour has greatly increased the evil power of the money-lender. It seems very doubtful whether a rural village, if it could give an opinion, would not rather be without our whole civil courts and civil procedure, and without our criminal law—preferring its old way of dealing with its own cases in village panchayet.[1] It is nearly as doubtful whether it would not be well advised in so deciding.

(S.W. has left off—yielding to the enervation of the mid-

---

[1] A traditional institution of local government at the village level. The *panchayat* was not an elected body but consisted of respected elders of the village community. It had neither a fixed membership, nor any settled rules of procedure, its function being simply to arbitrate in disputes referred to it and to manage festivals in the village. The *panchayat* was considered reflective of the collective will and wisdom of the community and, in an extreme case, the sanction behind its decision would be social ostracism. With the coming of the British and the introduction of an entirely distinct, centralized judicial system, there was a gradual breakdown of the *panchayat*. In independent India efforts have been made to revive this institution in a suitably modernized form.

day heat, and to the irritation from a screaming baby. I want him to sum up his impressions of the Economics of the British dominions in India—of which I have, without due thought or knowledge, somewhat grave misgivings—more than misgivings as to past stupidity and plunder—and misgiving *questions* even about our present Economic policy. Meanwhile I jot down one or two impressions of the purely personal side of our contact with Indian life.)

First there seems to be no typical "Oriental"—no qualities that seem to be common to the Japanese, to the Chinese, and to the Indians. There are, of course, *institutions* that are common to these three races, as compared to the institutions of the more advanced European communities. The "Joint family" with its reverence for the Parents' authority, its maintenance, without question, of even adult male members, its subordination of women, and its community of property, still exists in Japan as well as in China, and it is an equally common feature of Hindu and Mahommedan India. The small cultivator, and the small masters are characteristic forms of production throughout the Far East and India as contrasted with the great industry and capitalist agriculture of so many of the Western races and their colonies. There is even a certain community of Religious Experience, in all these three countries—the Buddhism of Japan and China arising in India and being, in one sense, a mere off-shoot of Hinduism. But after one has recited these obvious likenesses, in social and economic structure, one comes to the deep-down unlikeness between the men and women of Japan, of China and of India respectively—an unlikeness which is certainly greater in the case of the educated Indians, than the unlikeness of the Hindu Indian to the modern Italian and even to the Englishman. The Japanese are a race of Idealists, but these Ideals are fixed and amazingly homogeneous and are always capable of being translated into immediate and persistent action. They are, in fact, perhaps the most Executive race in the world—the most capable of discovering the means to the end—and the most self-contained and self-disciplined in

working out these means, and therefore in attaining their
ends. One sees, in front of them, the danger of becoming
vulgarised by their success as practical men—of losing the
substance of their Ideal, in the shadow of accomplishment.
About the Chinese I do not feel competent to speak as I dislike them so heartily. But the very fact that they excite our
dislike whilst the Japanese excite our almost partisan admiration and the Indians our real affection, shows how different
the Chinese race must be either to the inhabitants of the great
continent of India, or to those of the little Island of Japan.
What revolts us in the Chinese is, on the one hand, the absence of the idealism of the Japanese and Indian races, and on
the other, their present lack of capacity for the scientific
method, and for the disciplined effort of the Japanese. There are
doubtless qualities in the Chinese which we have not had the
sympathetic insight to discover—in fact the Chinese do seem
to us to be what all Orientals are assumed to be: "inscrutable". As for the Hindus, they strike us as an essentially
lovable race. Unlike the Japanese and Chinese, they have
the element of physical beauty—of fineness of feature, large
shapeliness of stature, and extreme spirituality and intellectuality of expression—they produce more aristocrats of
body, mind and manners and bearing than either the Chinese
or the Japanese. Then the fact that the cultivated Hindu has
more completely assimilated English thought and English
literature whilst possessing a real knowledge of his own clas-
sics gives him a broader base for intellectual intercourse with
the cultivated Englishman. Like the Japanese, the Hindu is an
idealist—but alas! for his political efficiency, his ideals are "all
over the place" and frequently he lacks the capacity to put
them into practice—he can neither discover the means nor
work at them with unswerving persistency. Then the aristocracy of India is dragged down by a multitude of lower
castes and lower races—embedded in a population which
seems strangely childish in intellect and undisciplined in conduct. The perpetually repeated commonplace of the Anglo-
Indian official "they are like children—you must treat them

as such" is ludicrous in its class insolence when you are thinking of the educated Hindu of higher caste, but probably true
at present about a great mass of the population of India—I say
true at present, because if you treated them persistently as
Men they would probably "grow up" to manhood. And yet
even in the hordes of humble Indian folk, who crowd the
third-class carriages, you see a spirituality and a bright intelligence—sometimes a beauty and dignity which you
altogether miss in the inhabitants of the Chinese village or of
Canton. And when you come to associate with the men who
make up the Arya Somaj or the "Servants of India" all your
prepossessions as to the lack of self discipline and persistent
self-devotion and even of executive force among Hindus,
dissolve into a mere prejudice of which you become ashamed.
But perhaps the most striking quality of the Hindus whom
we have seen, is their essential modesty—not so much a de-
preciation of *Things Indian* as compared to *Things European*—
but the modesty of Man against the Universe. That terrible
coarse-grained self-satisfaction and self-absorbed sensuality
and self-conscious respectability and consciousness of God's
own Englishmen as the King of the Universe—which makes
some good-hearted and capable Englishmen so horrid to
live with, or even to talk to, is not to be met with among
Hindus. All Humanity is a pitiful business to the philosophical Hindu—and the greatest one on Earth is inferior to the
humblest ascetic of the lowest caste on the straight way to
final emancipation from the wheel of Human Desire. It is this
quality of intellectual perspective that makes the Hindu a delightful and refined intellectual companion—whom one instinctively feels to be one's superior.

What strikes us as serious in the present state of feeling between the British Ruler and the Indian Ruled, is the complete
and almost fatuous ignorance of the bulk of British officials
of their essential inferiority in culture, charm, and depth of
intellectual and spiritual experience, to the Indian aristocracy
of intellect. That means that as the Indian aristocrat grows in
the power of self-discipline and executive force—and he *is*

growing very rapidly, the cleavage will become wider and wider, and co-operation between the actual alien governor and the potential native governor will become less and less possible. And as national feeling is bound to spread and intensify, the Indian aristocrat will have to work underground with the object of compelling the British Ruler to relinquish his hold. If, on the other hand, the English would recognise this new governing class—and would gradually take them into his confidence, with a view to making them party to the Government of India, then the British race might pride themselves on having been the finest race of school masters, as well as the most perfect builders of an Empire. The British Empire might endure until International Law makes all empire a practical anachronism though perhaps it would still remain as a much loved sentimental tie embedded in an ancient name for certain far distant parts of this earth.

Travelling in India, associating with educated Hindus, observing the life of the common people, raises one long series of questions—questions which keep one's mind perpetually busy and always baffled at not finding any explanation or answer. Sometimes these questions relate to the relations between an alien government and a subject race, sometimes they concern the results of an economic policy prescribed by an individualist and materialist people on an essentially communal and religious race. But the one problem that has been before my mind—as an almost morbid obsession—is the problem of the religious life of Hinduism. At the Temples of Benares and at the Magh Mela of Allahabad, I was revolted by the incontinence of the popular religion—the strange combination of almost hysterical and certainly promiscuous idolatry—with crude superstitions as to the physical results of "God-propitiation"—and behind it all the sinister background of revolting lasciviousness and gross crudity. This disgust reached its culmination in the grotesque lewdness of the Khajuraho Temples with their direct incitement to unnatural vice. Add to this, the exhibitions of the life of the ordinary Saddhu, with its self-indulgence, vagrant idleness and frequent hypocrisy and vice—or the equally nauseous imposition of the Brahmin family priest with horoscope and fortune-telling—and one is reduced to a state of cynical doubt as to whether the most complete Hedonistic materialistic atheism would not be preferable to the religious experience of the Hindu people. But this is only one side of the shield. The vision of the austere and pious domestic life of the Purdah ladies of Bhupendranath Basu's household with their unmeasured devotion to husband and children, their industry and frugality, and throughout the whole family life the intense reverence of the younger to the elder, all qualities based on the Hindu religion, relieves one's gloom, though possibly it does not make one more hopeful of the immediate progressiveness (in the Western sense) of the Hindu race. With this almost fanatical idealisation of wifely devotion, one might even see Suttee re-established in an "India without the English". Indeed the rite of Suttee ceases to appear barbarous if once you accept this atmosphere of pure idealism. If the body is a mere illusion, if the only reality is the spirit of devotional communion of wife with husband, then why retain the illusion—why not let the body dissolve in the flame of the funeral pyre? By this willing self-immolation the Reality endures—the spectators, far from taking part in a cruel custom, are witnessing the victory of the spirit of devotion over the physical fear of death. The only question that arises to the modern democrat is—Why not a suttee for the widower as well as for the widow?

Another and more inspiring vision is that of the Informal Religious Orders of social service arising in modern India—the teachers in the Arya Somaj educational institutions, or the members of the "Servants of India" or of the "Fergusson College".

Here the Hindu Religion is combined with a sincere and powerful self-discipline, a self-discipline with the express object of maintaining the mind and body in the fittest condition for the most perfect service of the community. These Orders seem preferable to the Religious Orders of Western peoples in two remarkable features—complete freedom of thought and the normal domestic ties for all members. Though the Arya Somaj has a definite doctrine and is almost fanatical in its propaganda of the Vedas, there seems to be no attempt to enquire into the particular faith of the individual member, or to shackle him, in any way, in the expression of it. There is no authority that can determine what shall be the intellectual faith of the Somaj. It is an interesting sidelight that the only dispute that has arisen is not on the question of faith but on the practice of meat-eating as against vegetarianism. "You can *think* what you like, so long as you *do* what is prescribed," is the universal attitude of the Hindu heresy hunter. And when you pass from the religious sect of the Aryas, to the Servants of India, you lose all trace of religious dogma— you are confronted with a Religious Order without any definite religion or even a definite metaphysics.

The other great advantage of these modern Hindu Orders is the absence of enforced celibacy for the adult men. The strictest chastity is prescribed for the boys and the most careful arrangements are made in the Guru Kula for the enforcement of it. But this chastity is with a view to "greater virility" in adult life—a more perfect fulfilment of the duty of parenthood. Directly the man is adult he is expected to marry, and his wife and family are maintained in the same modest and abstemious way as he is himself. These two characteristics—freedom of thought and normal domestic life— are a real contribution to the institution of religious orders.

In estimating the net result of the religious experience of modern Hinduism it is therefore essential to balance the superstition of incontinence of the Hinduism of the populace, by a realisation of the new development—of the healthy, virile and free service of religious orders, self-dedicated to the progress of the race. The only analogue in the European world is the Salvation Army, but that organisation is marred by the lack of broad culture or intellectual distinction. Moreover, the Salvation Army has the commonness inherent in an autocratic organisation dependent on the personality of one man. One of the outstanding charms of Hindu religious organisation is, in fact, its impersonal character, its independence of any one personality, its free and untrammelled growth from the soul of the whole people. Indeed the whole conception of service by an aristocracy of birth and intellect, for mere subsistence, and within a democratically managed community of social equals, is an entirely new idea to the Western mind. If only the British official with his insistence on high salaries, prestige, and elaborate arrangements for the pleasures of life, would recognise the existence, within the Indian community, of a moral and intellectual standard superior to his own, without necessarily desiring to imitate this standard, he might continue to assert the superiority of the British in other respects—without offending the susceptibilities of educated Hindu society.

A traveller, especially an elderly traveller, is liable to come back from his travel with his own general ideas confirmed. Observations of Hinduism in its baser and nobler aspects confirms my theory of the legitimate relation between the sphere of science and the sphere of religion. Most of the demoralisation of popular Hinduism arises from applying religious emotion to determine the *processes of life*—of seeking the help of the God in the illness of a child, in consulting the horoscope of a boy and girl prior to marriage, and accepting the magic of priestly rites as the determinating factor in every act of life. On the other hand, in much of the popular religion there seems no kind of attempt to purify or exalt the Purpose of Life as displayed in nobility of human motive. In the worst forms of Hinduism the individual may be impelled by the most vicious desires, he may even murder and bear false witness, without fear of religious ostracism, so long as he is true to the rites and ceremonies of his sect or caste. In his Pantheon there are Gods who will, if duly propitiated, help him to do evil things. In the lowest strata of Hinduism, superstition governs all the forms of conduct, whilst the lowest animal impulses are permitted to determine the motives and even the substance of conduct.

In the finest form of Hinduism, we watch an almost perfect relation between religious emotion and intellectual life.
Here all ratiocination is left free and untrammelled by religious dogma—you can think what seems to you to be true in
any particular case. Religion concerns itself with the purity
and nobility of your *purpose* in life—with the self-discipline
which will enable you to maintain it intact. Even the control
over your physical instincts which is enjoined, is to be guided
by a scientific knowledge of the laws of health, and is to be
varied and developed according to any new knowledge
attained by scientific discovery. Hence when we tried to explain our view of the relative sphere of science and religion to
the Professors of the Guru Kula and to Gokhale and the Servants of India, we found a complete and ready acceptance of
our theory, as the one which they had been themselves working out.

What is to be said of the economic condition of the three
hundred millions of Indians? It is an uncomfortable fact that
it should not be beyond controversy whether they are better or
worse off than a generation ago. The British official unhesitatingly says they are better off; and alleges the rise in wages of
his syce (groom) as proof. But as he will admit prices have
also risen enormously, and the wages of the lowest grades of
labour, and those in the remoter places and the Native States,
have gone up far less than those of the skilled domestic servants of the English. It is more to the point to assert that the
average Indian now enjoys a great variety of commodities
than before: he is said to be visibly earning more and spending more. The general consumption of umbrellas and shoes,
cigarettes and tea, gramophones and made clothes is de-
monstrably greatly increasing. On the other hand, serious
Nationalist thinkers declare that the Cultivators are (outside
Bengal) more impoverished than they were, and therefore
more easily brought into destitution by droughts, which are
thereby made into "famines" (for the famine of India is now
only a "money famine", a spasm of local "unemployment",
which might be weathered if the cultivator had his own sav-

ings to fall back upon). On the whole, I should infer that the average Indian both earns more and spends more, his Standard of Life has risen and is rising; and if he does not get rich he at any rate gets a somewhat wider life.

What is more important is to consider the economic influences at work. Here the biggest factor is perhaps the Government Land Revenue, which (outside Bengal and Benares, etc.) is not a permanently fixed rental. Every thirty years—sometimes every twenty years—the Settlement Officer comes and looks at each village, and (with all sorts of elaborate rules and safeguards) fixes, without appeal to any independent tribunal, *how much more* the cultivator shall pay for the ensuing term. Against this periodical "skimming off the cream", R. C. Dutt and all the Indian Nationalists declaim, and their objection has been supported by leading officials from time to time. But the India Office and the Government of India will not agree to concede a "Permanent Settlement", on the sole ground that the Government cannot and need not forego the continuous increase of the Land Revenue, especially in so far as this is of the nature of "Unearned Increment".

Now, on this point, I am converted to the Nationalist position. Safeguard as one may, the system comes essentially to that of the Irish landlord with his cottier tenants. It is worse because the Government is virtually in the position of a monopolist landlord. The cultivator has practically no option. He must have access to land, and the Government fixes its terms. The Settlement Officer is admittedly driven to get all that (subject to the rules) he can. He is told to take all that the cultivator can spare, over and above the limit (half the net assets) that the Government itself fixes. When the time for re-settlement approaches, land goes out of cultivation, houses are let go into ruin, wealth is hidden, etc., in order to get a lower assessment. All this comes essentially to the system that ruined Asia Minor, Korea, etc., viz. arbitrary taxation of those becoming wealthy. Only by the greatest care can the Government of India prevent its Settlements being actually oppressive and productive of starvation. It seems clear that, notwithstanding all possible rules about exempting improvements, the continuous raising of the Land Revenue wherever there is improvement in yield cannot fail to discourage thrift, industry, enterprise and even honesty in the cultivator. I conclude that, at whatever loss of future increases, the Government of India ought, in one way or another, to concede a Permanent Settlement to its cultivators—or, (as Lord Ripon proposed) at any rate make the Land Revenue vary only at intervals with the general price level. The "*Unearned* Increment" of agricultural land—apart from irrigation—reveals itself only in higher prices, and if this potential increase were retained by the Government, it might well regard all the rest as due to the cultivator's efforts. The Government would be recouped (as has been the case in Bengal) by the growth in the other sources of revenue payable by a population which, ex-hypothesi, has more wealth (e.g. licences, import duties, income tax, stamps, etc.). Thus, contrary to my prepossessions, I come to regard the Permanent Settlement of Bengal by Lord Cornwallis in 1793 as a wise measure. (The mere fact that the Zemindar landlords oppressed their tenants has nothing to do with the "permanence", or otherwise, of their own State Rent or Land Tax: they are not *more* apt to rack-rent their cottiers because their own head-rent is *not* increased! As a matter of fact, the same sort of legislative protection of tenants against landlords has been required in all the provinces). Similarly, I am convinced that the evil of the State Land Revenue has been greatest where the State has dealt direct with the individual Ryot, or small cultivator. He is, in Bombay and Madras, not in the least like a peasant proprietor. He is an Irish cottier, under an all-powerful absentee landlord. It is hard to resist the evidence that he has been much oppressed by the Government. He ought to be given the "Three F's" at once—Fixity of Tenure, Fair Rents and Free Sale—and the same status should be given to the actual cultivators elsewhere, both as against their landlords and as against the Government Land Revenue demand.

One other measure is required, viz. Credit legislation. The

peasant cultivator needs to be protected against the usurer and against himself in the way of borrowing, by an extensive "Homestead Law", which should prevent his holding and his cattle, as well as his plough etc. being seized for debt, or even mortgaged, or (as the Punjab law has it) even sold to anyone not being a cultivator. But this is to injure his power of borrowing. Supply this by a ubiquitous system of Co-operative Credit Societies, which the Government itself might well supply with all the capital needed, thus using its own credit to enable them to lend at low rates for legitimate purposes.

The Government of India (and the India Office which has been even worse than the Viceroys) clings to the growing Land Revenue, and pursues an extremely fainthearted economic policy—partly out of ancient prejudice but chiefly because the Government is horribly *poor*. Its revenue is small and precarious, and the customary sources of English Chancellors of the Exchequer are closed to it. The Hindu Joint Family system stands in the way of Death Duties, and increases the difficulties of an Income Tax. The consumption of popular luxuries is so small that no great sum can be got from alcohol, tea, tobacco, etc. English opinion won't permit any increase of the Import Duties against English goods. Under these circumstances we suggest a bold policy of Government exploitation—taking into Government hands all the railways, developing the 240,000 square miles of forest by Government paper mills, match factories, timber trade, etc., and perhaps starting Government tobacco works and spirit distilleries. The I.C.S. is aghast at this, and even Gokhale does not approve, because to the Nationalists, the position is rather as it was to the *Laisser Faire* Liberals a century ago. To the Indians the Government is a hostile force, and they are loth to see it expand in any way. This cripples them in political programme, because they are always urging retrenchment.

To resume my disjointed notes on Hinduism. What is the value of all that religious expression that is covered by the term Yoga—that self-study or contemplative concentration of thought to which Hinduism and Buddhism attach such immense importance, with its coincident aspiration towards a complete suppression of human desire and of the greater part of human faculty? In our *Industrial Democracy* we defined the desire for Liberty as the striving after an increase of human faculty and desire; a state of liberty as the maximum of desire and faculty, among all the members of a given society. Our western ideal is, in fact, the fullest possible development of human faculty among the whole people—assuming that we agree as to what constitutes the fullest development both in quality and quantity. But it is clear that the ideal is wholly antagonistic to the Eastern ideal of restricting activity and assiduously cultivating a state of mind which seems to us to resemble blankness. Was there ever any justification for the practise of Yoga—has any progress in the development of human personality been attained by it? Quite clearly the modern Hindu religious order, unlike the ancient Saddhu, either eliminates Yoga (as in the case of the Servants of India or the Professors of Fergusson College) or subordinates it, as a part of mental and physical discipline whilst insisting on the obligation of each individual to develop all the faculties of body and mind for the service of humanity. I had hoped that our journey to the East would have enlightened this fundamental question, but I come back as mystified as ever. Mrs. Besant's coquetry with Yoga and the sight of the Saddhus who are supposed to practise it, leaves me in a state of cold scepticism—testifying to my continued ignorance of what may be behind this old world wisdom.